Dating Secrets of the Ten Commandments

Dating Secrets of the Ten Commandments

Shmuley Boteach

Doubleday New York London Toronto Sydney Auckland

PUBLISHED BY DOUBLEDAY
a division of Random House, Inc.
1540 Broadway, New York, New York 10036

DOUBLEDAY and the portrayal of an anchor with a dolphin are
trademarks of Doubleday, a division of Random House, Inc.

Book design by Bonni Leon-Berman

Published by arrangement with Gerald Duckworth & Co. Ltd.

Library of Congress Cataloging-in-Publication Data applied for

ISBN: 0-385-49620-6

1 3 5 7 9 10 8 6 4 2

To Michael

who taught me of humility . . .

In loving appreciation for the music, the friendship, the

inspiration.

"Serve God with joy; come before him with music and dance."

—PSALM 100

And to Uri's magic, which makes it all possible.

c o n t e n t s

"Do not covet your fellow's house. Do not covet your
fellow's wife, his manservant, his maidservant, his ox,
his donkey, nor every thing that belongs to your
fellow."

acknowledgments

Why am I writing yet another book on relationships? Could it have something to do with my wish to create a new relationships canon, capitalizing on the fantastic success of my earlier book *Kosher Sex*? Could it have something to do with the fact that my other books on academic subjects like *Jewish Mysticism, Dreams,* the *University of Oxford,* and *Rabbinic Dream Psychology* had their sales doubled in the first year when my mother bought a copy of each for a friend? Is my obsession with sex and relationships just a cynical attempt at milking an irresistible subject for cheap profiteering? Am I a shameless author who seeks to regurgitate the same stuff he's written before, albeit repackaged like new for naïve, unsuspecting readers? You bet.

There are plenty of precedents for authors trying to rip off the public, especially when it comes to sequels. Take the *Chicken Soup* series of books. I still remember when the first book was published. It was this cool book called *Chicken Soup for the Soul.* It had warm stories about moving life experiences. Now, of course, it has been franchised into a major business. On a recent trip to Singapore I saw about fifty different versions of *Chicken Soup* at the airport. There is *Chicken Soup for the Soul at Work,* and *Chicken Soup for the Soul with Hemorrhoids, Chicken Soup for the Soul on a Viagra Drip,* and *Chicken Soup for the Marxist-Leninist Freedom Fighter Soul.* In the light of this I feel that I have a responsibility to continue to exploit the *Kosher Sex* success to the maximum.

Once again I have to first thank my wife, Debbie, even though she hasn't been spotted since the publication of *Kosher Sex.* ("If you publish that book, I will be so embarrassed, I'll run away and become a Sherpa!") Reliable reports have come back to me about a Jewish woman wandering around with a paper bag over her head in the foothills of the Himalayas, calling herself *Ms.* Smith, so I feel confident that once the Sanskrit edition comes out, Debbie will read my message of thanks.

Likewise, I must thank my six children. They all complained that their friends at school had told them that their daddy had written a "rude" book. Thus I have to return to the ranks of respectability by penning another book, only somewhat rude, but this time claiming that it is based on the Bible.

I especially want to thank Dan Williams, whom I first met as a student at L'Chaim at Oxford, and who has remained one of my closest friends ever since. Dan generously volunteered to do all the field research for *Kosher Sex* and went well beyond the call of duty. The odd thing is that although the book was published last year, he tells me he is still doing the field research—but that's the level of dedication that he brings to all his undertakings. For this book Dan, an English graduate with a double first, did all the initial editing—a truly huge achievement—and is responsible for putting my copious material into order. He also suggested many useful ideas and anecdotes, which I have lifted and claimed as my own. But heck, what are friends for?

I also want to of course thank my long-suffering editor at Doubleday, Eric Major. Eric and I have an interesting role reversal. He is a Briton living in the United States, and I am an American who spent eleven years living in the United Kingdom. What this means is that every time I pitch an idea for a book at Eric, he looks at me and says, "HHMMMMMM, yyyeeesss. Quite. Indeed." This response is standard and the beauty of Eric, as well as every other Englishman, is their utter predictability. So, whether I return from "holiday" and inform Eric about terrible bouts of constipation, or call him and warn him before a book's publication that I am about to be outed by a newspaper as a homicidal axe murderer, he always just looks at me with the same stoical glance with which the Queen greets Camilla. I have dedicated my life to ruining Eric's, and am currently succeeding beyond my wildest imagination, phoning him at all hours of the day and night, especially when he is in the shower. But good sport that he is, Eric has told me that I am not responsible for the nervous tic which he has coincidentally developed ever since I signed on with Doubleday. Well, too bad, I guess I will just have to try harder.

Finally, I thank the giver of the Ten Commandments, God Almighty and Creator of heaven and earth, whose loving kindness sustains and nurtures me every day of my life. If not for His infinite patience, would I still be here?

Hoping you all enjoy this book and the life-transforming profundity it contains.

You're all beautiful!

Shmuley

Oxford, England

September 1999

Rise of the "Relationships Rabbi"

I am often asked why I do it. Why give countless lectures, write so many books and essays, join in all those debates, even have the occasional argument with total strangers in the street—and all about sex, marriage, and relationships . . . ? Well, actually, I try to explain, there is a lot more to it than you might think.

"But, Rabbi," goes the inevitable next question, "shouldn't you be writing about something a bit loftier than sex all the time? Say world peace or prayer or charity . . . or the punishment God metes out to congregants who fall asleep during the Rabbi's sermon?"

The answer, quite simply, is no. There are few issues more important and complex than love and marriage, sex and adultery, family life and—the subject of this book—the starting point of the whole business: dating. I am concerned about today's singles. Whereas once upon a time, not long ago, people would date for love, permanence, and commitment, today they date for recreation. Going on a date is like going to a movie (where, not coincidentally, many dates take place)—a time to forget about life and simply have a great time, and maybe a bit of sex to boot. But what are the ramifications of what is effectively a ten-year job interview? Can people really cordon off their twenties for a decade of being evaluated by the opposite sex and still emerge whole and unscarred?

Please do not be put off, dear reader, by the liberal sprinkling of humor found throughout this book. I am so sick and tired of people who take themselves way too seriously. Dating should be an educated, yet pleasurable experience. You have to go out and have fun and make sure the other person has fun. Ironically, the harder you try at succeeding at dating, the more apt you are to fail. Paradoxically, the less you try to impress on a date, the more you eventually will. You have to just let go and be yourself and allow the full vibrancy of the human personality to be manifest. Nothing is more off-putting in a relationship than arrogance and we all have to learn to laugh at ourselves a little. Indeed, the human capacity to jolly self-deprecation is what makes us most attractive to the opposite sex. Consecutive surveys conducted among both men and women confirm what we all already know, that is, that the second most attractive thing about a person on a date is a keen sense of humor. The first most attractive attribute, of course, is their being filthy rich. So, unless you're Bill Gates, you better learn to see the lighter side of life . . . and quick!

Who wants to date anyway?

Generally speaking, there are four possible objectives for dating:
1. You want to have fun. You want an enjoyable day out with a member of the opposite sex. (Your pets no longer want you, in fact they have kicked you out of the house.)
2. You want sex. (You're male.)
3. You want a relationship, but not commitment. (Still a man, huh?)
4. You are evaluating members of the opposite sex for the possibility of lifelong commitment and marriage. (Ah! So now

you're a female . . . or a man who has had a sex-change operation. Or you've got a nagging Jewish mother who tells you that if she doesn't have grandchildren soon, she will impale herself on the nearest sharp object and leave you a lifetime of guilt.)

5. You are doing research for a book on dating (but that's enough about me).

I am often asked if a person should date for sex. My answer? Absolutely! I know *I* dated for sex. So did my wife. But the difference is that we dated in order to find a person with whom to have sex for life, a spouse. And believe me, that's the best sex of all.

You guessed it, my friends. I am one of those bona fide Stone Age religious prudes who believe that sex should be saved for marriage. But before you set fire to the book, hear me out. I do believe that sexual attraction and sexual gratification are essential ingredients for a successful relationship. It's just that sex is such a potent human activity that, if indulged in too soon in a relationship, it can actually be harmful. And the general consensus among relationships experts is swinging my way. For while no one expects to marry a virgin nowadays, most believe that sex should come later, rather than sooner, for the relationship to have any long-term prospects.

But let's give the other side a chance first. Basically, the arguments for having sex while dating, especially early on, are the following:

- You're male. "Get real!" you say. "I'm a man and I got a monster in my pants. What am I meant to do? Get castrated?" (What you're basically saying is "I can't control myself.")
- You're a woman and you have a boyfriend who "can't control himself."
- You're an Australian sheep and have an outback rancher who can't control himself.
- You *both* love sex, find it very pleasurable, and see no real

reason to hold back. "Hell, go for it. That's our philosophy. The more, the merrier!"

• You believe that by withholding sex you might lose your boyfriend or girlfriend, who is panting for it.
• You're a woman who feels that after all the money your boyfriend spends on you, and all the affection he lavishes on you, you have an obligation to "give back" by either having sex with him or doing his laundry. You find sex the less objectionable of the two options.
• You believe that having sex might solve the problems that keep creeping into the relationship.

Okay, enough. Here are the arguments for waiting until you're married, or at the very least having sex at some point *after* the first ten minutes of your relationship.

Sure, many men are indeed highly sexed. They want to have sex as much as possible, with as many different partners as possible. An evolutionist would say that a male looks for the widest possible distribution of his gene pool. Is it any surprise that in the current vernacular of American rap music men are referred to as "dogs" that like "dogging" all day long?

But men are still human beings. They can still exercise self-control and restraint. Your guy uses a knife and fork at the table, doesn't he? He even shaves and showers. He controls his animal instincts in most areas of his life. So why shouldn't he control his sexual urges too? Imagine that you marry him, and in ten years' time he has sex with another woman "because he can't control himself." Would that be acceptable to you? Of course not! Nor should it be acceptable now, when you are trying to build a serious relationship.

But it is a mistake to overemphasize the male sex drive, as if they're the only people who enjoy a bit of slap-and-tickle. The Women's Liberation Movement has led a revolution in women's sexuality, with a new awareness of just how powerful the female libido really is. This is consistent with traditional Jewish thought.

Two thousand years ago the Talmudic sages observed that a woman's sexual drive is actually *stronger* than that of a man. Commenting on God's injunction to Eve (Genesis 3:16) after she ate of the tree of knowledge, *"Your desire shall be for your husband,"* the ancient Rabbis wrote, "This refers to exceedingly strong sexual desire."

The chief difference between male and female sexual desire is that men find it easier to compartmentalize their bodies and their hearts. Women, being far more naturally sexually mature than men, find this compartmentalization difficult, and sometimes impossible. That's why in sexual surveys a huge number of women say that they don't enjoy sex with a man that they don't love.

There is something beautiful about not being able to separate your heart from your body. It means that you have fully integrated your emotions into your whole person. Why would you want to go backward? Why would you want to be as dumb as some men? In fact, I believe that exposure to a loving woman is actually a redemptive act for a man.

Commitment-free sex leads to the separation of our emotions from our senses, and this is why, I believe, so many people who may have been passionate enough in their single years often go off sex once they are married. Numerous meaningless affairs, in which sex is not about love, but just about pleasure, condition their thinking, so that when they want to feel loved, they shut off sexually and just want to be held. Later, the husband complains that his wife is too frigid in bed, when he is the one who turned her off sex by using her for his own selfish urge satisfaction.

There is another reason why sex without commitment causes huge problems in a relationship. Sex creates intimacy. *But only when it comes at the right time.* Otherwise it causes what has come to be known as "the intimacy gap." If you and your boyfriend or girlfriend have only been dating for a month, then you cannot yet be very intimate spiritually and emotionally. But if you have sex, you attain immediate *physical* intimacy. So, on a scale of one to ten, when you are emotionally only at three and you physically jump to a ten, doing things to each other which would make a great new chapter in the *Kama Sutra*, you have a vast intimacy gap separating your hearts and bodies. This creates an asymmetry between body and soul that is jarring and unhealthy. You suffer from an intimacy gap, with all its consequences.

There are usually two consequences that follow from the intimacy gap. The first is confusion, the second is obsession.

The intimacy gap leads to confusion about the relationship because a void has been created. Suddenly, questions arise as to where the relationship is going and what you really feel about your boyfriend or girlfriend. After all, you've had sex. So, do you love each other? This sort of situation is inevitable because your mind does not know how to handle the strange experience of having complete and intimate physical knowledge of a person who is still, essentially, a stranger. In trying to rationalize what you have done, you give yourself a false set of expectations. Well, if we are doing it already, then this relationship must be something special. He must love me, no?

This is why "the morning after" is traditionally such an unpleasant experience. The sex has generated expectations, but the fact remains that you are not really a couple, you have merely shared something very special without being ready for the commitment it should entail. This leads one person in the relationship to want to withdraw—usually the man. After all, he got what he wanted. He captured his quarry. It's time for some other adventures. This isn't because he doesn't care or doesn't love you, but because he feels phenomenal expectations pressing on him to get into a relationship when he himself is not yet ready. Even if neither of you bolts, you will still feel constrained by the strange relationship you have created, which is both intimate and distant, simultaneously.

His choosing to distance himself usually leads to the second consequence, obsession. The woman, still rationalizing that the sex she had is a sure sign of love, begins to pursue him more aggressively. She reasons to herself that sharing a night of sex means that she has found her soul mate. She begins to ask why he has not called, and why he has no time to see her. And the more persistent she becomes, the more elusive *he* becomes. This is not a healthy relationship.

The fact is, men more easily compartmentalize their bodies and their hearts, but women find it very difficult to do so. So, as far as he's concerned, you've only had sex. As far as the woman is concerned, you've experienced intimacy. Your different understanding of what happened is bound to lead to arguments. And if you suppress what you feel, it's bound to lead to resentment.

My advice would be to tell him that, for you, sex is the culmination of the journey of love, and he must first demonstrate his love and devotion to you by a strong act of commitment—a diamond engagement ring will do. When you tell him this, he will either (a) turn blue and pass out, (b) run away faster than a greyhound, or (c) respect you more for what you said and tell you he's happy to wait. Either way, you'll know exactly where you stand.

There are also many people who no longer believe that sex is an important part of a relationship. They say that communication, shared values, similar backgrounds, and similar interests are much more important than attraction or sex. This is nonsense. None of these things has the power to bring forth our strongest, most intense emotions the way sex does.

Therefore, by all means date for sex—but let it be your final destination, at the journey's end once you have chosen each other, not something you jump off for at the first stop. It is imperative that we respect our sexuality and develop its potency to maximize the intimacy and closeness that we feel within a relationship.

If your reason for dating is simply to have sex and fun, you need a video, not a book. You may get a few laughs out of reading this, but until you come to understand your need for something more serious, you're never going to have a real date.

Who needs to be told how to go on a date?

Don't let yourself become a paid-in-full member of the loneliest generation of all time. The greatest human need is to become a need. The truest and innermost human desire is to be desired. The pain of the vulnerability and loneliness of human existence is only assuaged when we find someone who depends on us. If you trade in true happiness, based on human warmth and companionship, in exchange for sexual conquest, material prosperity, or emotional independence, you cheat yourself of the most enriching experience of your life: having one person who wants, loves, and needs you.

Why did you pick up this book in the first place? Of course, you wanted to delve into my words of profound wisdom. Wouldn't anyone? But chances are, you are also reading this book because you are interested in dating. (All right, so you just picked it up at a friend's house because it happened to be the closest thing to the toilet. Okay, okay, don't rub it in.) Perhaps you are disappointed with what you have experienced in life so far. . . . Or perhaps—maybe, just maybe—you have come to recognize that you need something more out of life. You have decided that the time has come for you to look for love, to connect to a person of the opposite sex romantically, emotionally, and sexually. Cherish that feeling of need. It will help you to be a better date, a better lover, a better friend, and, ultimately, a better spouse.

When I told friends that I was writing a dating book based on the Ten Commandments, most of them smiled and some even laughed. (Others cried, "No, not another one of your books on sex. Ugh!") Most of them thought the idea sounded cute, but not real. After all, aren't the Ten Commandments austere laws about religious morality? What can they have to say about the very earthbound hopes and dreams of people trying to find their soul mate—or let's face it, any kind of mate—through dating? Well, the answer is, never underestimate human ingenuity when it comes to making an honest buck.

Okay. That's only partly true. The real truth is that the Ten Commandments were never meant to be a moral code, but rather the ground rules for an archetypal relationship, the love affair between God and people. And matrimony, the fullest expression of love between a man and a woman, is the closest parallel available to us. When a man and woman join in marriage, become one flesh through sex, and create new life through children, they are doing no less than emulating their Creator. As a Rabbi, I serve many functions: counselor to the confused, teacher to the curious, comforter to the sick, and advisor on a slew of different life issues. (Well, that's the idea anyway, even if I personally spend most of my time perfecting my tan.) After more than ten years in the job, I can say unequivocally that I feel closest to the Almighty when I am called upon to perform a wedding, or intervene to try to save a failing marriage. Therefore there is no higher or holier subject for a Rabbi to write about. Case dismissed.

Oh, there is one subject that is loftier, and that is the story of my early childhood. Basically, there is another, more personal reason for my intense preoccupations with marriage and relationships. Readers of my earlier books will know this. My parents divorced when I was eight. Ever since then I have been looking for a way to keep husbands and wives happy together under the same roof for the length of their lives.

At first, I believed that as a child of a broken home, I was cursed. I expected that marriage would be much more difficult for me, and it is a fact that children of divorced parents are statistically twice as likely to divorce themselves. I now know, however, that in a strange way I was blessed. Because I experienced a very turbulent childhood, with the base of my security—two loving parents under the same roof—torn away, I learned what it was to feel vulnerable at an early age. This is what caused me to embark upon a religious odyssey at the age of ten, a journey that culminated in my becoming a Rabbi at the early age of twenty-one. And it also impelled me to marry, also when I was twenty-one. Simply put, I was lonely and experienced the kind of loneliness that neither friendship nor intermittent romantic relationships could possibly assuage. Marriage to Debbie has been my personal salvation, even if she calls it her worst nightmare.

Debbie and I have almost nothing in common, save one thing. We are both peasants. A peasant is the opposite of an aristocrat. Where the aristocrat counts up what he has, and looks for a partner who can match it, the peasant begins with what he lacks. He looks at himself and sees a person who is weak, vulnerable, exposed to the whims and caprices of others. Not having faith in his or her own limited ability, he or she looks to date in order to find a lifelong companion who will make them feel worthwhile, even if the rest of the world dismisses them as unimportant. They are not afraid to tell their lover that, more than loving them, they need them and cannot live without them.

But apart from that—we have nothing in common. I'm quite an unassuming guy, modest and humble, who loves being in the background. Amidst all my other talents, I would say that it is my humility that sticks out most. There is nothing I hate more than recognition, while Debbie needs and craves it. I also hate divulging anything of my personal life, while Debbie is totally public about everything. I love doing housework—ironing, dishwashing, making the kids' school lunches—while Debbie adores clubbing and nights out with the girls. Debbie loves money, while there is nothing that I relish more than taking the last shirt off my back and giving it to the poor. (Okay. Reverse all those things and you'll get the truth.)

But we do share one thing. Lacking completion in ourselves, we find it in one another. Debbie makes me feel whole. She makes my life livable, and without her I could not continue. (Now, will you let me back into the house, dear?) Aside from that, there is absolutely no reason in the world why we should be married.

The Jewish wedding ceremony
and the Sinai Experience

Jews have always recognized the parallel between what happened on Mount Sinai, and the giving of the Ten Commandments, with what happens when a man and woman vow to share the rest of their lives together. What Jews call *Maamad Har Sinai,* the Sinai Experience, is commemorated during the Jewish wedding ceremony.

The wedding canopy, the awning spread over the bride and groom, known as the *chuppah,* symbolizes the way in which Mount Sinai loomed protectively over the Jewish people. The bride is escorted by her father (and in some traditions by both parents) to the wedding canopy, just as Moses led the Jews to Sinai, acting like a chaperone. And because Mount Sinai bloomed for the occasion with beautiful flowers and blossoms, the Jewish wedding canopy is decked in a rich variety of colorful flora.

The relationship guidebook

But there is much more to be learned from the Revelation at Sinai than how to lay on a traditional Jewish wedding ritual like you see in the movies. As you read on, you will discover how the Ten Commandments provide excellent lessons in how you can be truly attractive, poised, exciting, and engaging for your new date.

I won't be telling you "what to do" on your date, like some other self-help books. You know the ones I mean? The kind that are packed with prescriptions for success, insisting you should wear this, do this, remember to do that, and don't forget to say this, but whatever you do, never, ever say that! How can you "just be yourself"—which they all also say is the number one priority, by the way—when you are also trying to implement every other suggestion they make? How can you "just be yourself" when every rule book tells you that if you say the wrong thing your date will grab their steak knife and hack you into millions of pieces—or go home to Mom? It is all so unforgiving. If, God forbid, you call him instead of waiting for him to call you, you've blown it. If she spots your bald patch, forget it, she'll be washing her hair next time you call. If you agree to go out with him one Saturday night when he has only called you on Friday, then shame on you. He'll think no one else is interested in you. Who wants to go out with a girl no other guy wants to date? By the time you see him next, he will have married someone else and had ten kids.

This book is different. I say that for two reasons. First, to make you feel good about having bought it, and second, instead of giving you a long list of things to do when you are on your date, this book will show you how to prepare yourself. I'm telling you that by understanding the true meaning of the Ten Commandments, you can change as a person. Believe me—you won't know yourself. You will become a Prince Charming, or an Enchanting Princess. Most important, by reminding you of your relationship with the Creator of the Universe, and of your own importance in the big scheme of things, this book will provide you with the most important ingredient of all for successful dating: a sense of dignity and self-worth.

No cheesy pickup lines

I lecture to singles groups several times a week on the subject of marriage and relationships, and this gives me a lot of opportunity to observe the modern dating scene. What I witness is an unbelievable lack of confidence. People today seem to have no belief in themselves, and this causes all kinds of confusion and heartache in their search for love. So many young men, for example, find it impossible to muster up the courage simply to walk over to a pretty girl, introduce themselves, and talk to her normally. Instead, they say ridiculous things like "I hope you know CPR, 'cause you take my breath away." We think we've got to come along with all these bells and whistles, say the smart thing, wear the right perfume, have a trendy job, be unbelievably thin, or, at the very least, own a cool pet before anybody is going to be interested in us. Where did we get such a crazy notion?

The most seductive quality of all, by miles, and the most attractive to the opposite sex, is self-confidence. It is achieved when we start to feel good about the direction of our lives. The most attractive type of man or woman walks with their head held high. Not because they have a beautiful face, great figure, or bulging bank account, but because they are simply, quietly confident in their own ability to contribute something positive to life. That is the greatest turn-on of all. The basis of self-confidence is the belief that you have a precious gift to give to the world that cannot be duplicated by anybody else.

The Ten Commandments
summary

And that's where the Ten Commandments come in, because that's exactly what they—through me—are about to give to you, the greatest gift of all, confidence in yourself. Rather than some ridiculous pickup line, this book will give you the stamina to walk up to a woman and say, "Hi, I'm Archibald, but my friends just call me Bald."

I believe that you will be amazed by just how well the Ten Commandments lend themselves to being the ultimate guide to dating. You may never be as dynamic or as good-looking as Charlton Heston when he played Moses in the movie, but after finishing *The Ten Commandments—The Book!* you will be instilled with the mysterious power of the ten greatest secrets of how to make a great relationship:

1. Primacy
2. Exclusivity

3. Confidence
4. Sacred Moments
5. Gratitude
6. Compliments
7. Mystery
8. Sincerity
9. Trust
10. Contentment

Like the Israelites approaching the Red Sea, let's march straight in, and hopefully I will be your Moses and help you part the stormy waters of modern dating. This way, whenever you are experiencing relationship trouble or need advice prior to a really big date, you can simply take the "Two Tablets" and read everything that you will ever need to know.

Trust me. I'm a Rabbi.

Searching for a Soul Mate Rather Than a Partner

Learning to Date as Peasants Rather Than Aristocrats

What God wanted in a relationship

Having given you an earful about the importance of using dating to create the permanent relationship of marriage, I now address what you should be looking for in marriage. In particular, I want to focus on the erroneous modern search for partners rather than soul mates. What's the difference, you ask? Well, I'll tell you.

According to Talmudic legend, the Almighty did quite a bit of "dating" before He settled down into a loving relationship with the Jews. He offered the Ten Commandments to other nations, but was upset when each of them decided that the requirements were not to their liking. For example, the Chaldeans were interested at first, but when they were told that the Torah forbids stealing, they changed their minds. The Egyptians were put off by that pesky prohibition on adultery, and the Syrians were amazed that they were expected not to covet.

But the Jews were not so fickle. When Moses told them that God wanted to give them the commandments, they asked Moses how much they would cost. When he responded that they were free, they said, "Okay, we'll take ten." But humor aside, when Moses asked the Jews if they would accept the Ten Commandments, they responded affirmatively with "We will do and we will try to understand," signifying the need for every relationship to embody the right actions and the right motivations. No petty quibbles from these folks. They were committed to the relationship and they did not care about the conditions.

Okay, on the surface the Jews may not have been the best pick of the nations. They'd been slaves for two hundred years, and even after liberation, they griped continually about going back to the fleshpots of Egypt. And there were so few of them! Only six hundred thousand males of military-service age.

But none of that mattered. God did not choose to love the Jews for their attributes or skills. He chose to love them because they chose to love Him—unconditionally. This is why they said, "We will do" before "we will try to understand." The Jews reassured God that even if they didn't understand why He wanted certain things, they would still always accommodate Him.

The difference between a soul mate and a partner

Today, far too few people date in order to find their soul mate. Instead, they search for a "partner." Because of a fundamental confusion of priorities, these men and women want to find a person who will provide them with many different and superficial things, rather than a companion who will connect with them on the deepest level.

Of course, there is some logic to their thinking. It's very sensible and . . . *businesslike*. Imagine, for example, that a man named Stanley wishes to open a clothing store. Seeing the benefits of not undertaking this mammoth project alone, he seeks first to find a partner. He expects the partner to match his contribution in money, toil, creativity, and enterprise. For this, the partner will receive an equal share in the business.

So Stanley puts twenty thousand dollars into the business, and asks his new partner, Harry, to invest the same amount. Stanley spends fifty hours per week driving around representing the business to clients, and he expects Harry to do the same. This is why they are partners—because they each contribute an equal share to the business.

What if Harry is not as articulate as Stanley? What if his going out and speaking to clients will prove disastrous to the business? No problem, says Stanley to Harry. I'm good at some things, while you're good at others. So I'll put forty hours per week into sales, and I expect you to put an equal amount of time into accounts. Now we have a complementary partnership and that works out fine.

This is how most people go about dating. The first thing they do is determine that marriage is an enterprise that requires two people. Since you are only one person, you require a partner. And what kind of partner should you find? Why, someone who can either match or at least complement your contribution. Hence, all that men and women today aspire to in marriage is simply finding a partner. Not only do these people not *find* their soul mate; they're not even looking. They have settled for something far, far less.

To find the perfect soul mate, you should focus not on what you have, but what you *lack*

Here you have one of the biggest mistakes of all. The way people today look for a marriage partner is by sitting down and making a list of everything they have to contribute to a relationship. So the man sits down and he says to himself, "Well, I'm good-looking, well educated, come from a good family, have a good sense of humor, and have a great job. Therefore, what I'm looking for is someone who at least brings the same contribution to the party. I need a woman who is very pretty, highly educated, from a great family," etc. Although this is the most common form of modern dating, it is also the stupidest. Dating should never begin with a list of what we *have*. Rather, it must begin with making a mental list of what we *lack*. You don't go into a relationship because you *have* something. Rather, you go into a relationship because you are *missing* something. And only by identifying *that one big thing* that we are missing are we guaranteed to find someone who actually makes us feel whole.

In other words, a partner in marriage can give you many things. They can bring with them physical beauty, an income, some decent relatives who aren't all inbred, and an occasional laugh. (Forget about sex once you're married.) But although the partner brings many things, these things are superficial. A soul mate, on the other hand, brings you only one thing. But it is the most vital thing of all—namely, an end to your loneliness and a feeling that you are the most special person in the entire world.

A generation of aristocrats

In my work as a Rabbi at Oxford University and in London, I have noticed a curious phenomenon. The more successful the man or the woman, the more partners they date and the later they marry. They are convinced that their jobs provide them with satisfaction, and because they are good at what they do they hold out for the best. When they feel lonely, they simply go on a shopping spree or to some exotic holiday destination that serves as a distraction.

Our world is hardly recognizable from that of our grandparents, everything has changed drastically. But while most of us focus on technological changes—personal computers and the continuing conquest of space—we ignore the all-important social changes. Ours is a generation in which nearly everyone in the Western world is an aristocrat. Previous generations were not ones of empowerment. There was a small aristocratic class for whom everyone else worked and upon whom everyone was dependent. But while not everyone in the West today is wealthy, the vast majority are self-sufficient. We have our own jobs, own our own homes, can afford to take holidays and buy ourselves nice clothes. We can, thank God, employ other people to help us with the housework and nanny the children. We are the new class of nobility.

But a huge price is being paid by this generation of aristocrats. Whereas poorer classes have traditionally looked for one big thing in the person they date, aristocrats have always looked for many small things. Because people with earning power—aristocrats—have greater choice about their lifestyles, they tend to make a laundry list of things that they would like to find in a relationship and marriage.

These aristocrats, feeling smug about themselves, rarely look to share their lives. They don't feel any great need to search their soul for a soul mate. They earn their own money, own their own cars, have their own circles of friends, and have lived in their own apartments since college. To look for a soul mate would indicate a deep-seated inadequacy that few are prepared to concede. Instead, the aristocrat looks for a "partner."

Therefore, the very first move by the aristocrat who wants to find a companion is to take a look at themselves and list their attributes. A successful woman lawyer today will make the following mental list. I am (1) attractive, (2) well educated, (3) from a good family, (4) possess a good sense of humor, (5) am highly independent, (6) earn $80,000 per year, and (7) am fun to be with. Now, when she dates, she looks for someone to match this contribution in the relationship. She first goes out with a guy who is good-looking, but who earns less than she does. Now that just won't do. Why should he become a fifty percent partner with her in this relationship when the level of his contribution is less? Oh, but there are mitigating circumstances. His job, although it pays less, entails a lot of travel. Now he is back in the running because his contribution is achieving parity with her own.

The proud tradition of aristocratic dating

I know that these calculations may sound silly, but they have been practiced by aristocrats since the beginning of time. The King of England wants to marry off his son. Well, he brings a kingdom to the table plus *x* amount of riches and *x* amount of noblemen who pay him homage and allegiance. He is then introduced to the daughter of the King of France. She also brings a kingdom, but does she bring the same amount of cash and prestige into the relationship as does the Prince? How many ladies-in-waiting are at her beck and call? Well, this will depend on the last battle her father fought and either won or lost. France's navy is currently weak while the Spanish Armada is strong. It's settled then, the Prince will marry an infanta from Spain rather than a princess from France.

All of us are amused by the history of royal weddings over the past thousand years because they were all about business partnerships and political alliances and never about love and relationships. But I can't tell you how many people think this way today as well. I have known hundreds of young people who are university-educated, with good jobs, who go through a laundry list when it comes to managing their romantic lives. They wonder whether or not the person they are dating matches their own contribution to the relationship, or whether they are being cheated into going into a "fifty-fifty partnership" when the other person can only give thirty percent.

Cheated? Yes, *cheated.* This is how they describe it.

Greg met Simone in his first year at Oxford. They fell in love and dated for the next three years. Just before their final examinations they became engaged and seemed deliriously happy. At the engagement party, Greg's parents came over from the States, met Simone, and grew to love her like their own daughter.

But then something terrible happened. While Greg got a first-class degree and was immediately offered a high-paying job at Morgan Stanley, Simone just squeaked by and got a job as a nutritionist. Suddenly Greg's parents changed their tune. They started telling Greg that he might be making a mistake and to think carefully if this was the girl he wanted to marry.

Greg came to see me for advice. I called his parents and asked them what on earth they were doing. "Our son is being cheated," they told me. "This girl is nowhere near as bright as Greg, or as hardworking. Why should our son marry down?"

Why indeed? This logic is not flawed, for it is the thinking of aristocrats. But aristocrats can never be truly happy in love. At best, they can hope for a harmonious partnership. Those who wish to find a soul mate in their relationships are a completely different breed of person.

Indeed, they are the polar opposites of aristocrats. They are "peasants."

The needy, beautiful peasant

The peasant has an entirely different orientation in dating. Rather than begin with what he *has*, he begins with what he *lacks*. He looks at himself and he sees a person who is vulnerable, who is exposed to the whims and caprices of others, whose life turns on a dime from great joy to possible tragedy.

And he feels lonely. Not having complete faith in his own ability, he or she dates in order to find a lifelong companion who will make them feel profoundly worthwhile, even if the rest of the world dismisses them as unimportant. For him, love is a salvation, not a luxury. The nobleman who owns this person will insult and abuse him and tell him he's worthless. But when he comes home to his wife, she will refute the nobleman's words and make him feel like a king.

Whereas the aristocrat dates and marries for many small things, the peasant dates and marries for one big thing: someone who takes away the pain and makes life a celebration. In choosing a soul mate rather than a partner, the peasant is given the greatest gift of all, someone who holds him, takes away the pain of living, and gives him happiness and pleasure instead.

The peasant, with his shabby clothes and tiny hut, has a one-word advantage over the aristocrat that makes all the difference in a relationship—namely, humility. The peasant is not afraid to acknowledge his profound dependency on others. And this is what makes him such a great lover. He is not afraid to tell a woman that, more than loving or admiring her, he needs her and cannot live without her.

Confessions of a Hasidic aristocrat

I joined a Hasidic community of my own choice. Not having received the depth and breadth of Jewish education they had, I sat in the Talmudic seminary late into the night watching television, uh, I mean studying, long after most of the other boys were asleep or chatting in the dormitory.

By the age of nineteen, I had caught up and was rewarded by being chosen to go with nine other homegrown Lubavitcher boys as emissaries to Sydney, Australia, to found the city's first ever rabbinical training college. I was proud of myself and, little by little, it went to my head. It was there that I wrote my first book, a study on Jewish dream interpretation, which, thank God, sold so well that the initial printing of five books soon had to be doubled.

By the time I returned to New York two years later, I was more than a little convinced of my own importance.

I decided that the time had come for the prince to marry. A couple I had known in Sydney recommended that I take out their daughter, Debbie, and I agreed. She was nice enough, but did not have the qualifications that I felt someone of my standing deserved. She lacked "pedigree": her father, while a highly respected physician, was not a famous Rabbi, and she did not come from an aristocratic Jewish family. Hell, they didn't even have a television in every room of the house. The only thing going for her was that she was a thoroughly decent, modest, and kind human being who had an immense capacity to love.

But who gave a damn about that? This was not what my ego was looking for. It was looking for status. In other words, she was not "the best" and I felt that after all my hard work that was what I deserved. I wanted all my friends at the rabbinical seminary to admire and envy me for my woman of choice. But Debbie could not even drive, for goodness' sake! She had never written a book, nor could she get up in front of a public audience and give a great lecture. "Why should I marry her?" I asked myself.

I still remember the day when my aristocratic delusions crashed around me, when I realized my true neediness, the shocking fact that I was actually a peasant in this lonely world. I finally had a mature perspective on marriage, and appreciated my opportunity to grab hold of the one human being who could assuage my loneliness.

A day to give thanks for

It was Thanksgiving Day 1987, and Debbie was with me in Miami Beach. We had been dating for a few weeks, but I had already decided in my heart that she was not the one for me, that by marrying her I would be cheating myself out of someone far more prestigious. That day I took Debbie to a Thanksgiving lunch that was being given by my sister and brother-in-law, and was attended by all my immediate family. I felt sad but self-assured. I liked Debbie a lot and didn't want to hurt her, but now that I had made up my mind, I felt content. I had achieved a sense of clarity and was happy that I was going to get on with my life. I decided to dump her after lunch, and had prepared a characteristically compassionate speech. "Debbie," I was going to say, "thanks for the laughs and the good times, but I decided that you should marry someone of your own lowly standing. So long, adios, ta-ta, bye, later." That wouldn't hurt too much, I thought, and patted myself on the back for being such a gentleman.

As we sat and ate our Thanksgiving turkey, I suddenly felt an excruciating pain coming from my nether regions—the region of my anatomy that no self-respecting Rabbi would write about in a book. I had had surgery near the area back in Sydney (no, it was not a penile elongation procedure—thank you very much!). Well, they operated, and things came out much better than before.

So here I was six months later sitting in Miami having not had a hint of discomfort since. And yet I was now about to pass out from the awful pain I felt down under. I was sure that some primitive outback Australian imbecile doctor, whose mother was also his aunt, had left some minor surgical tool or the daily newspaper in my lower abdomen. It kicked so much I thought it might even be a kangaroo.

I did not want to destroy the festive lunch, so I whispered in my mother's ear that I was going to drive myself to Mount Sinai Hospital's emergency unit. You'd think that being a Jewish mother she would care, even a little. But no such luck.

"What's wrong, Shmuley?" she asked, chewing on a corncob.

"Ah, not much, Mom. I'm pretty sure I'm dying, but it's nothing too serious. I'm going to drive myself to the hospital. You don't have to come."

"Well, okay, Shmuley. Have a nice time."

"Thanks a lot, Mom," I moaned, as I crawled toward the door in agony. "Thanks for all the care and support. And if I never see you again, Mom, I just want to thank you for allowing me to live in the attic after I could no longer afford the rent in the house, as a little boy."

"Don't mention it, son. After all, what are mothers for. Goodbye," said my mother, as she poured cranberry sauce over her turkey. "Mom, what's wrong with Shmuley?" asked my sister, Ateret. My mother stared blankly at Ateret for a moment before she realized what she was talking about. "Oh, it's nothing, he may be dying. He's going to the hospital. Pass the gravy."

By now, I had reached the door. Seeing this, Debbie sprang to her feet. "Where are you going?" she asked.

I was embarrassed. I couldn't possibly tell her that the chances were that I was already a eunuch. "Uh, well, uh, I have this terrible pain in my lower abdomen from an operation I had in Sydney, so I'm just going to drive myself to the hospital," I muttered, trying to smile casually through gritted teeth.

"I'm a doctor's daughter," she told me. "Show me where it hurts and maybe I can help."

"Uh, thanks for the offer," I yelped, "but it's sort of private. Man stuff, you know." My family was now arguing over who would get my few private effects. I rushed to the car, Debbie chasing after me. "I'm coming with you to Emergency. I insist!" And she jumped into the car.

A few minutes later, I was being examined by a nurse who nearly passed out when she saw the grotesque inflammation of the region concerned. "Oh my God, oh my God." "This is no time for compliments," I told her. "This is an emergency." "I don't know what to do!" she exclaimed. "We have only a skeletal staff because of Thanksgiving. What you have looks really serious. Maybe it's even too late." She then took out some oil, gave me extreme unction, and asked me if I renounced Satan. I told her that she had the wrong religion. "Just get me a doctor," I hollered at the top of my lungs.

"Well, we need a specialist urologist and he's currently on the golf course and can't be disturbed," she answered.

"Surely there is someone in all of South Florida who can save my life!" I hollered, and that sent her scurrying off to the phones. I was sure that I only had a few moments left to live, and what a way to spend it, half naked on a cold bed in an impersonal hospital.

To increase the humiliation, the caring American health service then kicked in. An elderly woman, so old that she had advised Noah on which types of wood were most water-resistant, came into the room.

"Hi, I'm Agatha from Billing. Do you have an account with us?" she inquired.

"An account?" I screamed. "What kind of account?"

"Why, a charge account, of course. Do you come here regularly?" she asked.

"No," I explained, panting heavily against the pain. "It isn't every day that I expect my anatomy to blow up like the Hindenburg!"

*"Oh, I see," she answered calmly. "Well, let me tell you about our special charge options. You can go for the PPP, Partial Pain Plan. It's our special discount plan that gives you half the medication you need and entitles you to three monthly hospital visits, all for the low introductory fee of $700 per month, and we throw in a free manicure if you sign on today. Or you can always choose my own favorite, the DEAD plan, **Doesn't End** until **After** your **Demise,** for the special low price of just $57 per month. The DEAD plan also covers mortuary expenses."*

Now I knew I was in hell. "How much would you charge me for a single cyanide pill?" I yelled beseechingly. "I prefer death to this." Highly offended, she left the room.

I did not want to spend my last few miserable moments on this earth alone, so I threw something on and walked barefoot to the entrance, where Debbie was anxiously waiting and asked her to come back to the room. There I sat with her, tears started rolling down her cheeks, as she repeatedly asked if there was anything she could do. "Could you look after my pet goldfish?" I asked, momentarily forgetting in my delirious state that I had no goldfish.

In those few moments, I was a changed man and I understood exactly what life was all about. Gone was my arrogance. I was lucky to have this caring woman at my side. How much more miserable I would have been had I been sitting there alone. "Do you have a charge card?" I asked sensitively.

Why do we not want to die alone but are prepared to live alone?

It was at that point that I realized that none of us, NONE OF US, wishes to die alone, and yet we're prepared to live alone. And the reason for the discrepancy is that while alive we're full of ourselves, our own dreams, our own ambitions, and intoxicated with our own sense of success and independence, we don't seek to share our lives with others.

But at moments of infirmity, disease, and the prospect of death, God forbid, we suddenly feel what was true all along: that we're all vulnerable and in need of a warm human body to take away the pain. Debbie's capacity for giving at that moment completely overwhelmed me and made me forget just how ill I was. With her by my side, things just didn't seem that bad.

I turned to her and told her that I was sorry that I had to die but that it was nothing personal. She said not to worry, that dates die on her all the time—some by their own hand—and she wouldn't take it as an insult. She then said that we should both say a short prayer for my recovery, maybe I could live after all. I responded that life sucked and death was a better alternative. She could not know how much of this revolved around the potential loss of what Woody Allen describes as his "second favorite organ."

However, then Debbie smiled at me, and I suddenly felt a warm sense of optimism spread through my heart. Perhaps I would survive, after all. With Debbie next to me, I suddenly wanted to live!

It was then that one of the strangest marriage proposals in all history was made. "Look, Debbie," I said sheepishly. "If I get through this, and I mean not only survive but with all of me intact, then I pledge, God willing, to marry you—that is, if you will have me."

Still crying and not knowing exactly what I was referring to, she accepted. "It would be my greatest pleasure." Now I really hoped that everything would still hang on.

About thirty minutes later, a highly irate-looking doctor came rushing into the room, still with golf gloves on his hands, vanquishing any hopes I had of encountering the compassionate side of the American medical profession. "Where's the little jerk who ruined my Thanksgiving?" he shouted.

I apologized profusely for dying during his golf game. He refused to accept.

"Okay, show me the offending organ," he barked. "Organ?" Debbie asked. "You mean lower abdomen, don't you?" "Who is this woman?" he thundered. "Get out of here, unless you enjoy this kind of thing." Debbie quickly hurried out.

I undressed and he examined me. First he turned a deep shade of red, then purple, and finally blue. "That's what you brought me to see? You little sissy! That's nothing more than an inflammation, an infection. Most guys would be thankful. What's wrong with you?"

So my life was saved from illness, but there was still the probability that before the doctor left he would kill me himself. I pleaded for mercy. "But, but, even the nurse thought it was really serious," I stammered. "Nurse, shmurse, what does she know?" he stormed.

He quickly scrawled a prescription for medication. "Here," he growled. "Take two of these every day for a month. And don't ever call me during a golf game or the next ball I use with these clubs won't be a golf ball." I thanked him and promised to name my first three children after him. He rushed back to the golf course.

Debbie ran in, with a better understanding of what was truly going on. "Is it okay . . . uh, oops, I mean, are you okay?" "Yeah, yeah, I'm fine," I told her. And I really was. I had lived to see another day, and I now knew who I was going to marry.

But suddenly it was Debbie who was not so sure. "Shmuley," she said hesitatingly. "You know, about that marriage thing . . . Well, as I said, I have accepted and all that. But are you still capable of having children, or will we have to go to a sperm bank?"

Six months later we were married in Debbie's native Sydney, and the rest is history. Thank God, we never did have to go to the sperm bank. The fact that each of our six children looks totally different—the oldest Native American, the second Scandinavian, the third Asian, and so on, is entirely coincidental. Neither should any inference be drawn from the fact that each of our children has a different last name.

I really believe that had I not suffered this horrid episode, I would never have settled for someone like Debbie. Instead I would have been like most other people these days, the aristocrats who search for someone who will advance them in social standing and career. I would have continued to date and date always believing that by doing so I was slowly getting closer to "the best." This brief experience, all of which is true with only minor embellishments (and if you believe that, I have a really nice condominium in Bosnia that I'm looking to unload), taught me that marriage is about one big thing, and not twenty insignificant and incidental things. It is about addressing the human depth crisis. It is about having someone who appreciates you for what you are rather than what you can do.

But in order to appreciate your need for a soul mate, you must first go out into the wilderness. God gave the Jewish people the Ten Commandments specifically in the Sinai desert as He could not relate to them while they were still in the fleshpots of Egypt. They first had to experience their dependency on God for their very lives. You too will not find a soul mate until you feel yourself to be in the wilderness, dependent on another human being for earthly love and comfort.

Compatibility is overrated

A soul mate is someone who provides you with one thing—an end to life's loneliness, a feeling that you are now complete and can face the world.

I'm not saying that it's a bad thing to share commonalities with the person you marry. On the contrary, it's definitely an advantage. But having only that without having a soul mate who addresses our deepest need to feel whole and complete is like a man bragging about a beautiful car that he has on display in a personal showroom. It may have a beautiful body—but it has no engine.

So while being able to discuss which laxative works best, and which brands of chili dogs don't give indigestion, is highly important in marriage, this can never serve as a workable substitute for the simple need to find a soul mate who addresses our deepest human loneliness and pain.

This is why it is so stupid to avoid dating a person because they are not "compatible" with your superficial requirements such as good looks or earning power. A beautiful person can fall in love with Quasimodo, and a spiritual person can date a very materialistic person. For example, I have seen wonderful marriages between go-getter, investment banker types and very spiritual, deeply religious Christians. In fact, materialistic people often find something very redeeming and grounding in marrying spiritual people. And as far as looks are concerned, hell, if my wife (who is pretty) can love me, then there's hope for everyone!

The practical acid test

How do you know that you have found the right person for you? That you have found true love? How do you distinguish between having a partner and having a soul mate?

The difference is found in passivity and silence. If you always have to act in order to have stimulation in your relationship, if you feel you always have to talk and impress each other, regale each other with exciting tales, hot gossip, and funny jokes, then you have a partner. Your relationship is not so different from that of two business partners who work together and always try to prove to each other how much they are contributing to the business.

But if you can simply hold each other, saying absolutely nothing, and still the pain goes away, then you have a soul mate. He or she knows your thoughts and secrets without your expressing them, and shares a love with you that empty platitudes and clichés can never capture.

A woman sits at work, feeling overwhelmed by all her responsibilities. Her boss is nasty today and her colleagues make her feel inadequate. Suddenly she closes her eyes and thinks about her husband. It so happens that he is not in town at that moment. He is on a business trip. She can't even reach him by phone because he's running from city to city.

And yet, *the mere thought of him,* the knowledge that he exists, that he belongs to her, and that he loves her, is enough to take away the pain. She gains strength from knowing that he is out there and that together they are a unity, a couple. But for a woman who is in a partnership things are different. Only when he calls and soothes her does she feel okay. Only in his embrace does she feel comforted.

When you find your soul mate, you don't even need to hear their voice or feel their caress in order to find comfort. The pain goes away just by knowing that they love and care for you, even if you are separated by thousands of miles.

You know you have a soul mate when you want to share with them everything you experience.

One of the most important things to ask yourself in a relationship, to see if you really care about your girlfriend or boyfriend, is whether you miss them when you are not around them. Do you pine and ache and feel less complete? When you see something beautiful, like a sunrise, do you miss them and wish they were with you to share it? When something good happens, do you immediately want to tell them about it? When you see her smile, or hear him laugh, does that make you happy? If the answer to these questions is yes, then you have found your soul mate.

You will want to share everything with your soul mate. All of a sudden, living on your own will seem strange. Because now they complete you, and without them even when you're having a great time you still feel like something is missing.

One of the ways you can identify your soul mate is that they bring out the best in you. Your greatest attribute, whether it is being loving and compassionate, strong and disciplinarian, tenacity, intelligence, or emotion, your soul mate brings it out. They might not bring out all the little things, but they bring out the best in your soul.

A soul mate complements you in the deepest way. What you once lacked, he or she now brings to your life. Your soul mate improves you as a person, and enables you to accomplish things you only dreamed of.

Finally, when you find your soul mate, you will see his or her faults. Love is not blind. You will be aware that your soul mate lacks so much in so many areas of life. But that won't matter at all. Because you will know that you need each other, that you belong with one another, and that together you will overcome all obstacles. Like the love of a parent for a child, whereby notwithstanding whatever faults exist the parent can contemplate no other, when you find your soul mate you know that your search is over. In a strange and mysterious way, true love consists of the choice to give up choice.

A soul mate is not someone who is perfect, but someone who is perfect for you.

According to Jewish tradition, your soul mate has already been chosen for you, and is out there right now. That is why Judaism refers to a person's soul mate as his or her *bashert,* or predestined one. According to rabbinical legend, before we are born, an angel named Achzariel announces who we are going to marry. The Cabbalists, the Jewish mystics, took this a step further by saying that each of us came from a soul that was separated in heaven, with one half placed in us and the other in a member of the opposite sex. It is up to us to find that special person here on earth. Until we find them, we are only a half.

When you find your soul mate, being with them is the fulfillment of a promise made in heaven. You will want to be with your soul mate always, as you will know that is your destiny.

The dreaded cold feet in dating

Unfortunately, all too often men and women will pass up the opportunity to commit to their soul mate because they get cold feet. Suddenly you doubt whether you are truly in love. Sure, you "love" the person, you feel content with them, but are you sure that you are "in love"? "What if this is a terrible mistake?" you ask yourself anxiously.

Relax! That's your fear talking, not your heart. If your boyfriend or girlfriend matches up to the description of a soul mate in this chapter, then they're your soul mate. It's that simple. You are meant to be with them, and it would be a tragedy for you to ruin that by giving way to your anxiety. Marriage is not an undertaking based on certainty but is rather, as Dr. Samuel Johnson said, "the triumph of hope over experience."

Final words: marriage is not an occupation, but a calling

I often ask people, "Aren't you going to get married?" At that point I hear a strange response: "When I meet the right person." Sure, the idea is reasonable, but the sentiments are rarely so. Usually what I am hearing is a person telling me that they are waiting for a person to come along and impress them with their eligibility. This is the thinking of aristocrats, and leads nowhere.

In dating, you should always be a peasant. If you insist on being an aristocrat, you will focus entirely on what you want, what you deserve. In the process, you will overlook what you *need.* You are too self-centered, too focused on yourself, to truly evaluate the person you're with. You are sure to miss the person who is perfect for you. You blow it because you are so preoccupied with yourself. You will squander your time on endless dating—enjoying a variety of fleeting encounters and relationships. But you will never settle down. At least, not until social pressure and the desire to "settle down" take over. And by then, you'll be lucky if you have indeed found the "right person" to make a life with.

So, instead, forget about all your achievement, credentials, money, prospects, and expectations. Be a peasant. Be humble, and search only for that person who makes you feel needed, and whom you need in the deepest, most profound way. Pretend you have nothing to show for your life. Face up to the fear, loneliness, vulnerability, and despair that lie under each and every one of us, and embrace them. Your job is nothing but a job. Stop getting so much fulfillment from it. Look to people rather than career for comfort. For now, you know how much you lack, and how much you need another person to fulfill you. Go out there and find your soul mate.

o n e

Primacy

Make Your Date Know That He or She Comes First

To do something, say something, see something, before *anybody* else—these are things that confer a pleasure compared with which other pleasures are tame and commonplace, other ecstacies cheap and trivial.
  —Mark Twain (1835–1910), U.S. author.
  The Innocents Abroad

THE FIRST COMMANDMENT: I am the Lord your God, who brought you out of the land of Egypt, from the house of slavery . . . (Exodus 20:2)

That's one hell of an introduction, isn't it? No goofy pickup line, just straightforward, personal information—the *tachless,* as we say in Jew talk. We hear the confidence in this introduction and think, "Wow, this God is one cool customer . . ."

I was fifteen years old when I decided that God was cool and that I was going to be a Rabbi, and so I went to a seminary in

California. (Almost the only issue that united my divorced parents was mutual hostility to the path I had chosen in life. Becoming a Rabbi is no job for a nice Jewish boy. If you are really bright, you become an investment banker. If you have some gentile genes mixed into you, a doctor. If your mother smoked heavily while she was pregnant with you, you become an accountant. And if you were kicked in the head by a mule when you were two, you become a Rabbi. Hence, every Jewish parent who has a child who has become a Rabbi lies about it and says that he is a truck driver or a sheep shearer instead.)

At Yeshiva, the seminary, there were approximately fifty young men, and, being far away from our families, we soon bonded and made friends. My closest friend of all was a boy named David. On his fifteenth birthday we gave him a little party. Well, we went around the room and we each toasted him. After seventy-odd toasts he became very drunk. Then we took him back to his room and tried to put him to bed.

In the midst of this process, he suddenly became incredibly lucid. He got out of his bed, placed his hands on both my shoulders, and said, "Shmuley, I have something of the greatest importance to tell you." He spoke with the authority of a prophet. "You are the Messiah, Shmuley. I have been sent as a messenger of God down to this earth to reveal to you that you are the chosen, long-promised redeemer of Israel. I've waited fifteen years to reveal this to you, because the time was not yet ripe. Now, the age of redemption has come." We all laughed out loud and told him he was crazy. Then we took off his shoes and tried to stick him back in bed. But he resisted all our efforts. Light shone from his face. "I'm telling you, Shmuley," and here he started to cry, "you are the Messiah and your task is to redeem the Jewish people and remove iniquity from the earth—like trying to get Barry Manilow to stop singing. It's you. You can't shirk your responsibility. God has authorized me to provide a sign that what I'm saying is true." And with that he began to string together complex mystical names of God from the Hebrew alphabet. None of us were laughing anymore. The other boys were transcribing his words, letter by letter. It all made sense. He had revealed a holy new name for God according to the ancient cabbalistic formula.

Having accomplished his mission, David's soul was called on high, at least for the night, and he promptly fell asleep. The other boys looked at me with awe. I was the most special boy on the planet, born to bring deliverance to all the inhabitants of the earth. Everything my mother had always been telling me was true. My head swelled to the size of a watermelon and I couldn't fit through the door. The Messiah. Me. Right on!

I swore the other boys to secrecy. They were frightened and quietly withdrew. I paced the floor, wondering how to handle things. First I would probably have to retreat to some cave and fast for forty days and forty nights. No doubt Elijah the prophet would soon appear to me and provide further instruction. With this in mind I stayed up the whole night preparing a plan for what would have to be achieved for the perfection of the earth. I made a list. As far as I can remember, it was something like this:

1. End all conflict and usher in a period of world peace.
2. Rid the earth of disease.
3. Resurrect the dead (tough one).
4. Bring back John and reunite the Beatles.
5. Eradicate country music from the earth's airwaves.

Boy, was I going to be busy. I decided that the first thing that I would do in the morning was to call Ronald Reagan—who was our President at the time—and tell him I was the Messiah, but make sure he kept it a secret. Better to have him as an ally. I was a bit worried about all the innocent lives I might have to destroy in Las Vegas. It's hell being the Messiah.

By the morning David had sobered up and remembered nothing of the night before. The other boys rechecked the supposed new mystical name of God that he had revealed in the night,

*and discovered the letters actually came out as something like
IMFULLACRAP. All awe and reverence for me instantly van-
ished. I was the laughingstock of the school. My Messianic mission was over, having lasted a measly eight hours.*

But the point of the story is that I had stayed up all night, at the
age of fifteen, and was prepared to take upon myself an immense
amount of work and global responsibility, just because someone
had made me feel special.

It's something we all need and search for. The greatest human
need is to feel unique, distinguished and special. But the secret of
life is that you can never feel special on your own. It takes a
stranger with free choice to *choose us* in order to feel special. We
want someone who confirms our sense of uniqueness. This desire
to be accorded primacy, to be treated as Number One, at least by
one other human being, is one of the deepest human desires. So
strong is it that when we find someone who makes us feel this way,
we are sometimes prepared to give up everything else.

The First Commandment is the only one that commands . . .
nothing. But there is an important message hidden here. By simply
declaring His identity—"I am the Lord your God"—God is teaching us that primacy is the first rule of a new relationship. He does
not have to embellish this with any specific demands for devotion
or worship. Once primacy is given, love and respect follow naturally. It was through acknowledging God's essential, irrefutable
primacy in their lives that the Jews at Sinai began to build indissoluble ties in their relationship with Him—ties that bind us to this
day.

Primacy—the first rule
of dating

So that's where you start. Make the person you are dating know
that you think that there is no one like them. Give your boyfriend

or girlfriend precedence, make them feel that they are more important than everything else. Coming even five minutes late to a date is basically a statement that something more important than them came up. Don't do it.

> *One morning in synagogue I met with Max, a highly successful merchant banker. He looked unhappy, and confided that he had been arguing with his fiancée. "I've been coming home late from work a lot recently, and have canceled several of our dinner dates. I've tried to explain to her that with the economic problems in Asia nowadays, I have to stay at work until trading opens in Tokyo."*
>
> *"But it's not yet the end of trading in Asia. Why are you here and not at the office?" I asked.*
>
> *"Well, I have to make time for God," he replied, looking puzzled.*
>
> *I told him, "Your fiancée will soon be your wife, and that relationship is no less important than religion. In the Ten Commandments, God places our obligations to our fellow man alongside our obligations to Him. You should make your meetings with her as high a priority as praying in synagogue."*

I've noticed that women especially hate the feeling that their boyfriends compartmentalize their dating. "I'll see when I have time, but work comes first." Remember, boys—and girls—your date could become the most important person in your life. It's just plain silly to make them unhappy when they have so great a capacity to make you happy.

Giving yourself to your date

Notice that the First Commandment states, "I am the Lord *your* God," rather than simply "I am God." Here the Almighty demonstrates His closeness to us, His connection with us. He is not too far above us to say that He is ours. He belongs to us. It is the generosity and intimacy of this statement that persuades us to give Him primacy in our lives.

A woman may think that her boyfriend is handsome, kind-hearted, or a good earner, but this will not distinguish him in her mind. Indeed, she will know that there are certainly better-looking, kinder, and higher-earning guys out there. But only her man is *hers*. It is this basic fact that makes him the most important thing in her life. Nothing you can buy will impress her more than the gift of yourself. This is the giving that engenders commitment.

Spend time together

You and your date are important to each other because of the simple fact that you have decided to spend time together. Let's face it, singles have it good. Here you are, totally free, living in your own apartment, with a decent, well-paid job. You come and go when you want. You socialize with whom you please, you see the movies that you like most. You frequent the restaurants that best cater to your personal palate. You visit the friends and relatives you choose, whenever you wish. Why on earth would you want to ruin that ideal lifestyle by entering into a partnership with someone else, especially a commitment like marriage? Why give up your freedom? Have you lost your mind? Once you do that, you can no longer dictate your own schedule. You have a partner to think of as well.

Why are we prepared to do this? Why would we give up all our freedom and the power of directing our own lives merely in order to share it with someone else?

The answer is simple. We never really wanted freedom anyway. That was never our deepest desire. Deep inside, we all hope that we are somehow unique, irreplaceable. Feeling special is an essential part of our survival instinct. Moreover, it is actually true. It's real. God has counted the hairs on your head.

But the paradoxical thing is that while we feel on the inside that we are unique, it takes someone on the outside to confirm it. Don't believe the modern-day psychobabble that it's enough in life to love and appreciate yourself. Balderdash! We all need someone to give us a pat on the back and tell us we are wonderful. We are nothing without love and appreciation. Notice, I don't say approval. You have to have inner convictions in life, and you shouldn't just search for approval. But you do need appreciation and to be told by an external party that you are indeed loved, that time with you is what makes life worth living.

Being the one and only

From the first date, when a man asks a woman to spend time with him, she feels distinguished by the fact that he could have asked anyone—but chose her. When a woman agrees to the date, the man feels honored and gratified. She could have refused, but chose to accept. Paradoxically, in order to establish a relationship and thereby enhance our lives, we must first risk personal destruction. In other words, before bringing another person into our lives, we must be willing to risk rejection. When dating becomes a devoted and loving relationship, men and women constantly remind one another of this. They have chosen to be together, and the importance of making that first choice is immense. It makes worthwhile any loss of personal freedom and the challenges and worries about moving into a more binding relationship. But if you make your date subordinate to all other concerns, if you deny them their right to primacy, then they have little incentive to give up their freedom in order to make you happy.

Don't interrupt

The sages explain that when God spoke at Sinai the earth was utterly silent:

> *When the Holy One, Blessed be He, presented the Torah, not a bird chirped, not a fowl flew, not an ox lowed, not an angel ascended, and not even a seraph proclaimed, "Holy." The sea did not roll and no creature made a sound. All of the vast universe was silent and mute.* (Midrash Rabbah)

The lesson here is never to interrupt your date. One of the mistakes that some people make is that they don't stop talking on a date. They love the sound of their own voice. Women especially complain that men love talking about themselves, and rarely listen. Man or woman, yours was not the voice that thundered forth from Sinai. So start falling in love with the sound of your date's voice and let them be heard.

> *Carol told me about her date with a computer programmer, Simon, who talked for five straight hours about why the UNIX operating system is better than Windows. She was finally forced to take drastic action. She held a knife to his chest and threatened to cut out his heart if he said one more word. So take a breather.*
>
> *My friend Gary lost the opportunity for romance with a gorgeous woman. Gary is a brilliant Oxford scholar, and he asked a ballerina to have dinner with him. She accepted. Because he has a Ph.D., he assumed he was much cleverer and wittier than she was, so he talked down to her. After one hour at the dinner table, she asked him to please take her home. "What's wrong?" he asked.*
>
> *"I have never in my life met a man so full of himself as you. I'm going to leave now so that I won't come between you and your self."*

The date was over. Gary blew it. No matter how smart, rich, or beautiful you are, your date must be given primacy.

I have personally endeavored night and day to wean myself off this terrible habit of cutting people off when they speak. To be sure, what I have to say is so much more interesting and important. But even so, you have to show some respect to lesser mortals. Alas, I have failed miserably. But you don't have to. The most eloquent way to show your respect for another person is to let them speak and *listen*. Bite your tongue, chew on your lip, take a laxative—do whatever is necessary to suppress the urge to talk all about yourself and show your date that you are more interested in learning who *they* are.

"I am the Lord your God, who brought you out of the land of Egypt"

Ancient Egypt was a land obsessed with death, a place where the manner in which a man was buried was more significant than how he lived. You are familiar with the great pyramids, the tombs of the mummified Pharaohs, glorified shrines to death.

I want to use the metaphor of coming out of Egypt, as coming out of old, or dead, relationships. Egypt = Ex. When two people have fallen in love and become one, there can be no separation without amputation. A breakup is a form of bereavement. It represents death, in a sense, the death of love, and the pain it causes cannot be underestimated. A man or woman who suffers a breakup will often stop eating and sleeping. Some become suicidal. Even when they do recover, they often emerge from the experience burdened and scarred with the hurt and bitterness of the past, not elated by the hope and promise of the future.

Michelle came to me looking distraught. She had recently broken up with a man who, after three years with her, had refused to even discuss marriage. I knew she felt she had made the right decision, and was surprised to see her in this state.

"What is wrong with me?" she demanded. "Since the breakup I've gone out with lots of wonderful men. Yet, although I try to be pleasant, I can't help acting aloof and cynical in their presence. Already, two men I really liked have not invited me out again."

"You must understand what a huge trauma you've been through," I said. "A breakup demands a mourning period, like any other form of bereavement. You'll just have to be a little less sociable for a while."

Some people date and break up so frequently that they become hardened; they don't realize the harmful effect having their heart broken has on them. They pick up the pieces and glue them back together so they can go straight into the next relationship. But the cracks are still there and they are all too obvious. In this condition, it is hardly fair of them to expect the dating to go as well as it should.

If you have just ended a romance or are still recovering from a past love, you need some healing from the effects of coming out of Egypt. Even the Israelites needed forty years in the desert before going to the promised land. After the breakup of an ex, everybody needs a break. You have to achieve proper closure on your past life. The best way to achieve this is often to talk—endlessly. The right person to talk to is not your new romance. You need to have a patient Moses to talk to, someone to bring you out of Egypt. You need someone who brings a redemptive and soothing quality into your life, perhaps a professional counselor, religious advisor, or simply a good friend—someone who can help you get over the pain, lead you out of Egypt. So be prepared to spend time in the wilderness. Don't rush into the next affair.

The Jewish religion mandates a mourning period after a bereavement of social withdrawal, affording the individual the opportunity to recover before they have to smile at strangers and laugh at acquaintances' jokes. Grant yourself a healing period.

Coming out of Egypt can also be a metaphor for separating yourself from your old ways of life. If you are going to date seriously, you may have to drop some things that would make your date feel that you don't have the time to spare for a serious commitment. If you are too steeped in your own concerns, enmeshed in or enamored of your past, to ever want to share your life with someone else, this will soon show. You've got to first come out of Egypt.

The joy of dating

God is telling us in the First Commandment not only that He has taken us out of Egypt but also that He will help us out of our sorrows and elevate us to a plain of joy.

One of the most effective ways to win over someone's heart is to raise him or her above their everyday troubles. Life is painful and lonely for us all at times. Our problems can seem huge and unbearable, even if they seem laughably small to someone else. Be empathetic, no matter how trivial you think your date's complaint is. When she says how much she hates her parents for not making her trust fund available to her until her sixteenth birthday, don't give her a lecture on global poverty, just deliver a very caring and compassionate look and say, "I hate them already, the diabolical monsters." Always focus on entertaining your date.

If you give someone a thoroughly enjoyable time, make them laugh and help them to forget their worries for a while, they will always want your company. They will associate you with joy, and may come to think of the rest of their life without you as empty and meaningless. Conversely, if you only use your date as an opportunity to unload your troubles, don't be surprised if the next time you invite them out, they are too busy washing their hair.

Remember your date's name and use it often

In his First Commandment, God introduces Himself by name, and He calls His people by name. Someone who uses your name makes you feel warm, like a caress. Calling someone by name calls on something very deep in them. So rather than saying, "You know, I was thinking that maybe we should go to the sea on Sunday," try "You know, Dan, I was thinking . . ." (When he reminds you that his name is Tom, not Dan, just say, "Yeah, whatever. Anyway, I was thinking . . .")

Or you could try this:

"My what an unusual name. It's very beautiful. It just flows off my tongue. What does it mean?"

This statement will usually elicit one of the following responses:

(1) "Really, have you never heard the name Mary before?"

(2) "Thank you. My name, Mardisbapagolojurang, is West African and means 'She who cuts off the testicles of those who do not call her the morning after.'"

Or (3) "Yeah, thanks for the compliment about my name. I'm glad you like it because I hate it. Do you know what it was like to go through high school with the name Elmer?"

Try to use your date's name often. If you forget it for any reason, don't panic. Instead, cause some sort of distraction that will allow you to steal his credit card, or glance at her ID bracelet or organ donor card, and thus refresh your memory. If this is not possible, stay calm. I had a friend who managed to survive an entire evening by using the words "hey" and "yo."

("Hey, it's good to see you!"

"Yo, you wanna order some wine?"

"Hey, where ya going?")

He was, however, very rich, good-looking, and circumcised to boot. Unless the same is true of you, be more careful. Treat your date's name with the required respect, or else.

Boredom—the bane of dating

Why will a man end a relationship? Why will a woman dump one guy and date another? Whatever the reason you give for being dissatisfied with a relationship, the basic truth is that you are bored. It is not stimulating. The earth does not move for you anymore. You forget why you were ever interested in the first place. Sure, there are many other reasons that relationships break up, like too much arguing. But on the whole, the most frequent reason is that you slowly drift apart because you don't find your partner as compelling as they once were.

Why are people so fascinated by the stars and outer space? Because space is infinite, an inexhaustible source of wonder and mystery. We just don't know what is out there, so we never get bored by it. Unfortunately, most other subjects—including our fellow man—do not seem nearly as fascinating, because they are finite and limited.

This is a dating paradox. On the one hand, you continue dating in order to learn more about one another. However, the risk is that the more you are exposed to each other, the more likely you are to get bored.

If you are bored, the problem is usually with you, not your date. If you are interested only in what your date represents—their looks, their wealth, their glamour, or because they are a great dancer—you will definitely grow bored. I guarantee it.

You need to look into the soul of your date. This is why you must search for a soul mate rather than just a partner. All of us are comprised of two essential ingredients, a body and a soul, a finite and an infinite dimension. The body can be seen, touched, tasted, scented, and heard, but the soul can only be experienced. Your objective should not be to see how much you have in common— whether you share a taste in music, or agree about political is- sues—because if you agree about everything you are sure to get bored. Instead you should open your heart to them and show them your spiritual dimension. In return you will get a part of them which is infinitely interesting and provides endless opportunity for exploration. Look for your partner's soul.

> *The great Rabbi Dovber lay dying. He told his grandson on his deathbed, "Now that I am about to meet my maker, I am no longer a body. My whole being right now is merely the divine spark which vivifies me in my last moments." His grandson touched his hand, "Look, Grandfather. You are wrong. You have a body. I have just touched your hand." And the old sage responded, "Because you touch with a hand, you feel a hand. Had you felt me with your soul, you would see that I am nothing but a soul."*

The importance of this point cannot be underestimated. In the same way that a man and a woman cannot make love unless they are naked, similarly they cannot fall in love unless they are naked. So peel away all those layers. You must expose your soul on a date if you are really to connect on a deep level. Don't be afraid to discuss your fears, your greatest anxieties, and your lifelong ambitions.

Three practical suggestions

1. Discuss important issues on your date, rather than the latest movie you saw.

Speak about what your values are. Tell them important stories about your formative experiences. (Think twice, however, before you relate how you felt the first time you interrupted your parents having sex.)

2. Do good deeds with your date, rather than just going to karaoke.

Go and visit a forgotten grandmother together. Remind her to remember you in her will. Volunteer jointly for a drag charity car wash. Protest outside a Garth Brooks concert.

3. Show your date that you have some core beliefs by mixing some religious traditions into the date.

Sacrifice animals together in the comfort of your living room.

But seriously, if you are Jewish, invite your date to the Sabbath evening meal with your family. Go to church together, or even do something as simple as saying a prayer together for someone who is in the hospital, or who has lost their cat. These simple activities will show your date that you are interested in nurturing your soul and exploring theirs.

Don't try to change people

God has primacy over all Creation. He is the Master and Judge of the earth. But you are not.

Since you are not God, do not seek to be a judge. Nothing is more off-putting than someone who goes into a relationship in order to reform their partner. Nobody loves a critic.

My friend Mark went out with a beautiful girl on three dates. In that time she criticized everything about him, from the tie he wore to the restaurants he chose, to the cologne he splashed on.

("What is wrong with Seven Nights in the Stable, anyway?" he asked me. "And as far as the restaurants are concerned, I like Big Bertha's Boiled Brains Butchery. She's just too darned picky.")

The reason you should date is in order to find someone to love, with all their faults, not to change them. That's why we hug the people we love. We are showing them that we embrace *all* of them. Knowing that there is a God, man can never aspire to be anything more than number two. Therefore, be humble.

Be forgiving of your date's shortcomings. I know a guy who is still alone at the age of thirty-seven. He finds fault with every woman he dates. The last complaint I heard from him was that he gave up dating a great girl because her teeth weren't straight.

The Bible says that when Adam was first created, he was lonely. But why was he lonely when he was surrounded by millions of angels? The ancient Rabbis explain that he was lonely because angels are perfect. They could talk with Adam and share a joke, but they never needed him. No angel ever came over to Adam and asked for a loan. Nor did any angel named Alistair say to Adam, "I'm cold, and I need a hug."

It wasn't until God created Eve, who, like Adam, was imperfect, that Adam's loneliness was finally assuaged. Now there was someone who needed human warmth just like him, who occasionally became frustrated, just like him, and who needed encouragement and guidance, just like him. And in his capacity to give, Adam found meaning and purpose in his life. Be thankful, therefore, that the person you are dating is not perfect, leaving plenty of room for you to make your invaluable contribution to their life.

Oh, and by the way . . . you're not perfect either.

Summary of Primacy
1. Make your date know that they come first
2. Show your true self to them
3. Spend "quantity" time together
4. Make them your one and only
5. Don't interrupt
6. Come "out of Egypt"—take a break from dating after a breakup
7. Bring joy to your date
8. Remember your date's name
9. Don't try to change people
10. Don't bring your mother on the date with you

two

Exclusivity
Making Your Date Your One and Only

To gain that which is worth having, it may be necessary to lose everything else.
— Bernadette Devlin McAliskey (b. 1947), Northern Irish politician. *The Price of My Soul*

THE SECOND COMMANDMENT: You shall have no other gods before me. You shall not make yourself a graven image nor any likeness of that which is in the heavens or on the earth below or in the water beneath the earth.

You shall not prostrate yourself to them nor worship them, for I am the Lord your God, a jealous God, who visits the sins of fathers upon children unto the third and fourth generations. (Exodus 20:3–5)

When the Jews emerged from Egypt, a land steeped in idolatry, God required not only that they accept Him as their Lord but that they forgo their allegiance to all other deities. God, in so many words, was telling the Jews, "I won't be satisfied if you merely place me before Zeus, Jupiter,

Apollo, and Aphrodite. I want you to give up contemplating the possibility of any other god." He demands to be worshipped exclusively.

Get rid of past idols: keep your ex your ex

Your date may ask questions about your former lovers. Don't presume that they are nosy and prurient—they may just be making polite conversation because you've been staring at your shoes for the last fifteen minutes. But neither should you be drawn into this topic of conversation. If they ask you why you broke up, don't be tempted to start telling them. I know it's been preoccupying your waking and sleeping thoughts for the past year—but believe me, it's not healthy for your budding romance to talk about your former relationship. Say something like "It was pretty complicated, but I guess in retrospect it wasn't meant to be. Please excuse me for not wanting to talk about it." That's it. Don't add anything else. You should certainly not praise your ex at length. Neither should you disparage them, as this will seem mean-spirited. In short, the less said, the better.

There are those who believe that it is healthy, even advisable to discuss previous boyfriends or girlfriends on a date. The thinking is that by discussing previous relationships you can allow issues within this relationship to be aired. Many people also think that it's simply an interesting subject of conversation. You are happy to tell them every last little detail because

(1) it makes them jealous, and a little jealousy is always a good thing,

(2) it makes you sound incredibly desirable to have had all these previous paramours, and

(3) you can flatter them by always favorably comparing them with your ex.

But this is a terrible mistake. Your date should never be made to feel that he or she has won—or is still in—some sort of contest, or left feeling you might dump them the minute some newer, better "contestant" comes along. Talking to your date in this way is like the Jews telling God that He is their favorite out of all the gods, even better than Jupiter or Diana—rather than worshipping Him as the Supreme Ruler of the universe.

Because, let's face it, you probably had intense feelings about most of your former boyfriends or girlfriends. Your date already knows this, presumably the same is true of them. But when you reminisce about former partners, you betray the fact that they still occupy your thoughts. Your date will not feel at all flattered by the distinction of being "more special" than all the rest. In fact, there is a strong possibility that your date, if he or she has any pride, will refuse to play the comparison game and will become defensive and hostile. However they choose to respond, the end result will be that they will misrepresent themselves and deprive you of the opportunity of getting to know their true self.

The Jews did not drag Egyptian idols with them to Sinai. In the same way you should not involve old lovers in your new romance. The beauty of human relationships is the endless human capacity for renewal. Throw away the pictures of your previous lovers, including the mental ones. Take down that stadium-sized poster of your ex doing the full Monty. Any gifts they gave you, you can keep, as long as you treat them as useful items rather than holy icons. Of course, engagement and wedding rings don't count— you should return those immediately upon breaking up, or at least pawn them and go on a great holiday with the proceeds. Otherwise they might interfere with your chances of finding new love, just as idols disrupt our relationship with God.

My friend Larry was happily married to Laura—or so he thought. One day, after three years of marriage, he came home to find a note saying that she had left and was not coming back. He was devastated. After two years, he started dating Kelly. How-

ever, Larry did not put away the old photographs of him and Laura together that were on the wall of the house and Kelly was deeply disturbed and hurt.

I scolded Larry for this. "Come on," he responded. "I was once married to this woman. Should I pretend that this is not the case?" I asked him why all those baby photos his mom took of him, the ones showing his behind hanging out of his diapers, were not also on display. After all, that was also a stage in his life. "Because they're humiliating, that's why." "Exactly," I said. "And Kelly finds those pictures of a woman with whom she still has to compete with in your mind similarly humiliating."

Larry got rid of the pictures.

Never settle for a cheap likeness

Maimonides, the great medieval Jewish scholar, explains how idolatry came into existence. Ancient man came to worship things like the sun and the moon because he thought by showing respect to God's creations, he was ultimately paying homage to God, just as honoring a king's ministers shows respect for the king. Unfortunately, after a while, they thought of the sun as a deity in its own right, forgetting that it was God who created it. Similarly, at Sinai, when the Jews began to despair of seeing Moses come down from the mountain, they collected together all their gold and silver jewels and ornaments and built the Golden Calf—as an intermediary to God.

The Second Commandment reminds us that each and every man and woman is capable of having a direct personal relationship with God. The Revelation at Sinai teaches that God is not a remote Being, but is always accessible to us. A great Rabbi, Menachem Mendel of Kotsk, once asked his disciples where God was. They answered that He filled the heavens and the earth. "Wrong," he said. "God can be found wherever we let Him in."

Having never found this God, the ancient idol worshippers had many deities, none of which was sufficient. Why wasn't one idol enough? The answer is simple. What does an idol do? It just sits, and so you get bored with it after a while. Therefore, there was a need to change idols constantly to avoid monotony. The same is true on a date. If you date two-dimensionally, ignoring the all-important third dimension—the depth each person possesses that signals their unique connection to, and representation of, the Spirit of God—you will become bored. And then you will feel dissatisfied, so you start two-timing, three-timing, four-timing . . .

No two-timing—this means you

Simply stated, when you are in love, you want to be the center of the other's universe, not just one of several small planets orbiting around their sun.

Danny was a good friend of mine, a handsome and clever Oxford graduate who soon got a highly paid job with a firm of investment bankers. He spent all his free time wining, dining, and seducing one woman after another. He showered in the morning, dressed expensively, worked hard to make money, and bought a fancy car, all for one purpose only.

This was destructive, not only because of the bad reputation he was earning as a "player" within his own community but even more so because he was willfully destroying his own soul with every date, becoming more and more false, cunning, and cynical. By the time he wanted to become serious and settle down, he found he couldn't do it. He had come to feel that a happy marriage was impossible, because all his relationships were so shallow.

On the basis of the Second Commandment, I explained to him how he was responsible for his pessimism. His cheap flings had caused him to objectify beautiful women—like idols—and to lose his sensitivity to each as a human being, a potential life partner. Like an idolater, he had chosen a futile and destructive pattern of behavior, moving from the worship of one idol to the next. In the process, he had denied himself the possibility of having a profound, exclusive relationship with one soul mate.

There is another problem in two-timing. Although you may be the soul of discretion, eventually word will get around. Even if it does not, your date will soon sense your detachment and suspect that you are not exclusively focused on them. Then they will begin to withdraw, unwilling to reveal themselves to you. Why should they risk the humiliation of having themselves compared with someone else tomorrow or next week? No woman with any self-respect will voluntarily enter a harem, even if she is its Queen, and no guy will want to feel he's sharing you with the local football team. Exercise some restraint, and be sure to date only one person at a time. Moreover, be totally focused on your date both mentally and emotionally, rather than date with only half your personality engaged in the encounter.

The most important dating secret of the Second Commandment is to make your date feel that they are the one and only person you are interested in romantically and sexually. There is no relationship that does not involve some sort of sacrifice. The essence of romance is that you actually give something up for someone you love. You show your date that he or she makes you so happy you don't need anyone else. Do yourself a favor and forgo all those flings in favor of the real thing. Don't turn your schedule into a romantic traffic jam. Pace yourself, dating one person at a time and giving them your undivided attention.

Unless you focus exclusively on your date, you won't be able to ascertain whether or not you may have a future together.

It doesn't mean you will, of course. The first person you date is not necessarily going to be the soul mate prepared for you in heaven. But give each person you spend time with a fair chance to get to know the real you and to express their true character. Let them feel confident that you are fully present in the date, in body, heart, and mind.

Beware of image makers

Unfortunately, in dating we are all often attracted by graven images. Rather than getting to know and love someone's true character, we fall for their "image," their exterior personality. We fall for glamour and excitement, a beautiful face, or money, or for the status of their profession or family pedigree. The Second Commandment teaches us that—beautiful as they may be—in the end these "graven images" are a poor substitute for the warmth and wealth of the deep, true love of a human heart and soul.

Idolaters are never impressive. Even the woman who loves flattery and sets out to attract you with her beauty will ultimately resent being treated as an object of lust. It is degrading to her because it denies the richness of her being. Men of power or great wealth may enjoy all the attention they get from women, but they don't fool themselves about what the women are really after— a share of the limelight and cash for themselves. Neither the idols nor their worshippers give one another anything of any value.

> *Robbie called me from Central America. "Shmuley, I am so happy. I met the woman of my dreams. We're going to get married."*
>
> *"How can you be so sure?" I asked him—especially since he told me they had only known each other for five days.*
>
> *"You know the way that I love horse-riding? Well, she loves horse-riding as well!"*
>
> *"Let me get this straight. This is the perfect relationship because you both love sitting on the ass of a horse?"*

Mae West once said that she'd rather be looked over than over-looked. But, guys, please don't take this to heart. Don't make the mistake of gawking at every curve and limb. She knows you want sex—after all, you're male. But by making it so obvious, you are announcing the shallowness of your interest in her and your true intentions for the date. Think smart, or at least think of yourself. You may be convinced that she doesn't notice you staring. Trust me, she does. Your eyes are popping out of your head. And soon even you will catch that look in her eyes that will tell you that she knows all, and thinks you're nothing but a lech. You will feel like a schmuck, and all that self-confidence you radiated, that carefully mastered charm? Gone. The date will be a disaster.

So if you feel your eyes wandering, redirect them to her eyes. That is where the truth lies, and that is where you'll find the real person. A great pair of legs may be alluring but you can't converse with them. A pair of eyes is different. A person's eyes can tell you so much, whether or not she likes you, feels comfortable with you, enjoys your company. Truly, the eyes are the windows of the soul. And the first message you'll see in her eyes is appreciation of the fact that you are taking the time and trouble to discover her truest, deepest self. There is nothing wrong with glancing occasionally admiringly at her body, as long as you avoid staring and always come back to her eyes. She may feel good when you look at her body, but only looking into her eyes can make her blush. By staring at her body you will make her feel that she is a molten, golden image. But by staring at her eyes you will bring out her humanity and distinctiveness. Studies show that women love conversing with gay men, and the main reason is that they speak to their eyes, and not their chests. They recognize women as people with personalities rather than as objects with curved surfaces.

Don't ever date for money

Warren Buffett, America's most successful investor, once said, "To marry for money is probably a bad idea at any time. But it's especially stupid if you're already rich."

There are few people in the West today who aren't rich. Yes, that includes you, although you were probably too cheap to buy this book and are now perusing it at a friend's house. But in all seriousness—are you starving? Do you have only rags to dress in? Of course not. To marry for money, then, is simply dumb, dumb, dumb. I could understand impoverishing your soul in order to save your body from starvation—but just to dress your body in Gucci rather than Gap? That's just plain silly. I know that they say that "happiness can't buy you money." But I would still encourage you to put your happiness first.

The perils of self-worship

There is a deliberate play on words in *"You shall not make yourself a graven image."* It contains a second prohibition, against turning ourselves into an idol, a warning against self-worship.

There is no single greater lesson in dating. Do you hear me?

I said, THERE IS NO SINGLE GREATER LESSON IN DATING. ARROGANCE IS THE DEATH OF EVERY DATE.

Self-love creates insuperable barriers in any relationship. Nothing is so off-putting as a man or a woman who worships himself or herself. How can you devote yourself to your boyfriend or girlfriend when you love yourself so exclusively? The egotist has no room for anyone else. He is incapable even of appreciating love that is extended to him. Everything he gets he takes for granted because in his own high opinion of himself, he deserves it. Similarly, a woman who feels that only her opinions are valid and only she has good taste, will never be good company on a date. She will have no capacity for sharing, or listening.

Rob and Charlene dated for eighteen months. They were very happy together and spoke about marriage. Then Rob's fledgling technology company suddenly got a massive investment from a Japanese bank. Overnight, he was the talk of the town. As his shares soared, however, his relationship soured. Charlene found him aloof and distant. Within two months, they had broken up. And all because Rob now thought that he deserved someone better. He got invitations to all the modeling shows and was hailed as one of London's most eligible bachelors. I called him up on the eve of the Jewish New Year, wished him health and blessing in the coming year, but pointedly omitted any reference to his business.

"Don't you want what's best for me, Shmuley? Aren't we friends?"

"Of course we're friends, Rob. And that's why I won't bless your business efforts. Because the best thing that ever happened to you was Charlene. But you have taken God's blessing of financial prosperity and made it a curse to you."

(To counteract the curse, I encouraged him to give all his money to me. When he did, I promptly dumped Debbie and ran off with Dr. Ruth. But her book sold so much better than mine that she left me. So now I'm back where I started.)

You must learn to eradicate all traces of arrogance, ego, and selfishness in yourself if you are to enjoy dating. (If you find that difficult, as I do, then at least fake it.) My advice is not that you should be an insincere person or a liar. Rather, my words are based on a famous Jewish teaching—namely, that inner change comes about through external action. So, for instance, if you know that your besetting sin is to be miserly and uncharitable, then instead of pretending to feel greater compassion, just go out and find a needy person and give them some money. Force yourself. Do it again, and again, and again. Repetitive action becomes second nature. After a while, you will find yourself unable to pass a poor person on the street without giving them something. It will have become part of your character. Instead of just giving charity you will have *become* charitable.

The same is true of arrogance. If you are a puffed-up little man or woman, then be self-deprecating on a date. Tell jokes against yourself—even if it hurts! (My wife always tells me she understands how easy I find it to laugh at myself.) People will think you are almost as great as you do yourself. Get into the habit of doing little things on a date to demonstrate your selflessness. Offer to hang up your date's coat. Buy him a copy of my book. Tell her that you'll be happy to take her grandmother to fit a new pair of dentures. Do the little things that show that you are considerate and selfless. But don't offer to take her sister out to a movie.

Dating, not "relating"

There is another similar, but more insidious, problem: that of dating for personal growth rather than to discover another human being. People who date merely in order to learn more about themselves, to deepen their relationship with the most important person of all—"me"—are just practicing another form of self-worship.

> *I considered Steve promiscuous. He pursued women indefatigably, and with great success. I met a few of these ladies, and was always struck by the fact that they seemed to regard Steve without any rancor or resentment.*
>
> *I asked Steve to explain this strange phenomenon, and he smiled wistfully. "Shmuley," he said, "I have sex in order to communicate."*
>
> *"With all those women?" I asked incredulously. "How much 'communication' can one man need?"*
>
> *"You don't understand," he responded, growing serious. "What I mean is that every woman I am with allows me to open up more, to feel easier in expressing who I am, to explore and know myself better. I look into their eyes, and see my own reflection."*

"Steve, if that's the case," I said, "a reflection is all you will ever see. You treat women as a means rather than as an 'end,' and you thereby deprive yourself of ever being enriched by an equal."

Steve is not alone in his self-absorbed attitude toward dating. The ethos of our age is, essentially, selfish, promoting self-realization, self-actualization, and personal growth above all else.

Don't make the mistake of joining the hordes of emotional drifters who are only concerned with their own personal development, who deprive themselves of the triumph of true self-completion. You are incomplete. That is a fact of life. You were created by God to find a person who will complement you, to whom you can devote yourself and with whom you can achieve inner growth. Rid yourself of your desire to be emotionally independent. You will be vulnerable, yes. But this vulnerability will lead to intimacy, and there is nothing more rewarding.

Knowing when to call it quits

"A jealous God, who visits the sins of fathers upon children to the third and fourth generations."

Why would God want to punish innocent children? In reality, all of us know it's the other way around—God gives us children as a punishment. Because we are iniquitous, He sends these freeloaders into our life, who sponge off us through their adolescence, get dents in our cars, and leave a mess wherever they go, only to grow up and accuse us of destroying their lives. And once we run out of money, we never hear from them again. It's the parents who suffer.

But seriously, as I've said before, Judaism teaches that when we do something once, it is just something we did. When we do it twice, it is still just something we did. But when we do the same thing three times, it becomes something we are. Our action becomes embedded in our character.

Unfortunately, the same rule applies in less lofty circumstances, with anger, for instance. If you lose your temper once or twice with your date, they will make allowances—maybe you had a bad day at work, or perhaps you didn't get enough sleep. But the third time, they will realize that you are an angry person. That's what this second commandment teaches us.

The trick here is to change the behavior, never excuse it, and always say you are sorry. Did you catch that? Always say you are sorry when you are in the wrong. By saying you're sorry you don't give repetitive action a chance to build up resentment. Even if you have done something really hurtful or offensive to your date, you'll be amazed what the word "sorry" can achieve. And don't say, "Sorry, but . . ." If you just find excuses for yourself, and talk all night about how much you hate your parents and how much they messed up your life, you will portray yourself as immature and irresponsible.

Everyone knows that your parents screwed you up. So what! Just because they did it to you for the first twenty years of your life doesn't mean that they have to do it for the rest of your life. When dealing with your faults, cultivate an attitude of "the buck stops here." There comes a time in the life of a family when destructive patterns must be broken. Your problems are *your* problems. Deal with them. Let your date marvel at the fact that amidst great adversity and with every excuse to be screwed up, you have triumphed. They will have great respect for you.

Sure, the woeful chronicles of your family may earn you a place on Jerry Springer, but you should in no way allow them to ruin your life. Seek to break any negative patterns that have become ingrained in you. If your parents spent a lot of their lives screaming and shouting at each other, go to the opposite extreme. Find another way. Speak gently and achieve your objectives with grace.

The role of jealousy in dating

It may seem odd that God refers to Himself as "jealous." But the Hebrew word for jealousy, *keen'a,* is related to the word for nest or abode, *ken.* So the concept of justifiable jealousy is predicated on the idea that there are certain things that we have every right to claim as our own and that should not be shared with anybody else. When someone is dating us, we have the right to claim exclusivity. We all have our nest and we have every right to protect it.

If we are afraid of insisting on exclusivity, it is a sign of insecurity. It is amazing to me that so many people view jealousy as a weakness. Precisely the opposite is true. To have no jealousy is unhealthy and unnatural. You go on a date to feel good. Trying to suppress your most natural emotion of outrage when you are with someone who can't stop flirting with other people is a big mistake.

A woman recently told me how she allows her boyfriend to go out with other women because he would do it anyway, and it is far better that it is done with her consent. I told her that this was like saying that she lets robbers steal from her apartment with her consent, because if she didn't go along with it, it would happen anyway.

I once appeared on a television program with a group of men who claimed they were addicted to sex. They all had girlfriends who put up with their indiscretions. One woman, a stewardess, spent a considerable amount of time away from home, and had told her boyfriend, "I know that you have to have sex, and since I'm not around, I don't mind what you do so long as you never become emotionally involved."

I was flabbergasted by this misplaced sense of tolerance. A woman who tolerates her boyfriend's infidelity is not entirely dissimilar from a woman who tolerates being beaten. She is degraded by both. Both constitute an abusive relationship. In both she gives affection and receives pain in return. It is a legitimate and absolutely healthy response to expect love and devotion from one's partner, and this should be sustained throughout the relationship.

If you are in a relationship that generates more pain than pleasure, get out.

What can you do if your date is flirting with someone else? Show him what it feels like. You don't have to overdo it and degrade yourself. But if you go to a party and your man starts speaking a bit too close and a bit too long to another, don't stand around being an appendage. Walk away from him and enjoy the party. Seek out someone else's company. And if your man doesn't come to find you soon, if he isn't afraid that some other guy is trying to win you over, then he doesn't love you—guaranteed!

Without jealousy there can be no exclusivity. One of the best ways to gauge whether or not you are in love with someone is to see whether you are jealous when other people show interest in them. To be sure, you don't have to take this to an extreme and many people would say that this isn't love but possessiveness. But they would be wrong. Jealousy is an intense and useful human emotion, so long as it is harbored in moderation. You have a right to insist on exclusivity in a relationship. So do it.

Be patient

An important lesson of the Second Commandment is one of patience. God says that he waits three and four generations for people to repent. Do not be impatient to receive proof that all the time and effort that you invested in your date has been worthwhile. All too soon you may find yourself thinking about the downside of the relationship, and will feel tempted to call it off rather than work it through, to go and find someone else rather than confront the problems. But to do so would be a tragic mistake. Don't be like the Israelites of the Bible, who jettisoned God's laws and built the Golden Calf because they could not wait for Moses to come down from the mountain. Their idolatry was a direct result of their impatience.

It is interesting to see how the episode of the Golden Calf was resolved. God was infuriated with the people and threatened to destroy them. Yet Moses interceded on their behalf, begging God to give them another chance. And God relented.

The lesson: if your partner asks you to forgive them for causing you pain, and shows genuine remorse for their indiscretions, rise above your pain and sense of rejection and learn to forgive.

Confront your problems

In your relationships you must learn to deal with things directly and always ensure good open lines of communication. It's okay to talk about the things that bother you. Don't be the kind of person who avoids confrontation. Those people who constantly give in, in order not to have to confront an issue, end up either exploding with rage or withering on the inside, with little left to offer.

A fear of confrontation often results from low self-esteem. When you avoid painful issues, you are saying you feel you have no right to raise the issue or you fear coming across as being too hard to please. You are forgetting that in a relationship both of you have the right to be happy.

Bernice was a devout Christian who began dating Nathan, an atheist. She loved him because he was considerate, intelligent, and funny. However, all too often Nathan would make snide remarks about Christians and about religious people in general. He basically believed that people of faith were nonintellectual, morons even, and he did not hesitate to say so.

This bothered Bernice, but she never said anything because she thought it would jeopardize their relationship. But it came to the point where she began to lose respect for Nathan. By saying something, she could have turned it around, but she kept quiet.

Eventually, Nathan broke off the relationship because he felt that Bernice was cold and indifferent to him. At that point, I told Bernice that she should discuss it with him, tell him what he had done to hurt her. Finally, she spoke to Nathan and saved the relationship.

(Because he was so sorry for having offended her, Nathan went to the other extreme and became converted. But like many new converts, he went off the deep end. He was circumcised and baptized on the same day, all the while meditating in the lotus position and smoking ganja. He was later eaten by lions on a mission to convert natives of New Guinea to Islamic Buddhism. But at least his heart was in the right place.)

When you find yourself dissatisfied with your date, instead of taking the "quick fix" route of breaking up, try talking it through instead. Never allow yourself to become intimidated or fearful of your date's reaction to what you say. However, be sure to choose the right time and place to bring up difficult issues. Don't reveal your admiration for Richard Nixon on the first date.

In short, remember the importance and the value of the exclusive relationship you have established with your date. Since you have both invested so much in one another, the least you can do is see it through.

As for me, I will always be indebted to an elderly, white-bearded Rabbi because of whom Debbie and I are happily married today. After dating for some time we got engaged. But from the beginning, the engagement was stormy. Forget stormy, there were daily hurricanes, earthquakes, and volcanoes rolled into one. The problem, of course, was not me but Debbie. As I've told you, she is just impossible. I was so kind and loving, but she never stopped making demands. I had always been a very easygoing kind of a guy, shy and retiring, loving the background . . . But Debbie? Jeez! She always needed to be in the spotlight. When we were fighting terribly, I went to this wise-man Rabbi friend of mine and told him it was over. I was going to break the engagement that very night. And I will never forget what he said:

"Shmuley, in the same way that you can break the engagement

tonight, you can also break it next week. Let's see if things can't be worked out."

And he spoke to both of us individually, and we are married today because of him. Can you imagine what Debbie's life would have been like had she married some ordinary guy? It's too horrible to contemplate. Her debt to him is infinite.

So, before you lose your patience and rush to end a good thing, think it through. Speak to God. Speak to a friend with wisdom and speak to your partner. Remember, not all of you are like me. Some of you have faults. Perfection is rare and only comes to one short, bearded Rabbi in a generation.

Avoid astrology

Finally the Second Commandment teaches us to avoid superstition. Superstitions are, basically, beliefs that forces other than God have power over our lives, and the Second Commandment tells us to discard all false gods. Superstitions which rule our lives, making us refuse to alter daily routines, or forcing us to avoid people with a certain name or date of birth, should be eradicated from your life. People in the grip of superstition often suffer such distorted outlooks that they lose the ability to connect authentically with another human being. Debbie originally told me that she would not marry me because she had read somewhere that short men with beards are inevitably sex-obsessed. Just shows you how silly some superstitions can be.

The great Talmudic commentator Nachmanides decreed that the words *"likeness . . . in the heavens"* in the Second Commandment are a reference to the constellations, specifically to the superstitious practice of astrology. Surprising as this may sound, a preoccupation with the zodiac, star signs, and the like is considered idolatrous because it distracts us from focusing on God's supreme power.

How many times have you heard this sort of thing on a date:

"Oh, you're a Scorpio, no wonder you are so lustful," or "Libra? Good, then we're compatible." These games are degrading to your date. Rather than giving them credit for their passion, or their attraction to you, you rob them by attributing it to uncontrollable heavenly signs. Suddenly, even the attraction you harbor for each other is not of your own doing, and the relationship is taken outside your control, both for better and for worse. Far more dangerous is that you give up the possibility of a perfectly happy relationship simply because the whole thing doesn't add up from an astrological point of view. "James, you're a nice guy and all. But today's *Daily News* says that men with red hair are bloodthirsty, and I fear that if we marry you might slit my throat during the night." Or, "Hilary, I do love you but I had a dream last night that we were strolling in the park when the Mir space station suddenly fell out of orbit and crushed us into the earth. Having calculated the chances of that happening and discovering that it is .0003492, I do think we'll have to part."

The Second Commandment tells us not to take any of these signs or dreams seriously. Why even mention your astrological sign on a date? Focus only on whether you are spiritually and physically compatible and leave the stars to the cosmonauts. Don't play games concerning heavenly matters. You have enough troubles here on earth.

Summary of Exclusivity
1. Make your date your one and only
2. Keep your ex your ex
3. Don't settle for a cheap likeness
4. No two-timing—this means you
5. Beware of image makers
6. Don't date for money
7. The perils of self-worship and arrogance
8. Don't use dating as a self-improvement course
9. Knowing when to call it quits
10. The role of jealousy

11. Be patient
12. Confront your problems
13. Avoid astrology
14. Eat, drink, and be merry for tomorrow they may cancel your VISA.

three

Confidence
Believe in Yourself and Others Will Believe in You or: Why Bulls--t Is Blasphemy

Trust thyself: every heart vibrates to that iron string.
  —Ralph Waldo Emerson (1803–82), U.S. essayist, poet, philosopher. *Essays,* "Self-Reliance"

THE THIRD COMMANDMENT: You shall not make wrongful use of the Name of the Lord your God, for the Lord will not absolve anyone who takes His Name in vain. (Exodus 20:7)

Women who date bad boys

The commandment not to take the Lord's name in vain is primarily a commandment about confidence. People only speak vainly—bragging, lying, namedropping—when they feel insecure and inadequate. You only say, "I swear to God that this is true" when you fear that you will otherwise not be believed.

At the beginning of this book, we commented at how impressive it was that God simply introduces Himself to the Jewish people. "I am the Lord your God." He could of course have done it differently. He could have used various chat-up lines to break the ice. He could have come to the Jews and first said, "Say, don't I know you from somewhere? Weren't you the guys who were enslaved in Egypt? Yeah, I think we met when I last went down to see the pyramids." Or, he could have said, "Hey baby, do you know that you Israelites look exactly like those famous actresses, the Chaldeans." Or he could have said, "Your place or mine? Heaven or earth?" But He didn't. He introduces Himself with great presence and confidence.

I lecture to singles' groups several times a week on the subject of marriage and relationships, and this provides ample opportunity for me to observe the modern dating scene. What I witness is an unbelievable lack of confidence. Both men and women who are involved in all stages of the dating scene today seem to lack a real belief in themselves. People today have an unjustifiably low sense of self-esteem, and this causes confusion and heartache in their search for lasting love.

Men, for example, find it difficult to muster up the courage simply to walk over to a woman, introduce themselves, and ask her for her name. Instead, they say ridiculous things like, "I hope you know CPR, 'cause you take my breath away." They hope that by offering a colorful witticism they will be able to compensate for their own colorless personalities. What they don't realize is that the best chat-up line is to simply and sincerely walk over to the girl or guy, introduce yourself, and ask them for their name. But because we have such low self-esteem, we are convinced that this is not going to work so we have to come along with all these bells and whistles. We've got to say the right thing, or wear the right perfume, or work in the right profession, have the right looks, or have the right pet. Where did this false notion come about that a woman is going to be more interested in what you do for a living than who you are as a person? And don't give the excuse that this is the way women are and there is no way to change them. Change them you must, with the force of your own personality. Sweep them off their feet, man.

That women today also lack confidence is easily attested to in the explosion of anorexia and bulimia, the proliferation of fashion magazines each of which promises to make you look like a model, and, most importantly, the fact that women today date in herds. Did you ever notice how women walk into clubs or restaurants in packs of three or more? They enter together, sit down together, and powder their noses together. When they need to move, they announce together, "Okay, we're moving right." And they do this because they believe in security in numbers. But this makes it even more difficult for a guy to brave those numbers and walk over and introduce himself to one of them.

To be sure, the most seductive thing of all about any man or woman, the most attractive to the opposite sex, is confidence. When a man walks over to a woman confident in his ability to contribute something positive to her life—not arrogant or full of himself but simply self-assured and resolute—that is the greatest turn-on of all. Indeed, it is the quality of confidence which explains the otherwise strange phenomenon of why so many good girls get involved with the wrong kind of guys. The one thing the bad guy has is confidence. He is a rebel who doesn't care what anybody thinks. He asks you to dance at a party and his voice never flinches for a minute. Attractive women are especially aware of how most men feel intimidated by them. Men treat highly attractive women like celebrities. And in a way, they are, *genetic* celebrities. Their great looks put them in the spotlight. Men stutter around them and are afraid to meet their eyes. They get nervous meeting them as if they're about to meet the President. But the bad guys who are indifferent to social ridicule just look her straight in the eye and ask her out. Women find this kind of confidence incredibly seductive. In a recent poll women rated a sense of humor and self-confidence as the two most attractive attributes in a man.

But how can men and women make an impression in today's

dating scene when they walk over to someone, shy and feeling low self-esteem?

No boxer can win a match with one hand tied behind his back. Dating is like boxing. You're trying to win someone over against all the other potential people who want to do the same. How can you possibly be effective in wooing them when half your personality is tied behind your back? By the time you walk over to the girl in question, you are stumbling with an artificial smile, and trying to overcome your projected sense of rejection. You are defensive before you even open your mouth. It's like trying to have a conversation with someone when you are half-asleep, because half your personality is asleep. You're going to come across as incoherent and boring. The most important thing in this first interaction is to make an impression. How can you make an impression when you aren't even impressed with youself?

This is why so many men compensate with cheesy chat-up lines. As Rabbi at Oxford University for eleven years, I collected from the students a host of favorites:

1. Pardon me, but I am writing a phone book—can I have your number?
2. Do you have a **boy**-friend? Well when you want a **MAN**-friend, come and talk to me!
3. My place . . . eight o'clock . . . bring a friend.
4. [Look at her shirt label. When she says, "What are you doing?"] "Checking to see if you were made in heaven."
5. Inheriting eighty million bucks doesn't mean much when you have a weak heart.
6. Is it hot in here or is it just you?
7. I lost my phone number. Can I have yours?
8. Your body is a temple. [To which she responds, "Well thank you. But unfortunately, there are no services today."]

The guys who can't think up these great lines make up for it by picking her up in a Ferrari or wearing an Armani suit. But what all this does is further betray your insecurities.

Goodness, purpose, and dignity are what give us confidence

The modern answer to this question is this: look your best, and you will be confident, because now you are attractive, or go to the club with friends so you will gain confidence from the herd instinct. But all these responses don't deal with the core issue. Real confidence is an inner experience and is achieved when we feel good about our character and actions. It is attained when we bring meaning into our lives. Confidence comes to us when our external and internal selves are in sync; when our outer actions are a reflection of our innermost convictions. The men and women that have the most confidence are those whose lives have a purpose and a direction. But those who don't feel good about who they are on the inside will always have to resort to artificial enhancements on the outside.

This is why the Ten Commandments, and what they teach about religion, morality, and our relationship with God, are so important. The most attractive type of man or woman on a date is a *dignified* man or woman. One who walks with head held high because they feel confident about the direction of their lives. The Bible says that every man and woman was created by God in His own image. Their real infinite worth is that within every single one there is a fragment of the divine. They have Godliness inside them. If we can tap into that, we can feel infinitely important. The soul that we possess dwarfs by far any material achievement that might attract someone in the field of dating. If we allow our soul to shine through our fancy threads, we will warm our date with the fire of vitality.

Profanity is passé

One hilarious scene in Monty Python's film *Life of Brian* depicts the ancient Israelites dropping huge rocks on anyone who even peeps the ineffable name of God.

Put most of us in Monty Python's ancient Israel and we'd be squashed bugs within a few minutes. Many people use God's name lightly every day. As often as they use the "s" and "f" words, they mention God in their expletives ("God damn it!") and their promises ("I swear to God . . ."). We no longer intend to blaspheme when we speak this way, but the use of profanity is offensive not only because it *is* blasphemous but because it is harmful to our relationships.

Most swear words are overused and drearily repetitive. Colorful language it isn't. Profanity is above all proof of unoriginal thinking and a boring mind. If you don't like the dish you ordered, don't call the chef "You! You . . . ratbag son of a b--ch." Your date will wonder what you might say about their mother one day. The chef will perfectly understand what you mean if you tell him that the last time you tasted anything like this was when you were a Boy Scout eating your first worm omelette. If you must swear, do it in some exotic language like Swahili or Mandarin. With any luck, your date will be impressed by your urbanity . . . or merely think that you are choking on your food. However, the Third Commandment is about much more than just not swearing.

Be as good as your word

Rashi, an eleventh-century Jewish scholar and one of the greatest Rabbis of all time, maintains that the Third Commandment is really about not making false commitments that we do not really intend to fulfill. God commands us not to use His name in vain for promises that we never intended to keep. In other words, it's a commandment about integrity.

In dating, it is imperative that we do not get carried away with excitement and make outrageous claims. Do not promise to do something that is clearly beyond your ability. This may not seem like much, but it is blasphemy.

The Rabbis state, for example, that a person must not swear in God's name not to eat for seven days in a row—even if the only choice is British cuisine—or to refrain from sleep for three days in a row. And that would include saying that you can sit through two French art-house films in a row. It simply cannot be done. You will end up looking like an unreliable guy who can't make good on his promises.

But there's even more to this commandment than an imperative to tell the truth. Why do people lie? Why do people exaggerate? Why do they stretch the truth? In short, because they lack confidence. And confidence is the third most important ingredient in a date.

On "stretching the truth"

On a date, it is a very common temptation to exaggerate or embellish the truth about ourselves. In the very insecure times in which we live, so many of us feel inadequate and end up trying to impress by inflating the importance of our jobs, our attributes, or our academic achievements. We brag about sexual conquests that, deep down, give us little to feel proud about. While all this may seem harmless enough (what's wrong with a little PR?), in fact it is duplicitous and, ultimately, endangers our relationships.

Making exaggerated claims about yourself and your prowess will never work in the long run (except on a male-bonding weekend where you head-butt in the woods). Sooner or later the truth will come out, and you will be more diminished for having lied than for not being the great success you claimed. You will have betrayed your lack of self-confidence, your own deep dissatisfaction with yourself and your actual achievements. And if you do not respect yourself, then why should your date?

> *Susan dated Rick for more than six months. He regaled her with stories of the success of his air-conditioning business. Although he never spent much money on her, he attributed this to the huge outlay in investment he was making to expand his business ever more rapidly. They got engaged and were happy.*
>
> *I was therefore saddened to receive a call late one night from Susan telling me that she needed to see me because she was calling off the engagement. "The whole story about his air-conditioning business was false. He lied to me. He has a tiny business selling used fans and old kitchen appliances, and it's gone bust twice already. Rick is completely broke."*
>
> *Susan said that she couldn't care less whether or not he had money. She was leaving him because he had lied about his finances. "I love Rick, and I would have taken a second job on the weekends to help make ends meet. But how can I marry someone who lies to me before we are even married? What will I do when he comes home late one night and tells me that it was because he was working? I will just never trust him. I can't spend my life on tenterhooks."*

Another story involves Rob who was dating Marie. It got off to a great start until Rob abruptly terminated the relationship. "I like everything about Marie," he told me, "except one thing: she never stops name-dropping and I find that incredibly distasteful. Why does she lack so much confidence in herself?"

So, guys, if you are five foot four and about to set off on a blind date, don't describe yourself over the telephone as "just shy of six feet." When you see the look of shock and disappointment on her face you'll wish you hadn't done it. Trust me on this one. It won't be your appearance that bothers them, but rather the fact that you lied about it; you only lie because you lack pride in yourself.

Be yourself

God wants us to be confident, to be ourselves in a relationship. Don't dress up your words. Don't use ridiculous pickup lines. Walk over to her with broad steps and beaming with confidence that you, just the way you are, are good enough to win her heart. You require no artificial embellishments. Put away the Ferrari and the pet chimpanzee. Nothing is more impressive on a date than a man or a woman who believes in himself or herself and radiates confidence. Be natural, be you, rather than relying on artificial gimmicks. The harder you try to impress, the more unnatural you will become.

Barry and Norman, two old men living in Miami Beach, were talking.

Barry said, "Norman, I can't figure it out. Here you are in your seventies, yet every gorgeous babe on the beach goes out with you. Every night I see you with a different woman."

Norman responded, "Of course they run over to me, Barry. It's because I have a gimmick. I drive around town in my beautiful red Ferrari. Your problem is that you have no gimmick. That's why you have no luck with the girls."

"What a great idea. I'll get a Ferrari too."

"No, no, you can't do that. That's my accessory. Go and get your own."

So Barry went and bought himself a camel. And every day he would ride up and down the beach on his camel. One morning he was horrified to awaken and discover that someone had stolen his camel. He ran to the police station to report it.

"Now this camel of yours," the officer said as he took the report, "Was it male or female?"

Barry was stumped. "I don't really know. I never checked . . . Uh-oh, I just remembered. It was male."

"How do you know?" the officer asked.

"Because every time I would ride it, all these beautiful young

girls would point at me and say, 'Hey, look at that schmuck on the camel.' "

Where do I get confidence?

To answer this question, there is a second aspect to this commandment. It also prohibits using God's name for a vain oath, not a lie, but a *vain* oath, a useless oath, an oath which states the obvious, like swearing that gold is gold or that Bill Clinton is heterosexual. Therefore, I cannot simply swear to God that two plus two equal four, because that is obvious.

On a date, never state the obvious. Don't borrow other people's opinions because you are unsure about your own. The most interesting people around are those who are unpredictable, whose personalities offer constant surprises. People loved Alfred Hitchcock movies because of the surprise twist in every plot. Arrive at the date with a great story to tell. Open your heart and express your emotions. Think of great new things you can do together that doesn't involve her taking her clothes off.

Being a dullard is blasphemy. God made you a unique individual. One of the biggest problems in the age of mass media is that people are becoming predictable and boring. We all drink from the same fountain of prepackaged ideas and goods. I often hear from people that although they went out with three different people in one week, it appeared to them that they had been out with the same person every night. Differentiation is increasingly uncommon among people today.

There was a time when a man would memorize lines of Tennyson or Byron before going on a date, so he could impress a woman with the depth of his personality. He wanted to be perceived as a sensitive, well-educated, and above all else, highly interesting young man. Today, he just goes to the gym so he can impress her with his imposing biceps. Conversely, women spend an hour in front of the vanity mirror getting ready for a date, and virtually no time at all reading up on the latest news to show they have something fascinating to discuss, an opinion on an important issue. Modern society worships form at the expense of substance, and the ephemeral body at the expense of the eternal spirit.

One of the biggest problems in society today is that people know they are becoming boring, so they try to compensate for their deficient character and opinions by buying expensive pieces of art for their apartments. This way they make the statement "You see, I now come with all these accessories. I am interesting." There is a morass, there is a popular consensus, there is the CW— Conventional Wisdom.

You have an obligation to use your mind, to have a personal view, a personal take on the world. Every person has a unique gift to give to the world. Discover what it is and offer it to the world. By this I don't mean that you should share your one great hobby with your date. Showing her your extensive Sardinian stamp collection is sure to have her impale herself against your front fence. Don't be surprised if she sticks her head in the oven as you show her your collection of Precambrian rocks. By being an individual I refer to the development of your mind and your emotions.

If you have a big date, read for a few days beforehand. Broaden your horizons. In today's world, if any of us were to disappear from the earth tomorrow morning, we would be easily replaced because there are no essential individuals. There is no one person who is really interesting and whose presence makes a colossal difference. Winston Churchill was an essential individual, right? Roosevelt was an essential individual. Who would say today that any person today is essential? To be a success in dating, you must become irreplaceable. For when someone chooses to date you, they are simultaneously closing off, forgoing the possibility of romance with everyone else. Be worth the sacrifice. Be stimulating.

Here is the answer to our earlier question—where does one get confidence from? True confidence comes from feeling special, from knowing that there is no individual on the planet quite like you. Confidence does not come from feeling that we are the best, but rather that we are unique.

The ancient Rabbis said that a person should walk around with two pieces of paper in their pocket. On one it should be written, "The whole earth was created for me." On the other it should say, "I am but dust and ashes." These are the two paradoxical aspects of a relationship. On the one hand you have to believe that you have something essential to contribute to someone else, which is why they need you. On the other hand you have to see yourself as being fundamentally deficient, which is why you need someone to give you love and affection. So remember . . .

No macho talk

The Third Commandment prohibits us from swearing to act in contravention of God's laws. So, for example, you cannot swear that you will steal tonight because one of the Ten Commandments prohibits you from stealing. A lot of men think it's macho to talk and behave like a maverick. They think getting into fights, breaking the speed limit, or drinking and driving will impress. In fact, this is rarely the case. Most girls will just see a guy who has no principles. She may even think, "What happens if we get involved, and he doesn't abide by *my* rules?"

Swearing it is so don't make it so

Why do we need to add swear words to our everyday conversation? Is it because we are so insecure that we have to strengthen our words with bold claims? If you are buying a car from a crooked used-car salesman, he will probably tell you, "This car can go from

zero to sixty miles an hour in 2.4 seconds. I swear it's true. I swear
on my pet hamster's life that it's true." And sure, it is true . . . if
you push the car off a cliff.

The more we use expletives about something, the more we betray our own insecurity and fear that we are not going to be
believed. If you were to say something and be confident that it
would be accepted, you wouldn't need to swear. The more you
swear, the less you will be believed. As someone once said, let your
yes be yes, and your no be no.

Courtesy counts

Avoiding foul language is a basic exercise in good manners. It's a
good idea to keep manners in mind at all times. For example,
don't pick up your date by parking in front of their home and
screaming their name at the top of your lungs. And no, beeping
the horn incessantly won't do either. Get your lazy rear end out of
the car and go and greet her at the door. Do the same thing when
it's time to drop her off. Don't drive by her house and say, "Okay,
get ready to jump on three . . ."

Furthermore, don't telephone at the wrong time. Calling your
date at unsociable hours, especially in the early stages, is disrespectful and shows that you are not considerate of their work commitments or their need to rest. Calling in the middle of the night is an
especially bad idea. If you call her at 3 A.M. to say, "I just wanted
to tell you—there was one more thought I've had about Luke
Skywalker as a role model for today's young . . ." This will not
impress.

I know. I've been there. While dating Debbie I would always set
my alarm to wake me up in the middle of the night so I could call
her. I reckoned that if I wore her down sufficiently and broke her
stamina through fatigue, then she couldn't resist me when I pro-
posed. Indeed, when I did finally ask her to marry me, she threw
her hands up in the air and said, "Only if you promise never to call

or speak to me again." And being a good husband, I've kept my promise in all these years of marriage.

Name-dropping—another no-no

Name-dropping is another classic betrayal of insecurity. "Loretta, I know you've said that you would prefer to drown at sea than go on a date with me. But will you change your mind when I tell you that I once used the same urinal as Harrison Ford? And only three weeks apart!" By name-dropping you may elicit some initial excitement on the part of your date, but this will pass. The fact is, if you were truly in cahoots with the celebs, you wouldn't think about it much. They are, after all, just normal human beings. You are good enough on your own. Don't go for the "greatness by association" shtick.

And no tittle-tattle

Be very, very careful of how you discuss your date behind his or her back. Remember this Third Commandment, of not taking the Lord's name in vain. That also means not taking anybody's name in vain. It's a prohibition against what we call gossip. If you don't plan to see the person again, fine, but there's no need to disparage him or her to your friends.

Your experience of the date was completely subjective. Who knows? Probably that very same train-spotter will make a great husband for some lucky gal. There are plenty of women out there who admire a man whose green trousers end at the top of his ankles and who think a bright red shirt a perfect match. And there must be thousands of girls who would enjoy meeting a guy who turns up in Vulcan ears and tells her to live long and prosper, before stunning her with his phaser. Don't ruin it for him. Also, remember that you yourself might be the subject of such invidious conversation, and who's to tell what damage that will do to your own future dating prospects?

But what about dates that were successful, that left us looking forward to the next meeting and wanting to tell everyone about our newfound joy? The answer to this is also in the Third Commandment. According to the sages, even using God's name to swear to something that is absolutely true is counted as blasphemy. Why? Because something that is true does not require the authority of the divine name to prove it. In other words, the name of God should not be used wastefully, should not be used in vain.

In all our relationships, good or bad, we must be utterly discreet. Don't use dating as the subject for great stories to entertain your friends. Don't share stories like "We were doing it on the couch and suddenly Paw walked in and pulled out a shotgun and Tommy tried to escape through the fireplace doggonit! We were scooping up parts of him right until the morning."

We quickly tire of anything in life that is overly exposed. A secret shared with too many people loses its special quality. God's name is holy because He is hidden, beyond our grasp. A relationship closes off two people into a world of their own. Keep it that way. Treat your date as a private experience, something sacred. Let the relationship retain its mystery.

Candor is key

By prohibiting false declarations, the Third Commandment also encourages us to make truthful statements. If you find yourself falling in love, then don't be afraid to say it. Declare your love when you know it to be genuine. In this day and age of excessive pain in relationships, many people refrain from proclaiming their real affection for fear of being hurt or of their feelings not being reciprocated. Cast this fear to the wind. Only losers are afraid of rejection. Strong-willed people understand that one must take risks in order to fall in love. It can't be much love you feel if you are not prepared to expose your vulnerable dimension.

I still remember that unforgettably tender moment in which for the first time I told Debbie I loved her. I leaned over the table at Hennie's Hamless Haven, looked her straight in the eye, and said, "Debbie, I love you."

And she ever so gently replied, "That's nice, Shmuley. But why not take your tie out of my soup." We went Dutch on the dry-cleaning bill.

Don't talk about commitment and then withdraw

Sooner or later, your love will bloom to the point where you feel ready to commit. You will begin seeing your date as your life partner. Thoughts of living together, engagement, and marriage will whirl through your head like a merry-go-round. You must feel that the rudiments of the relationship are proper and secure before you suggest any of these things. Otherwise you risk losing everything.

Rachel was dating Jeff for a couple of years. Jeff was very keen that they should move in together but Rachel was against it. She said that she was an old-fashioned girl who would only move in with a guy once they were married.

He promised her that they would get married, although he couldn't yet give a date, and finally she relented. They lived together for three years and the more Rachel pushed Jeff to honor his word to set a date for their wedding, the more he complained that the pressure she was putting on him was unreasonable and "claustrophobic." Finally, Jeff broke off the relationship and moved out.

Don't claim that you and your date are "serious" when in fact she is still trying to remember your name. If she gets wind of it, she'll run for the hills. Similarly, don't overinflate your expectation of the relationship, even in your own mind. If the one you love cannot bring himself to state—unequivocally—that he loves you, and wants to marry you, and wants to set a date for it, then assume that he doesn't. To do otherwise is to invite disappointment and resentment. While you should never be shy or inhibited with your date, neither should you be pushy. Give things a chance to develop in their own time. But if someone proves to be totally commitment-phobic, rather than pressing them endlessly, withdraw yourself completely and wait and see if they come a-runnin'. If they don't, you must draw your own conclusions. And whatever you do, don't move in with a guy before he gets down on a knee. Once he has you, why should he undertake any further commitment when he won't get any more of you. That's a bad deal. Men are shrewd businessmen and they will not willingly enter into a bad deal with little profit.

Keep God—not yourself— in mind

There is another play on words in the Third Commandment. The Hebrew for "take" (in "You shall not *take* the Lord's name in vain") is *ti-ssa*. An alternative definition of this is "to carry." The sages offer an homiletic interpretation for this: Do not carry God's name—that is, don't set yourself up as God's representative. You are not worthy of the mantle so stop setting yourself up as the Judge of all the earth. Be forgiving whenever your date makes a mistake. If they apologize for it, never bring it up again. Put it permanently behind you. Let them know for certain that they can throw themselves on your mercy and expect to be forgiven. (You may even make the occasional mistake yourself.) If they feel you are totally implacable, they might be tempted to start lying about what they did, just to avoid your rage and condemnation. People will commit great sins for the sake of a quiet life.

The great Moroccan Jewish commentator Rabbi Chaim Moses Atar, in his book *Ohr Hahayyim,* wrote that the essence of taking God's name in vain is to pretend to be more correct, more righteous, and more holy than other people, more righteous, and holy than we really are. Sanctimonious dates are everyone's worst nightmare.

And don't keep looking for a fight

Self-righteousness has been the death of many a relationship. This almost always comes to light when there is disagreement. You find yourself on a date with someone you really like, enjoying yourself tremendously, and hoping you are embarking on a phenomenal love affair. Suddenly they express an opinion with which you don't agree. (This will invariably be about politics, religion, or my books.) Perhaps they subscribe to conservative beliefs, while you are more liberal. Whatever. If you immediately dismiss them because of their viewpoint, a potentially beautiful relationship may be destroyed for good.

You cannot allow this to happen. Get off your high horse! Don't convince yourself that God is on your side and that you have a natural right to be right. It is blasphemous in the extreme.

Don't make the mistake of looking for a doppelgänger on a date. You are in a relationship with someone different from yourself, who has had different experiences and who can make a valuable contribution to your thinking. They will bring you new ideas and ways of looking at things. Don't squash their individuality. Keep the overbearing side of your personality in check. Who knows? They may even be right.

Your own opinions and those of your date will change with time. Chances are that both of you will become more moderate and reach a happy compromise. So relax, and be open to whatever your date has to say. Don't be a knee-jerk jerk.

Believe in yourself

Nevertheless, as I have said before, and will say again, self-confidence is one of the most important factors in successful dating. While you should be aware of your need for human love and appreciation, you should also remain assured that you are a valuable person, with a great deal to contribute to your date and to the planet at large.

It is beneath you to have to lie, exaggerate, or accessorize in order to feel valuable and worthy. There is no need to resort to vanity and lies. If you find yourself feeling excessively shy, or becoming reticent because you are afraid of saying the wrong thing, or of not being clever or witty enough, then your date may never get to know the real you. You may lose them forever.

God created you with so much to offer. Take heart. Take yourself seriously, and others will too. Believe in yourself and your date will believe in you too.

Summary of Integrity

1. Bulls--t is blasphemy
2. Be as good as your word
3. Don't exaggerate or stretch the truth
4. Be yourself
5. Remember the rules of self-confidence
6. No macho talk
7. Swearing it is so don't make it so
8. Courtesy counts
9. Name-dropping a no-no
10. And no tittle-tattle
11. Candor is key
12. Don't talk about commitment and then withdraw

13. God is the Center of the universe. You're not. Don't judge.
14. Don't keep looking for a fight
15. Believe in yourself
16. Secret to why women gain weight after marriage: A single woman comes home at night, checks what's in the fridge, and then goes to bed. A married woman comes home at night, checks what's in the bed, and then goes to the fridge.

four

Sacred Moments
The Gift of Time

As if you could kill time without injuring eternity.
  —Henry David Thoreau (1817–62), U.S. philosopher,
  author, naturalist. *Walden,* "Economy"

THE FOURTH COMMANDMENT: Remember the Sabbath
Day to keep it holy. Six days shall you work and accomplish all
your tasks; but the seventh day is Sabbath to the Lord, your
God; you shall not do any work—you, your son, your daughter
. . . your domestic animals . . . for in six days the Lord
made the heavens and the earth, the seas and all that is in them,
and He rested on the seventh day. (Exodus 20:8–11)

TGIF

Chances are that most of your dates take place on a weekend,
on a Friday or Saturday night. Why not? The weekends are our
free time, away from work, when we indulge in recreation and
meeting friends. Saturday is our day of rest, ordained in the Ten
Commandments.

But is that it? Was the Sabbath (Saturday for Jews, Sunday for Christians) sanctified by God simply to afford us some party time? In part yes! You should enjoy the freedom of the weekend and the opportunity it provides for relationships and meeting people.

Making your date a sacred moment

However . . . (However did you guess that there would be a however?) There is much more to it than that. The first three commandments have been about our relationship with God, and the last six, which we are still to get to, are largely concerned with our social behavior—in other words, how we treat each other. But this Fourth Commandment, about keeping the Sabbath, is a bridge between the first part and the second part. It is about our relationship both with God *and* with other people.

Our dating mirrors this. When we start dating we are combining our public, social selves with our private, innermost selves. Our date isn't just another pal, a fun companion to relax with. They are also, or we hope they will become, our soul mate, our other half, the one who makes the deepest, innermost part of us complete. That's why the Sabbath commandment teaches us to turn our meetings into *sacred moments*.

Maintaining a loving relationship in these difficult times is never easy. You have so many commitments to juggle. You have your job, the need to be attentive to parents, your desire to grow as a person, through reading and study. How then can you really give quality time and attention to your date? How can you afford them primacy when you have so many other urgent things that demand your time and attention?

The answer is that you must create special moments. To win over the heart of the man or woman of your dreams, you must make them into your Sabbath. You must make them the important thing, the thing that takes precedence over all the urgent things. A

Jewish businessman may be working on the biggest deal of his life, but come sundown on Friday evening, he stops whatever he is doing. There isn't an amount of money in the world more important than the Sabbath.

Could you imagine how it would be if you treated your date in the same way? No more "Sorry, honey, but I'm gonna have to cancel our plans tonight because the boss is sending me to Hong Kong." No more "Sorry, sugar, but this is the last day of the Anne Summer's sale and that rubber French maid's outfit I've always wanted will go if I don't get it." No more "Baby, you know that I want to see you tonight, but I haven't spoken to my houseplants in weeks." In short, it would be heaven on earth.

What is urgent and what is important?

The problem usually is that we let the urgent things rule our lives at the expense of the important things. To combat this, God in His wisdom gave us the Sabbath. The best way of summing up the Sabbath is this: a twenty-four-hour period in which there is nothing urgent.

Let's say your telephone rings. Right . . . *now*. You will almost certainly answer it rather than continuing to read this. How will you justify this act of heresy? "It might be urgent," you think as you rush to the receiver, dumping the book behind the couch, crushing the pages as you kick aside my deathless words of wisdom. But one day out of every week God has set aside a time where there is simply nothing to be done, one day of the week in which the important things come before the urgent things. For twenty-four hours a Jew is immersed into the Sabbath, a time when there is no television, no work, and no preoccupation with money. On the Sabbath we liberate ourselves from our enslavement to work. The only thing there is time for is family, prayer, and community.

"It might be urgent" has become a guiding axiom in our lives. We get caught up in the rat race of professional and social obligations, putting business trips before family holidays, and meetings with our business partners before meetings with loved ones. What insanity!

We humans are not morons. We all know what's important in life—money, fame, power . . . er, uh, I mean family, charity, and acts of loving-kindness. A recent study in the United States maintained that the average parent gives their children only fifteen minutes of quality time per day. That is what makes children grow up feeling insecure. Their parents allow things like work, television, and shopping for clothes to supersede the time they spend exclusively with them. To use a commercial analogy, upon being born, children are like an I.P.O. When the shares are first released to market, their value will be dependent on how much is invested in them. And when parents invest little to no time in their children, they end up feeling worthless.

It happens all the time. You promise to read your children a bedtime story, but then you remember there is an important client waiting for your call, and that it is urgent. You make the call. But then, the seven o'clock news is on and there is a report on the budget that you have to hear. So you watch the report. Then you need to call a colleague to see if he's heard it. Then you quickly scramble to catch the last few moments of female mud-wrestling on the Family Channel. Now it's time for the kids to go to bed, and you've blown another night with them.

We reach the age of seventy or eighty, we look into a mirror, and we discover that we have become something that we never intended. We are as small-minded and narrow and lonely as all the old people used to be when we were young, when we vowed we would never, ever become like them. But we have. How come?

We simply never accorded the important things in life any primacy. Suddenly we are not as close to our children as we should be, and they rarely call us. We never put enough time into study or communal projects. We look at our lives and they lack meaning and purpose.

Having the time of your life

It is interesting to observe just how important the concept of time is in dating. We always try to give our date "a good time" and we "spend time together" having "the time of our life." Even the word "date" suggests that romance is a space on our calendar, an entry in our timetable.

This itself is curious. Isn't it amazing that we use such strange and superficial euphemisms to describe finding our life partner? Sadly, our generation simply does not understand what our real needs are. We are educated to believe that our greatest need is to get a good education, a university degree, a high-paying job, and the respect of our peers. The need of the soul to latch on to its mate and find fulfillment, companionship, and deep meaning is made secondary or ignored. We are deaf and blind to the reality of the fundamental incompletion of our own existence.

Many people today go into relationships for much the same reason that they go to a movie or a good restaurant—namely, to find pleasure, enjoyment, and happiness. But few self-respecting men or women ever admit to actually needing someone, to being so dependent on another that they would feel diminished by their loss and therefore sacrifice something important in order to keep them. On the contrary, this would be all too depressing and contradict the value we cherish most—namely, our independence.

Hence the modern-day euphemism "partner" to describe our other half in the relationship. The man remains who he is, strong and independent. The woman remains who she is, self-assured and financially self-contained. And their relationship, based primarily on common interests, represents their commerce. They exchange things. They make each other laugh, they jointly pay the bills, and they have sex when it suits them.

Modern relationships are about being close and distant at the same time

In other words, relationships today involve distance rather than intimacy. Ideally, a relationship should cause two people to cease being strangers to each other. It seems incredible, then, that the idea of distance is actually *built into* modern-day dating. For example, people date today with little or no intention of tying a knot, at least not before a few years have elapsed. Closing the distance between each other, becoming one flesh, is not one of the goals of the relationship.

The very language used to describe modern relationships is designed to convey distance. We're all afraid of using language that would imply commitment or dependency. My friend the great Jewish thinker Manis Friedman got me thinking about this in a lecture he delivered to our students in Oxford.

It all started in the early part of the century, when terms like "courting" were still being used. Even courting can have some ring of intimacy. If you're in the same court, at least you're united by space. Moreover, "courting" gave women the upper hand in dating since they controlled whether the boy would be admitted into their "court." He would present his card at her door and hope to be admitted. But today that has all changed and women are at the mercy of men who must ask them "out" on a date. Now couples speak of "going out," which invokes images of being anonymous, in public, rather than alone together. So you're no longer even in the same court. Going out indicates the fact that even though you find yourself in the same geographical location—this place called "out"—it is only temporary and elusive. Soon, after you come back from going out, you reclaim your independence.

From there it became "dating." No longer are you united in space. That represents far too much commitment. For goodness' sake, it's like moving in together. Get me out of here! At most I'll give you some of my time, I'll give you a date, but get out of my space. So we supplanted the words "going out" with the words "dating each other," an expression that says that we sometimes find ourselves united in time. But while I give you some of my time, my private space remains my private space. I need my own life. In fact, many men and women not only refer to the act of interacting as dating, but they even refer to each other by a time euphemism, "my date," or in other words, "the guy/girl I occasionally spend time with when I'm not doing something more important."

From there, it descended to today's most common euphemism for dating, "seeing each other." Now, no longer are you even spending time together. It's not even that serious. Rather, you are merely, sort of . . . looking, or *staring* at each other. You are united in neither space nor time. You are now completely in your own sphere, but can still "see" the other person when and if you choose to.

It's fascinating that of all the senses, the metaphor we use is that involving "sight." People don't say, "Yeah, I've been *hearing* Sarah for three months." Nor do they say, "I've been touching Simon for a week" (maybe that's because in all likelihood Simon's been trying to touch you for a week). Nor do they say, "I've been tasting Claire for five months." Nor do they say, "I've been smelling Tim for a year" (even though you probably *have been* smelling Tim for a year).

This is significant, because the only one of the five senses that really works from a distance is sight. You can't smell from very far away nor can you touch, nor can you really even hear a far-off sound. But you can *see* for miles and miles. And with this euphemism we're conveying a sense of distance that is part and parcel of the relationship as it develops. We're afraid of getting too close, afraid of compromising our individuality. The dating scene today involves a collective fear of intimacy.

But tell me: How does this work? How can you possibly grow closer by "seeing" each other? Isn't the very idea of a relationship that you slowly become one? Why, then, does the most important metaphor for a relationship convey distance?

Because, ultimately, the idea of finding a true loving union has become so far removed from dating that it is no longer a real consideration. Instead, dating is an act of recreation, a leisure activity, in which we hope for the best but do not expect very much in the end. Therefore, we can learn so much from the Sabbath about how to bring sacredness back into dating, and treat the subject with the holiness and earnestness it deserves. And one of the first things that has to be recaptured is a lesson from the Sabbath about how to respect and apportion our time in the best way possible.

Before God created the universe there was only an unstructured, timeless eternity. The metaphor of God creating the world in six days introduces time as a measure of productivity. But on the seventh day God rested, showing us that time is also for something deeper than just doing and making. This is why Rabbi Abraham Joshua Herschel writes that "the Sabbath is spirit in time . . . [an opportunity] to put everything in its proper place." So the Sabbath is about setting priorities in our lives, and a proper order of priorities is vital if you are to achieve satisfaction in your dating.

Your money or your life?

So many people make the mistake of thinking that gifts—jewelry, tickets to the ball game, a blowup rubber doll—are what will win over your date. In truth, the greatest thing you can give is the gift of your precious time—time from your life.

In this commandment, therefore, God teaches us that time is more precious than any possession. For example, many parents make the mistake of thinking that the best they can do for their children is "to provide them with all those things that I never had." A man runs a successful business and gives himself a coronary working hard, so that everyone will want to marry his daughter because she is the daughter of a wealthy man. He wants to give his son a business that is ready-made so that his son doesn't have to work. He wants to give his family money and holidays and presents. In doing this, he does not empower his children but weakens them.

God teaches us that the essence of a relationship is not what we *do* for each other, or what material objects we give each other, but how much of *ourselves* we give. Judaism has always believed that the essence of our relationship with God is distilled from cathedrals of time rather than from cathedrals of space. Most religions have their great cathedrals, their churches, mosques, and temples, and even little country graveyards, places sanctified by prayer, where you meet God in the holy place. In Judaism, the emphasis is much less on the holy place and much more on giving God your time, on the annual festivals, and, above all, on the Sabbath. The essential Sabbath message is that time supersedes space. That the gift of oneself is greater than the gift of a flimsy material object.

Men and women, too, need to show that they always have time for each other, by planning special dates, by establishing special occasions. You must not miss your anniversaries. These cannot be compensated for with expensive gifts.

People today believe in expanding time to acquire space. They work themselves to the bone for material comforts and waste their lives in the process. The Sabbath teaches us to do the opposite. We are meant to use space to acquire time. We should use our hard-earned money not to acquire fancier clothes or flashier cars but rather to buy quality time with the people we love.

Your date tells you that he has to be away for a lot of the time because of his work. But then he tells you that he is making so much money that he has bought two round-trip tickets for a vacation in a month (or six or nine . . .); or a beautiful diamond for you to look at when you're not with him; or he leaves his smelly socks under the bed for you to remember his aroma always. None of these things is going to work. Not in the long run. God has taught us that giving our time is the only thing that matters.

Quantity vs. quality

It is tempting to place the emphasis on *how* we spend our time on the dates, neglecting to ensure that we spend *enough* time on them. The amount of time we devote to our dating is just as important as the quality of the date itself. The Sabbath teaches us that we should devote, at a bare minimum, one-seventh of our lives to the truly important issues. Likewise, we should give priority to spending the proper amount of time with our dates. Do you spend at least one-seventh of your time with your potential soul mate?

Don, a successful management consultant, was in town for an important conference. On my recommendation, he invited Jenny, a local girl, out on a date. Later, he told me that although he thought the date went well, Jenny had told him she was not interested in taking the relationship further.

"I don't get it!" he exclaimed. "I took a whole evening off so I could see her, and planned everything. We took a walk in the park, followed by dinner in a classy restaurant. I made sure that our conversation flowed smoothly, and even invited the violinist to our table to serenade her. Afterward we saw a play, and I took her backstage to meet one of the actors, an old pal of mine. Then we all went out for drinks.

"I got her home in time to make it back to the hotel to prepare my presentation the next day. I thought she had fun with me—how could she not? I dedicated the whole evening to her!"

"Perhaps that's the problem," I answered. "It's possible Jenny felt that you were so organized about your date merely because you didn't want her to take up too much of your time. I think you may have overwhelmed her with all your arrangements. Busyness is for business, not for romance. You should have made her feel that you had all the time in the world for her."

Taking my advice, Don called Jenny again and asked her to join him for a long, leisurely picnic in the park the next time he'd be in town. She told him that she had to floss her teeth that night, and when she finished doing that, she was going to watch professional wrestling. Don called again the next day and asked Jenny if she was free. "I'd love to go out with you," Jenny said, "but my apartment was painted today, and I'm going to stare at the walls and watch the paint dry. If it wasn't something really important, I would have gone out with you."

Feeling dismayed and rejected, Don threw himself in front of an oncoming bus.

(Okay, okay, so the latter part of the story isn't true. But I'm just so sick of all these dating books that always have these silly happy endings that you just *know* aren't true. The average story that I have come across in every dating book I have read goes something like this: "Peter was a born loser. An entire month would go by, and he would only get one message on his answering machine, and invariably, it would be his landlord calling to evict him from his apartment. One of the reasons that he never got any messages was that he was home all the time. In school, he had to pay other children to be his friend, and even then he could only write to them calling them friend in quotation marks. He was bald by age ten. He held a part-time job testing experimental drugs for the British medical council. Seeing an attractive girl on the bus one day, he introduced himself and asked her name. But she responded, 'Go drown yourself, creep. And I say that with all due respect.' Feeling lonely and dejected, he took out a single's ad in the local newspaper that read, 'Lonely, miserable, and depressed. Looking for romantic evenings and friendship. Nobody else wants me, including my own mother. Even my pet rock ran away. Please call me. Guaranteed that the line won't be busy. I hope life isn't one big joke, because I don't get it.' One day a woman named Helen called from the telephone company to shut off his line. But rather than getting dejected, Peter, having just read my book *Stop Being a Loser and Start Being a Winner,* remembered to say to her, 'Hi, sugar. I'm not a loser. I'm the one for you. Don't look elsewhere. Come on baby, light my fire.' Well, that was enough for Helen. She had always been looking for a man who spoke with confidence and believed in himself. She ran over to Peter's apartment, and after regaining consciousness from the smell of moldy Chinese take-away, grabbed Peter, and they made passionate love. Her affection changed Peter and, after changing from boxers to briefs, he ran for public office and became the President of the United States. The last I heard of them, they were making love fifteen times a night, and all of Peter's hair grew back, unfortunately all of it on the back of his neck. But they are so happy. And if you read my book, you can be just like Peter too." Right, and if you believe that story, then you'll believe all the stories which I've included in this book as well. And good luck to you.)

Many of us still believe the myth that "quality time" is more important than "quantity time" in our relationships. This notion was promulgated in the 1970s, based on the flimsy supposition that by dedicating fifteen minutes of uninterrupted time to their children, parents could compensate for being away at work the rest of the day. This has long since been debunked. In survey after survey children were asked whether they preferred to have their parents spend half an hour of "quality time" with them every day, or to have them present for four hours in the home, but distracted by work and other activities. The children invariably chose the latter, the "quantity time." They want to see their parents and know that they are not home alone, to feel secure even if they do not receive undivided attention.

It is no coincidence that 74 percent of extramarital affairs begin in the workplace. A man often spends more time with his secretary than with his wife, and a woman might find herself eating lunch with a male colleague more often than with her husband. Even a man and a woman who are not attracted to one another will, given enough time together, develop a strong affinity which can develop into sexual chemistry.

The fact is, there is no such thing as "not having enough time." (If you are spending all your time being busy, you are probably not working very effectively in any case.) Take control of your life. Just as God created the Sabbath as a day away from work, so should you "make time" to spend with your date and deepen your relationship. According to Jewish tradition, those who keep the Sabbath are blessed with good health and financial well-being. By dedicating time to your date you will earn their gratitude, love, and respect, and a wealth of happiness in your future together.

Regularity vs. spontaneity

There are two kinds of festivals in the Jewish calendar: there is the Sabbath, every week, and then the other festivals—Passover, Tabernacles, etc. These festivals do not have any specific time in the calendar. According to tradition they are appointed after the new moon has been observed and only when this is reported to the Jewish court. The festivals take place at different times every year, while the Sabbath is a fixed and regular date. So the days for the festivals are arranged by humans, the Jewish courts, while God Himself decrees the Sabbath day.

Similarly, while occasional acts of spontaneity can spice up your dating life—and of course she'll just love coming with you to the football game your boss has given you tickets for—far more important is the underlying sense of routine. This is counter-intuitive and is therefore a point which must be strongly emphasized. While your date might be excited at the prospect of meeting you on the spur of the moment, they will also want to know for sure that they have a place in your regular schedule.

By appointing a set time to meet your date during the week—by making regular "Sabbath" intervals—you will prove that you have incorporated them into your life. If it can't be a meeting, at least make it a telephone call. You are then saying that he or she is a part of your regular, essential schedule. If you only do things when the spirit moves you, who is to say you'll stay in touch when you're not in the mood? Give your date a regular "Sabbath" in your dating, not just an occasional series of "festivals."

Two ways of observing the Sabbath = two styles of dating

So now that we have agreed that both the quantity and the quality of the "sacred moments" of dating are important, let's explore some specific ways of thinking to help you bring the magic of the Sabbath into your date. There are two distinct and different approaches, both of which must be put into practice.

The Ten Commandments appear twice in the Bible, once in the book of Exodus and once in the book of Deuteronomy. However, the phrasing is slightly different in each case. In Exodus God commands the Jews to "observe and guard *(shamor)* the Sabbath day," and in Deuteronomy He enjoins them to "remember and honor *(zachor)* the Sabbath day." According to Jewish tradition, the commands *shamor* and *zachor* were heard simultaneously by the Jews at Sinai, hence Psalm 62: "Once has God spoken, twice I have heard. That strength belongs to God."

These separate requirements address different aspects of this special day. In *shamor,* guarding, we refrain from any activity not in the spirit of the Sabbath, such as working, or even discussing business. *Zachor,* honoring, means celebrating the holiness of the Sabbath with prayer, song, and festive meals. So one is a commandment to refrain from behavior that would desecrate the Sabbath, while the other is an active commandment, to undertake activities that make the day special and holy.

These two elements are absolutely crucial in our relationships. To be successful in dating, you need to "honor" *and* "guard" the relationship, on each encounter. You must go out of your way to make your date feel distinguished and honored by your attentions, and you must guard against doing anything that might disrupt the harmony and enjoyment of the date. So, for example, as well as complimenting your date on their appearance, make sure to avoid being distracted from the conversation. Don't daydream or think about all the things you have to do tomorrow, and worry about how you can do them if you're tired and get home late, etc.

Compare the honorable "aristocrats" . . .

Wealthy people find it relatively easy to "honor" the person they are dating. Free of financial constraints, they can afford to buy the best gifts and to take time off from work in order to devote more time and attention to them. As they usually feel confident and good about themselves, they are adept at complimenting and supporting their boyfriend or girlfriend.

However, "guarding" their dates is more difficult for these aristocrats. Accustomed to privilege and free choice, they often balk at committing themselves entirely to one person, are unwilling to sever ties with old lovers, or change their bad habits in order to please someone else. For them, success means never giving anything up. Although they have so much, they are hindered by their reluctance to sacrifice. These aristocrats must learn the lessons of *shamor* if they are to find happiness in their love lives.

. . . with the faithful "peasants"

"Peasants"—that is, most people, like you and me—value their dates because they view relationships as vital to getting through life happily. They are not accustomed to and don't expect ever to have, financial independence, nor are they interested in a life of emotional independence. So while these "peasants" may—and should—aspire to gain the means to introduce more *zachor* in their dating, spiritually they have much to offer to their dates.

. . . and the workaholics

In his book *Jewish Literacy*, Rabbi Joseph Telushkin describes how ancient societies tended to value people only for the work they did. Leading Romans ridiculed the Sabbath, citing it as proof of Jewish laziness. He describes how, in the ancient world, the Bible teachers struggled to establish that human beings had worth even when not producing.

The great gift of the Sabbath is its ability to liberate us from the preoccupations of the week and to connect us with something sacred and profoundly joyful. It provides an especially important lesson for those who have been conducting their dates with the same aggression and competitiveness with which they pursue their professional goals, making their dates feel as mundane as a weekday, a prize to be pursued rather than the fulfillment of a sincere and true connection between two human souls.

To invest your date with the sanctity and joy of the Sabbath, you must begin by actively distinguishing your time with them from a standard workday. There will be two benefits. Not only will you receive a far warmer response from your date but you yourself will start to feel much better about life. Your date will be a person with whom you can find a haven, a brief respite, from the demands of your job. You will have found your own walking, talking "Sabbath" in this special human being. Workaholics rapidly become boring, robotic, and monolithic. Make sure that you work to live rather than live to work.

The Sabbath calls for a reappraisal of values

All too easily we make the mistake of valuing people for what they do instead of what they are. Too often a potentially great relationship is destroyed in the first few exchanges between a man and a woman. They are introduced and the first thing they ask each other is "What do you do?" And depending on the answer, and that alone, many immediately reject the new person as not worthy of them.

The Sabbath teaches us that the human heart and soul are far more valuable than material wealth. One of the most sensitive things you can do when introduced to someone new is to consciously avoid asking about their profession. This is a great dating secret which will endear you to strangers.

Get over your curiosity about his earning capacity, or the possibility that she might be a compulsive shopper. I know your mother told you to look like a heat-seeking missile for a good provider—but show them that money is not so important. You want to get to know them better no matter what they do or don't do.

(Later, when you have lulled them into dropping their guard, you can check if they have a gold, silver, or platinum American Express.)

Living in the moment

So much of our professional life involves careful consideration of our past and our future. Witness the stock market, a huge gambling game predicated on past events, with hopes for future profits. In contrast, the Sabbath teaches us to focus on the present. It provides a twenty-four-hour period in which to live only in the moment, to enjoy simple, immediate pleasures like good company, fine food and wine, and the chance for private contemplation.

So when you are out on a date, relax. Too often people destroy a good relationship by becoming obsessed by future problems. How will we marry without money? Where will we live? Will he ever get over his attraction to farm animals? Will I have to give up my job? Will he mind having six children? Her grandmother is locked up in an asylum, so maybe she has defective genes? Will he soon be bald? Will she look like her mother when she turns fifty? Will she run off with Mick Jagger?

Get all these silly thoughts out of your head. Don't worry so much. Your mother will do enough worrying for everyone. Instead, focus on the moment, and be totally engaged in the encounter. Don't be nervous or jittery on a date. Stop tensing up those muscles. Hum elevator music to yourself and relax. Ask her what she thinks of the Carpenters. Sing with her at the table: *"Every sha-la-lah, every whoa oh whoa oh, so fine . . ."* Ask her what the words mean. Show your date that you are totally immersed in the sensation of her company and appreciate and cherish every moment. Get everything else off your mind and have a good time.

The virtue of patience

Once again, this commandment teaches us the virtue of patience. Nowadays, we have very little patience. In work and in play, we expect to progress, achieve results, and move on. We are profoundly impatient. The Sabbath, however, temporarily suspends our capacity to achieve results. Thus, we are forced to look around us rather than ahead, and to appreciate what we have rather than get anxious about what we hope to receive in the future.

Patience is a virtue vital to any relationship. You and your date are, potentially, embarking on a lifelong journey. This should feel exhilarating, even daunting. It should definitely not be rushed. Take your time. Go slowly. Do not be too demanding. Don't rush each other into emotional commitment. Don't rush into sex. Keep a bucket of cold ice on hand during every date. If you must be impatient, direct these feelings toward your own inadequacies and hurry to improve them.

The joy imperative

The Sabbath is a time of great joy. The Rabbis mandated that joy must be expressed through festive meals, good drink, singing and dancing. Nothing is allowed to interfere with that joy, and men and women are commanded on the Sabbath to banish from their minds all material concerns and worries and all sad and mournful thoughts.

Practice the same on dating. Be joyful. Be cheerful. Stop telling all those depressing stories about your early childhood. "My dad screamed at me, 'This will teach you never to wet your bed again,' and then he ate my pet rabbit." Don't roll up your sleeves to show her the cigarette burns your stepfather's uncle left on your skin. Instead, tell humorous and inspiring tales, like the time you rescued forty nursery children from the fifty-seventh floor of a burning building. As she gushes over you, just say, "Ah shucks, it was nothing. First-degree burns and all. But they were such cute little critters."

> *Sharon, a friend of my family's, went on a blind date with Gary, a devout animal lover. In an effort to "bond" with him, she described how her favorite cat was run over by a truck when she was seven. Then she gave a detailed account of the many days she had spent scraping up every last bit of the cat, so she could give the beloved beast a proper burial in her backyard.*
>
> *Gary did not call her again.*

So often in romantic literature we hear of a person who is "radiant" with joy. Having an inner light is one of the most attractive things about a date, and you should do your best to achieve it. You could go into a nuclear power plant and eat toxic waste for a week—or you can smile and be happy and show exuberance. This inner glow is contagious and will make your date smile too. (At least he will until you tell him that he won't get sex that night, at which point a dark depression will overcome him and it is best to move all metal objects away from his immediate vicinity.)

Mold the relationship, not your date

Six days a week, we exert our mastery over our environment. We dig and delve, we build, we color, and we shape. We need to feel at the end of each week that we have been creative, accomplished something, that we have made a difference; otherwise we cannot feel good about how we passed the time.

In contrast, the Sabbath teaches us to let the time pass, to sit calmly and passively (yet joyfully!) and enjoy the experience. While the seven days of the week are about mastering the world, the Sabbath is about becoming one with the Universe. Similarly, you must allow yourself to be calm and reflective when dating. Do not try to intervene in the life of your date. Don't try to build and shape them. Rather, be at peace with them, at one with them.

A week of preparation

Carrie went out with Max. As she told him about how much she loved her job as a tree surgeon, she could see his eyes slowly drooping, until he literally fell asleep. She watched him for fifteen minutes, then gathered her things and left. When Max awoke he had nothing but the restaurant cleaners to keep him company.

The Sabbath is an obligatory day of rest, while the remaining six are intended for work. The six—or five—days that we do our work are gifts from God, too. We must ensure that at the end of each week all the odds and ends of our business have been taken care of. We must look on what we have done and see that it is good.

The Sabbath was God's opportunity to rest from Creation, in order to return to it refreshed, with a sense of opportunity and hope. You should make your date feel that their company reinvigorates you. That they give you the sense of joy, stamina, and perseverance that you need in order to take on the world. Be alert and well rested on a date. If you find yourself nodding off, be sure to have country music playing in the background.

Bring peace into the date

The Sabbath is a day of peace and serenity, a break from the cutthroat work world where "it's business, not personal" is used to justify a whole range of nasty behavior and where problems are dealt with aggressively.

So many relationships don't have peace. They lurch from crisis to crisis. They thrive on tension and disputes. Although this fiery kind of love affair can seem exciting and dynamic, especially to outsiders, it reads better than it lives, and after a while the wounds and scar tissue build up. People become battle-weary, and even if they are in love, they give up, because they can't take any more pain.

Don't allow your relationship to be destroyed in this way. Bring peace into your dating. Don't complain about how much you hate your job and your family. Don't bring up your terrible experiences in Vietnam, or your grudge against Matron for all those episodes with the thermometer. That's for later.

People hate complainers. Try not to be a schmuck. If you feel angry and confused, keep it to yourself. Notice that although the Jews—world experts at whining—complained to Moses repeatedly after they left Egypt, when they arrived at Mount Sinai they shut up. No complaints were offered at Sinai. They recognized that they were having a "date" with God and had to put on a positive face. And so must you.

Be careful what you say

The ancient Rabbis decreed that on the Sabbath there was to be no discussion of any subject inappropriate to the sanctity of the day. Apply this rule to your dates. So often a guy and a girl go out and end up discussing the silliest things. Can you really think of nothing better to talk about than celebrity sex addictions and weight problems?

Here are some of my guidelines for avoiding empty chitchat:

Never talk about movies. Speaking authoritatively on 3,678 different films will expose you as a couch potato and a dweeb. Get a life.

Never talk about the weather. Every shmendrick with nothing to talk about talks about the weather. You are an international man of mystery. If she brings up the weather, look her in the eye and say something like "Even on cloudy days I think of you and it is as if the sun is shining." Having heard you utter the ultimate platitude, she will never want to see you again. (You see, I *told* you not to talk about the weather.)

Don't ever talk about your sex life. This is because you have no sex life. She knows this because of the way your tongue has been hanging out throughout the date, and because of the dark red blotches all over your skin.

Don't talk about other people's sex lives either. She'll think you're a pervert. She will begin studying your face intently, to help later on with the police lineup.

Never talk about your parents. You hate your parents. You know you hate your parents. Your date knows you hate your parents. You know that your date knows you hate your parents. And your parents know that you hate your parents. Why waste time stating the obvious?

Don't bring up your childhood, or any other truly depressing subject. Do you want your date to use the steak knife to slit their wrists at dinner? My friend Hymie spent an entire night telling his date how as a little boy he used to love eating ants. His date did not find the conversation appetizing.

Don't talk about your friends. Since everyone you know is much more attractive, rich, and successful than you, your date is bound to compare you unfavorably with them and wonder why she isn't going out with one of them instead.

Never talk about *Star Trek,* and don't offer to do your Bart Simpson imitation either.

After all these things you mustn't talk about, you may well ask what you should talk about. Why, *life,* of course. What else?

Attention, all single parents— with children, pets, or plants

You may have noticed that the Sabbath prohibition includes one's children. *("You shall not do any work—you, your son, your daughter . . .")* Many single parents are afraid to leave their children at home with a babysitter when they go out on a date. They worry that the children may feel abandoned if they see their parent spending time with a stranger. Some single parents don't go out at all; others insist on including their child in the date, as if to gauge your readiness to get involved with their "complicated" family arrangement.

This is a big mistake. If you are a single parent, make clear your situation to your date, without burdening them with it. Let their sense of commitment emerge with time. Remember always that just as every person has a right to rest on the Sabbath, you have a right to your date. In fact, you have an *obligation* to seek love and companionship, not only for yourself but also for your child.

Children need and crave a sense of hope in the future above all else, even more than parental love. By showing your child that you are searching for and finding long-term companionship, you are assuring them that there is always hope for happiness in the future, even after the trauma of a breakup or bereavement.

While we're on this subject, even pets *("domestic animals")* are included in the Fourth Commandment. Believe it or not, some people will hesitate about leaving Fluff while they go out on a date. What's worse, some people become so attached to their houseplants that they'd rather spend a quiet evening in, polishing their leaves, than connecting with another person. Wake up! You need human company—go out and find some before it's too late! He who spends too much time with his plants develops the personality of a cabbage.

Specific ways of celebrating

Jewish law forbids using electrical appliances on the Sabbath, and you should avoid mass-media entertainment for your date. Televisions, computers, mobile phones, and E-mail get far more of our time than people do as it is. Turn off the television, forget about going to the movies. Your companion is far more beautiful and interesting than any movie star, and they are there for you, if you only take the trouble to reach out to them. Let your date know that you'd much rather speak to him than watch Leonardo DiCaprio drown.

Apparel and appearance

Dress up for your date as you would on the Sabbath, or any other important occasion. When in doubt, always err on the side of looking more formal. Guys, that means a suit or at least a smart jacket. Ladies, go for a dress, or perhaps nice slacks and a blouse. Your date will be flattered that you have taken all this trouble. Also, if you turn up dressed more casually, your date may feel that your time with them is no more special than a trip to the dentist. Forget "grunge" and "heroin chic"—if you're a mess, your date will lose both their appetite and their interest in you. Heroine sheik will make you look bleak.

Fragrance

The way you smell is especially important. Jewish thought holds that the sense of smell is the most mystically significant, as it directly affects your emotions. That's why incense was such a vital feature of ancient Jewish worship. God loved it when the people would walk into the Holy of Holies, on Yom Kippur, and bring a beautiful scent. God refers to the sacrifices as a "sweet and savory offering."

This means, of course, that you should put on good perfume or cologne, and smell nice for your date. Don't buy any of that cheap stuff. If there is one thing you should never skimp on, it's the perfume you wear. Stay away from the bottle marked down 85% and named *Must and Mold in the Synagogue*. Also, women, stay away from the all-time favorite perfume *Aunt Martha's Tasty Waffle*. Never buy five bottles for the price of one. And, guys, don't believe that she loves the good old macho smell of perspiration mixed with dirt from your most recent football game. Invest in deodorant, cologne, body lotion, sulphuric acid, whatever it takes to make your aroma agreeable.

Oh, and if you intend to do any kissing, then oral hygiene is key. Brush your teeth long and hard before the date. On your way out, test your breath on your pet dog. Blow on him; if he shudders, howls, and promptly drops dead, then go back to the bathroom, floss, and gargle some mouthwash.

Candles

On the Sabbath, Jewish couples light two candles—one for her and one for him—to create a beautiful and romantic light. When you take two flames and put them together, they burn brightly as one. This provides a wonderful visual metaphor for the way the souls of a man and a woman can unite passionately, entirely. Try always to have lit candles ready for your date. The romantic glow is both beautiful and spiritual.

This is especially important if you are meeting for a meal in a restaurant. Desmond Morris, the famous social anthropologist and author of *Manwatching*, observed that almost all fast-food restaurants use bright lighting. This is because customers, feeling vulnerable and exposed while eating in this light, will finish their meals and leave sooner, clearing the way for other diners.

In contrast, candles at your dinner date will immediately engender a feeling of intimacy and comfort between you. Your date will feel less threatened by the soft light, less self-conscious about their appearance, and will be at ease in your company.

If you cannot find any candles, then set your shirt alight and tell her, "My whole being is aflame with love for you." Continue muttering this until she calls the fire department.

Meals

Meals prepared and enjoyed in the home with guests are central to the Sabbath experience. So, instead of always eating out, try cooking something at home and inviting your date to join in the preparation. Women especially love men who are somewhat domesticated. They will be impressed that you are going to all this effort for them, and that you have a love for the domestic life. Secretly, you will both enjoy the opportunity to interact in a home setting without all the pressure of bills and pets and wondering who left the cap off the toothpaste.

Wine

Jews sanctify the Sabbath with a special blessing over a glass of wine, which is then passed around to each member of the family and guests. By blessing every individual with a valuable beverage like wine, we demonstrate the importance of both the occasion and the person.

On a date, this is an extremely important concept. If you take your date out to a restaurant, order a bottle of wine to show that it is a special occasion. Make a big fuss of choosing the label. Reduce the waiter to tears by tasting and rejecting three bottles before finally making up your mind. If you don't know anything about wines, just order by number. Ask for number fifteen. The waiter will return and say, "Excellent choice, sir. The Bronx—April 1999, a very good month." Tell her that you are happy to splurge for her and that the wine cost seventy-five dollars. She doesn't have to know that that's the price for the whole truckload.

There is a Hasidic tradition of pouring your companion's wine for him. On a date, take turns pouring for one another. Toast each other frequently. Say a whole bunch of L'Chaims, toasts for good health and pleasant tidings. Make your toasts lighthearted but dignified. Wish your date good health and much success in all his or her endeavors.

Remember, the wine should enhance your date, not ruin it. It is significant that the Bible instructs the High Priests never to approach God's temple while drunk. You too should not allow drink to get the better of you on a date. It's hard to make conversation when you can't string together a proper sentence and spend all night drooling on your tie, and he won't be impressed when you get up on the table and sing "Material Girl."

Singing

Devotional songs are an important part of the Sabbath experience. If you both love music and are not utterly tone-deaf, try singing together during your date. It sounds a bit corny, I know, but you will find that a song will bring out good feelings in you both, especially if you manage to harmonize. Also, if you happen to be in a restaurant at the time, it will ensure that you receive exceptionally speedy service. But make sure the song you choose is tasteful. Don't serenade her with "Like a Virgin" on the very first date.

Dancing

The social warmth and energy of the Sabbath is often expressed through dancing. If you go dancing together on your date, choose the slow songs which allow you to enjoy the intimacy of your embrace. Avoid the loud and heavy music that turns dancing into an unimaginative sexual display. Unless you are Michael Jackson, you'll just end up looking like a fish floundering on the dance floor. If you are going to try and complete a scissors split on the dance floor, ensure that your trousers aren't on too tight, or everyone will hear a big RRIIIPPP and will laugh at your Tweety Bird boxer shorts.

Prayer

Every year in Oxford, many of my student friends have to go through the rigors of final examinations. Knowing that their entire degree rests on the results of these tests, they become understandably nervous and irritable. At this point, their girlfriends and boyfriends become frustrated, because they have no way of allaying their loved one's distress. My advice to them is always this: "Call them up and bless them for success in their exams. Say that you are praying for them." People who pray for you endear themselves to you through their prayers.

On the Sabbath we pray for many things, but essentially the act of praying is a communication with God. Similarly, communicate to your date how much you care by praying *for them*. If he is having a difficult time with his boss, tell him you will be praying for him every night before you go to bed. While they may be surprised by this gesture, they will also find it profoundly moving and flattering. Because, in praying for them when they are undergoing something traumatic, you are stating implicitly that they are worthy of God's attention as well as yours.

Charity

Another romantic gesture is giving something to charity in each other's name. Jews always give to charity just before the Sabbath comes in, because on the Sabbath we do not handle money. More important, Judaism teaches that by giving generously we can expect higher rewards from the Almighty. By taking care of God's needy children, He reciprocates by taking care of us.

Your date will feel blessed by your act of dedicating charity to their name. They will understand that they are so important to you, and to the world in general, that they warrant this special honor. They will not forget your consideration and generosity, and will reward you with affection and devotion. Just imagine how beautiful it can be. It's Shelly's birthday and her boyfriend Matt turns up with her present. While she is expecting gold earrings, a diamond, or even a beautiful Mediterranean cruise, Matt pulls out a beautifully laser-printed certificate from the Jewish National Fund telling her that a cactus has been planted in her name in some forlorn desert for her birthday. Can you see Shelly's face? Can you see the tears of joy and happiness? Can you see Matt's face as Shelly tosses her wine into his face and knees him in the groin?

Study

On the Sabbath, Jews study important texts of the Bible as a group. You'll find that studying is a beautiful way to spend a date. It was one of the things that Debbie and I did much of when we were first dating. She was studying Jewish texts in a women's seminary in New York, so I thought I could show off to her my encyclopedic knowledge of the great classics. Unfortunately, she was unimpressed that I had memorized all of *Portnoy's Complaint.* After I demonstrated my mastery of that great text she stopped shaking my hand. Of course, this does not mean holing up in the library together. Rather, do something that is intellectually edifying, like attending a lecture or a debate, or an exhibition in a museum or art gallery. Study a great religious text together, like the Bible. Jews read a portion of the Bible every week. Before you set out, though, be honest about what interests you and what does not. Otherwise, you might find yourself moaning, "Are we going home yet? I'm *tired . . .*"

I am consistently impressed by how many happily married couples I know met while still in their teens. My theory is that, because they spent their formative years together, they learned about life together. They developed and grew as one, and this formed an indissoluble bond.

When your date recalls how much they learned when they spent time with you, they will forever associate you with this personal growth. They will feel deeply drawn to you, as you have opened their eyes to the world. The other dating secret which can be culled from here is to find more wholesome and educational venues for dating. I suggest book shops. First, a higher caliber of individual hangs out in a book shop. Second, when you see someone holding a book, it provides an opportunity to walk over, introduce yourself, and ask them what they're reading. In an age where so many people lack confidence, this can really break the ice and make it so much easier to initiate a conversation.

Blessing each other

A rather beautiful Jewish custom is to bless the children at the Sabbath meal on a Friday night. You bless your sons to grow to be like the patriarchs, Abraham, Isaac, Jacob, and your daughters to grow to be like the matriarchs, Sarah, Rebecca, Rachel, and Leah. Indeed, much of the Sabbath meal is punctuated by men and women blessing each other and saying *"L'Chaims"* to each other. *L'Chaim* is a toast with wine. I run an organization called the L'Chaim Society in Oxford, London, and Cambridge. We invite hundreds of students in three cities for the Sabbath meal each week, and we encourage the students, who come from all parts of the world, to bless each other by toasting *a L'Chaim* in their native languages.

Over dinner, raise a glass of wine and toast each other. Bless her to do well in her big meeting the next day. Bless him to get that modeling job he's been dreaming of since he was twelve. Bless her to recover quickly from her breast enlargement surgery. Bless him that providence should help him get over his allergic reaction to Viagra . . . OK, OK, don't get carried away.

Going for walks

Because of its prohibition against using motorized transport, it is a Jewish family tradition to go for a walk on the Sabbath. Walking allows you to achieve intimacy in your conversation, without the trapped feeling of being confined in a room together. Especially if you are telling your mother that you want to leave home and move in with six Australians.

Suggest to your date that you take a long, leisurely walk in a scenic area, preferably one devoid of muggers, flashers, hungry wolves, or toxic waste. Some of the greatest dates of all time consist of nothing more than a moonlight stroll, holding hands and exchanging views about life and your feelings for each other.

(It is also the perfect date for a guy who is really cheap since it costs nothing. So if he insists on taking you on a walk every night of the week, you can be reasonably assured that you're gonna starve once you marry this loser.)

And talking about marriage . . .

Dating your spouse

A man and woman have been married for thirty years and the husband says to his wife, "Let's go back to Atlantic City, where we got married, to the same hotel and relive our honeymoon."

So they went back and while they were out for a walk, they came to a fence. The man says to his wife, "Do you remember this fence? It's where we first had sex."

They decide to have sex by the fence again. He's not as young as he once was. The spring is gone from his step, and as he kisses her he feels his arthritis flaring up. But she is alive like a young bloomer. The more he touches her, the more she is yelling and screaming. She recaptures her youth, she is yelling at the top of her lungs. Soon she has even ripped out the last remaining strand of hair on his head. He says to his wife, "Honey, this is amazing. It's like we hadn't aged at all. This is just like it was thirty years ago!" And she screams, "No, it isn't, dear. Thirty years ago the fence wasn't electrified."

Uh-oh, just when you thought it was safe to sit back, add fifty pounds to your girth, and ignore everything your husband or wife says to you, the Bible comes to your spouse's rescue. Did you know that in the entire Bible there is no word for husband or wife? Sarah is described in the Bible as the *"woman* of Abraham" and Rebecca is called "the *woman* of Isaac." They never became wives. They always remained women. Similarly, Abraham is referred to as "the man of Sarah," and Isaac as "the man of Rebecca."

There is great significance in this. We must not take our spouse for granted. We cannot stop dating or trying to impress, just because we married them. We must always make sure that we are pouring time, imagination, creativity, and feeling into our marriage. The rule is simple: whatever level of commitment you have shown your date to persuade them to marry you in the first place, put at least as much effort into persuading them to remain in the marriage—that is, to remain happily, out of choice. The only happily married people are those who get married every single day.

We need to renew our marriages at every stage of the relationship. We dare not take each other for granted, because our spouse will always be an autonomous and independent human being, who can choose to leave.

Marriage involves a fundamental contradiction. On the one hand, it is about comfort and removing oneself from the rat race. The whole beauty of marriage comes from finding somebody with whom we can be fully ourselves, totally natural. On the other hand, complacency is often what causes marriages to fall apart. Husbands and wives grow bored with each other and don't make the effort to be loving and affectionate. Very soon the marriage is on the rocks, as no imagination or creativity is ever used to shore up the relationship.

Zelda and Jacob have been married for twenty years. One night Zelda says to her husband, "Jacob, before we were married you used to take me out to dinner, to the movies, you used to buy me flowers. Now that we're married you don't do anything for me anymore."

Jacob responds, "Zelda, did you ever hear of a fisherman who gives the fish the bait even after it's caught on the hook?"

How can we reconcile these opposites? How can comfort and the need for renewal coexist?

The answer is that marriage thrives on the irreconcilable tension of having, on the one hand, found your soul mate, and on the other, having to continually renew your feelings for each other, so the love does not die like a neglected potted plant.

This is the reason why it is imperative that we continue to date even after we are married. Everything that has been mentioned so far in the book applies just as much to married people as to singles. A husband should make just as elaborate plans to take his wife out to dinner as he did when she was his girlfriend. A wife should seek to look beautiful for her husband, just as she did when she met him on that first blind date. Complacency and taking each other for granted is marriage enemy number one. You won the affection of your spouse, but you can lose it as well.

Sigmund Freud once wrote, "Despite my thirty years of research into the feminine soul, I have not been able to answer . . . the great question that has not been answered: 'What does a woman want?' " Well, Sigmund, I'm here to tell you that the answer to the question is, every woman wants to be the Sabbath.

The greatest gift you can give each other in marriage is to make your spouse your Sabbath, give them the gift of your attention and your time—in other words, the gift of yourself. When a man and a woman who are in love with each other have had the courage and the dedication to hand themselves over to one another for the duration of their days, they are foolish if they throw such a beautiful thing away. God created you to look after one another on His behalf, and consecrated you to each other with His holy blessing. Show Him how thankful you are by making your spouse feel divine.

. . . and, last but not least, sex!

Chill out—this probably does not apply to you. At least, not yet.

Judaism considers the Sabbath an especially propitious time for married couples to make love. With the heightened spirituality of the day, and the calm and relaxation which the Sabbath ushers in, man and wife can reach new heights of intimacy in their physical contact. After making a special occasion for your spouse, feel free to finish it off with unhurried, leisurely lovemaking that will strengthen your bond and make you look forward to your next "date."

If you're still single, go take a cold shower. Otherwise, pretend it's Monday.

Better to marry the right person at the wrong time than the wrong person at the right time

An old folk story describes Satan sitting around with his minions, devising ways of destroying the sense of meaning in human life. "Tell them there is no God," offers one devil. "Tell them to believe that there is no consequence to any of their actions," pipes in another. A third suggests, "Tell them that they've strayed so far from the right path that they will never be able to come back, because people aren't capable of change." "No," says Satan. "I will do this. I will simply make them believe that there is plenty of time."

This satanic notion of having all the time in the world, of not making the most of the time we have, of not making sacred moments, is what undermines our quest for goodness and righteousness. There is not plenty of time. Time is of the essence. All too often we take our time for granted. The Sabbath teaches us the importance of time and of the need to consecrate it rather than squandering it.

One of the great tragedies of modern-day dating is how often a man and a woman will pass up a good date, or refuse to marry their date, because they have prior commitments or they think the timing is wrong. How can they be sure that they have not lost the chance to meet their life's partner? I have a saying: "Far better to marry the right person at the wrong time than marry the wrong person at the right time." It seems incredible that in modern-day relationships we have put "good timing" before the truly essential. So many of my student friends whom I have known throughout the years have dated a wonderful guy or girl, only to break it off because they were afraid that they were too young to marry, or too involved with their careers. Needless to say, they were later riddled with regret for having passed over the opportunity of marrying someone perfect for them only because the timing wasn't perfect. That is why the lesson of always putting the Sabbath first is so important. If you find someone who is your Sabbath, who is right for you, now and always, then don't lose them. Grab them with both hands and hold on!

Summary of Sacred Moments

1. The gift of time
2. Making your date a sacred moment
3. What is urgent and what is important?
4. Having the time of your life
5. Being close and distant at the same time
6. Give your date both quantity and quality time.
7. Regularity is more important than spontaneity
8. Two styles of dating: honoring and guarding
9. Compare the honorable "aristocrats" . . .
10. . . . with the faithful "peasants"

11. Beware the workaholics
12. A reappraisal of values
13. Living in the moment
14. The virtue of patience
15. The joy imperative
16. Mold the relationship, not your date
17. A week of preparation
18. Bring tranquility and relaxation into your date
19. Be careful what you say
20. A warning for single parents: your kids understand that you need love.
21. Specific ways of celebrating
22. Better to marry the right person at the wrong time than the wrong person at the right time.
23. Women: Have yourselves declared legally blonde.
24. Dating your spouse
25. Sex on the Sabbath
26. Men's idea of romance is a candle-lit football stadium. Remember to light candles on a date.

five

Gratitude

Being Grateful for the Gift of Life

The art of acceptance is the art of making someone who has just done you a small favor wish that he might have done you a greater one.
—Russell Lynes (b. 1910), U.S. editor, critic. *Reader's Digest*

THE FIFTH COMMANDMENT: Honor your Father and your Mother that your days may be prolonged in the land which the Lord your God gives you. (Exodus 20:12)

Do you remember the first word you ever said? I remember mine. It was "mine." But then, I'm special. Probably your first word was "Mama" or "Daddy," and it was directed at those big, smiling people looking over you.

God commands us to honor our parents. The Fifth Commandment tells us that it is through our parents that He gave us life. It is a debt that we can never repay or reciprocate. It is enough, but also absolutely necessary, that we show them gratitude and respect for the rest of our lives.

So many of us focus on what our parents *didn't* do for us, feeling angry because they didn't understand us, were too critical of us, or didn't give us enough support and love. In most cases, however bad though they may have been at showing it, your parents will have loved you very much, all their lives, even if you never knew it. So be positive, don't keep telling them they screwed up your life. Try saying, "Mom, Dad, I just want to thank you for placing me in a *cushioned* basket when you left me at the orphanage doorstep. I think that was incredibly sensitive of you." But this is what the Fifth Commandment is all about: an obligation to show gratitude.

A heavy burden

The Fifth Commandment does not tell us to love our parents— it commands us to *honor* them. Most of us do actually love them, in spite of all their faults. You can't help yourself. However, unlike love, feelings of honor, respect, and gratitude do not come so naturally to us. Rabbi Shimon bar Yochai, the thirteenth-century Jewish mystic, believed that the Fifth Commandment is the hardest to obey. Indeed, the commentators went so far as to link the Hebrew word for honor, *kahbeid,* with the word *kahveid,* which means a weighty burden.

The Talmud recounts the extraordinary efforts the ancient Rabbis made in order to honor their parents:

> *Rabbi Tarfon's mother was walking in the courtyard one Sabbath day when her sandals tore and came off. Rabbi Tarfon hurried over and placed his hands under her feet as she walked, until she reached her couch . . .*
> *Rabbi Abahu asked his son Avimi for a drink of water. But when Avimi brought it, Rabbi Abahu had fallen asleep. Avimi waited, bent over his father, water in hand, until Rabbi Abahu finally awoke . . .*

Don't panic!
Before you contemplate running away to a monastery, let me

assure you that no one expects you to go to such lengths for your parents, or even for your date. The Talmud offers extreme examples of human selflessness as ideals to which we should aspire. The Talmud also provides specific rules for dealing with parents that are very applicable to your dating. Jewish law requires that we honor our parents by:

a) Not sitting in their seat
b) Not interrupting them and always letting them speak first
c) Always being polite and deferential when disagreeing or contradicting what they say

The power of forgiveness

One of the problems of honoring our parents is that often we feel great resentment toward them in later life because of the way we think they let us down. When we were young we thought that they were infallible superheroes, but later we came to learn that they also make mistakes. They can lie, get behind with payments on the car, cheat on each other, be mean with presents, listen to the Spice Girls, or they can even forget your twenty-first birthday. All of these can be enormously disappointing experiences. We start to see that many of our own character faults had their starting point in moments when our parents hurt us or neglected us or failed to stand by us while we were still learning about life and making our own mistakes.

We may come to feel ill will toward our parents, which becomes especially pronounced as time goes on and we bear the burden of looking after them in their old age. The Rabbis teach that this is one reason why the Fifth Commandment promises long life to those who obey it. We need extra time to learn to forgive, to let go of our bitterness and resentment. We must learn to love them again. The same is true if we take upon ourselves the onerous yet highly virtuous responsibility of taking care of elderly parents, which will demand a lot of our time and attention. Even if it takes you hours a day, God says, "What are you complaining about? I have given you so many extra years because you're looking after your elderly mom." God also compensates us for any time "lost" in honoring and caring for our parents by giving us long life.

Honoring people who are not perfect

My friend Roy told me that when he was a little boy, he saw his father as Superman. His father could do no wrong. He was, therefore, devastated one day when he discovered that his father had lied to him about something. Suddenly, he saw his father, warts and all, and he didn't know how to deal with it.

After thinking about it, however, he realized he loved his father even more for being flawed. Before, he had thought his father was the greatest father in the world because he was perfect. Now he could see that being a good and loving father had been achieved in spite of personal weaknesses and internal battles. And so he loved his father even more for making the effort.

God commands us to love our parents, not in spite of the fact that they aren't perfect, but precisely because of their imperfections. If our parents were perfect models of loving kindness, then the sacrifices they made for us wouldn't be any big deal. It would be expected. But in spite of being selfish so-and-sos, in spite of their own troubles, and in spite of their own weaknesses, they still changed our diapers every night. They loved us, read us stories and taught us how to read, helped us cheat to get by with our homework, worked long hours to clothe and feed us and send us to school. Now that's impressive.

The same is true of your date. There are times when you have to love people, not in spite of their faults, but because of them.

John was a guy who always came hours late to meetings. On his first two dates he kept Melissa waiting for twenty minutes. She was appalled and refused to see him a third time. I called her up. I said, "Do you know, Melissa, that he is usually at least an hour late everywhere? He was only twenty minutes late for you. Don't you see the effort he's making?"

You may have to deal with all sorts of disappointments and unmet expectations when you first begin dating someone. She might sound perfect on the phone, but when you meet her you find out that her velvety voice is due to her three-pack-a-day smoking habit, or that he makes such good conversation because he lives in a library and never sees the sun. Don't let your initial disappointment ruin the possibility of meeting a nice person. Once you've realized that your date has flaws, just like you, just like everybody except me, let that help you to appreciate their good points all the more. For all their shortcomings, they are trying to please you.

Getting along with our parents is a weather vane for how we will get along with our date

Your first significant relationship was with your parents, and, most likely, they will always retain an important place in your life. Your parents—love them or loathe them—were your creators and sustainers and, as such, represent God, the grand Creator and Sustainer of the world. That is why the Fifth Commandment comes first of all the commandments that deal with personal relationships. Only if we honor and respect our parents can we show that we can be trusted to honor and respect anyone else.

Your dating will eventually turn into commitment and dependence, which will replace your dependence on your parents. And, for better or for worse, you will bring many of your attitudes toward your parents, and the ones you learned from your parents, into your love life.

Honoring our parents is a sign of our gratitude to them for creating us and raising us, bringing us to life. Your date, too, can "create" you—spiritually and emotionally. Your date opens your heart and soul to new experiences—literally, makes you feel "alive."

The ancient Rabbis point out the parallel between the Ten Commandments and the Ten Utterances with which God created the world *("Let there be light," "Let there be a firmament within the water,"* etc.). God's word created the universe, and God's word, in the Ten Commandments, created human relationships. Communication is the secret of life itself. When someone pays attention to you and takes your desires seriously, you then feel alive. When people ignore you, you feel like you're dead.

And so it is for us. Being told you are wonderful changes everything. Seeing love shining in someone's eyes is better than life. All it takes to make someone feel alive may be to listen to what they have to say and to take their opinion seriously. Through praising our date and listening to them jabber on endlessly about how awful their day has been, or what a deadbeat they are, we can bring them back to life.

Eventually the two of you may quite literally "start a new life" together, when you get married and have children. The sense of renewal and vitality you enjoy in your relationship is reason enough to feel thankful, and want to do them honor.

How to behave on a date

The rules of courtesy and respect should be followed on a date. Of course, all this will seem very burdensome to you because your instinct will be to make an impact, to be remarkable, to show them what a unique and fascinating human being you are. You will want to tell them all about yourself rather than just be yourself. You must fight this. You will lose nothing by being a bit more quiet, pliant, and passive. Indeed, if you allow them to get a word in edgewise your date will be far more impressed by you and have a far better time than if you go through your entire repertoire of funny stories.

Every date involves an active and a passive dimension. You must actively seek to entertain your date, without overwhelming them. Give them time and space to express their own personalities.

I remember when Debbie and I first started to date. Having been a student in religious schools and rabbinical seminaries from the age of fourteen, I had had no real contact with women (apart from the blowup dolls that some of the guys kept in their closets, but I don't count them because they had zero personality). In fact, I viewed women as a nuisance, a distraction from our round-the-clock studying, people who got your hormones going but, unfortunately, about which you could do nothing at all.

For our first date, I picked Debbie up in my brother's Nissan 300ZX, a great little sports car, which he was kind enough to lend me for the occasion, in return for my signing over to him my share of our parents' inheritance. Before Debbie could even put on her seat belt, I zoomed off and she was clinging to the dashboard for dear life, her eyeballs sucked back into her skull.

We went straight to a kosher restaurant because I thought she would be hungry. Hell, I was hungry, so why wouldn't she be? When we got there I jumped out of the car and ran straight up to the restaurant. Debbie came chasing along behind me as I walked through the swinging door without bothering to hold it open for her. As she caught up with me, it slammed back in her face.

Clutching her nose, Debbie staggered into the restaurant, following me to our table. I didn't pull her chair out for her. I simply yelled, "Shotgun!" and leapt over the table to grab the seat closest to the salad bar. As soon as my food was brought to the table I tucked in. While earnestly shoveling, chewing, and swallowing, I engaged Debbie in a fascinating conversation about myself—giving her a pleasant view of my digestive tract. She was regrettably ill informed on the subject of me, so I was forced to do most of the talking. Anyway, I figured she'd be content just to listen.

Eventually, however, Debbie took advantage of a lull in the conversation to raise her hand and ask me if I'd mind calling an ambulance. Her nosebleed had turned into quite a hemorrhage, so professional attention was called for. While the ambulance drove away, I waved goodbye to Debbie, then began to haggle with the waiter about the bill. ("What do you mean full price? The hamburgers had blood all over them!" It was Debbie's blood but he didn't know that.) Thus ended our first date.

And so it would have continued, another once or twice maybe, before Debbie dumped me like a sack of fertilizer. However, as luck would have it, she was crazy enough to see something of value in me, and mature enough to do something about it. She sat me down, slapped me a couple of times, and told me how badly I was behaving. My first instinct was to scream and yell and call the police. But then I calmed down. I listened to what she said, and learned my lesson.

Although I felt humiliated, and not a little frightened by this Amazonian display of feminine aggression, I am forever indebted to Debbie for teaching me the importance of chivalry. Had she not done so, I might still be pigging out at that restaurant—alone.

Likewise, you should never be afraid to insist that your date treat you with respect and courtesy. It is your right, and actually your duty, to let them know if they are on the wrong track and headed for a lonely life. Can you imagine how sad it would be if a wonderful relationship were nipped in the bud, only because you never spoke to your date about what they were doing wrong? Imagine if Debbie hadn't slapped me down. She would have missed the opportunity of being married to one of the truly influential personalities of modern times, a legend in his own mind.

The three g's: gratitude, generosity, guidance

To show gratitude, adopt a positive attitude. Notice their efforts to please you rather than forever pointing out how miserably they fail. Focus on the fact that your date is giving you their time, and is trying to be pleasant because they like you. Pretend not to notice his hunchback. Focus on the positive: it will be great for the kid's piggy back rides. Look away when her glass eye rolls across the dinner table. They may not be perfect, their jokes may be terrible, they may have that annoying little tic, and their voices may grate on your nerves, but stop being so fussy and unappreciative. You have to think about the other person's feelings. You break down barriers when you show gratitude for and appreciation of their efforts to please. This will show them that your heart is in the right place.

Do your best never to be too hard to please. Men feel masculine when they succeed at pleasing a woman. And nothing turns a man off more than a woman who is impossible to please, especially if she has a mustache to boot. When you go out to a restaurant, don't complain that you don't like the food, or the canned music, or the way they serve the wine. Is that why you're dating? To have a great meal? Don't answer that question.

When she wants you to go with her to some awful, sentimental film and lets you kiss her afterward but won't allow you to go any further, don't complain that she is a prude. She's already proved that she's attracted to you, so be patient and don't rush her. Be happy that you have a girl that you can respect, even though you have to keep an ice bucket on hand during every date.

Basically, try not to be difficult. It all comes down to getting to know the person you are with, rather than just aiming to have a good time or thinking about what he or she does for you. The beginning of a relationship is especially nerve-wracking, and if even gorgeous, intelligent, and sensitive guys like me can make a stupid mistake in the early stages, what chance have lesser mortals got?

Always be generous and open-minded. With a little imagination and a positive attitude, you will see that he actually looks quite good in his fancy Italian-cut suit—it completely hides his rotund belly. Naturally, you'll make a mental note to tell him one day, after you are married, not to pull that one strand of hair across his bald patch. And eventually you'll find a nice way to tell her that her legs are so great they are a temptation to every man in the room, but it might be better if she wore a skirt that came at least an inch below her belt. But these minor adjustments to your date's style will come later. For now, be grateful that they want to spend time with you.

Also be generous—with praise, with sympathy and understanding. Your parents were generous to you when you were young, and it will soon be your turn to be generous with them when they are old—giving them your time, patience, and understanding, and perhaps helping them financially as well.

As for guidance—well, as I've said, a little goes a long way. But young men and women do make mistakes, especially in the early stages of dating. Don't give up on them if they appear a little crass at first. Tell them if they do things that badly disappoint you. Didn't your parents give you guidance? Would you have known how to live life if they hadn't helped by showing you the way? Then do the same with your date. Teach them what will make you happy. They aren't mind readers, you know.

Grateful—but not indebted

There is a big difference between being grateful and feeling indebted. Some people, women especially, feel that they have to reciprocate generosity by "putting out," having sex with a date just because he picked up the dinner bill. This is a big mistake. A woman reciprocates a man's generosity best by simply showing gratitude, saying "thank you" and telling him you had a lovely time. This will make him feel good about himself, his ability to please, and feel good about her. He'll want to be with her again.

Funnily enough, reciprocating by "doing things" for him often deprives him of some of the satisfaction he feels in pleasing you. One of the most important lessons on a date is to learn how to receive without feeling indebted.

As for any guy who expects a woman to "put out" for him just because he's spent a few dollars on dinner? He's just a schmendrick and you owe him nothing. Steal his wallet as a token of your indignation. Ladies, insist on dating gentlemen, the guys out there who were raised by their moms to respect and cherish a woman. If any man treats you as a means to the satisfaction of his sensual urges rather than an end in yourself, stop wasting your time. Go out and find a "mensch."

Never burn your bridges

Unless your family inspired *The Brady Bunch,* you will have had conflicts with your parents. You will have had arguments about everything from your choice of clothes to your choice of career. But very, very seldom do people turn their back on their parents. Willy-nilly, they are too dear to us. Hostile as we might feel toward them, we would never think of cutting off from them completely. The fact is that your parents, however much they drive you crazy, are important to you.

And so your date should be, even when there is tension between you. Force yourself to recall the good things he or she brings to your life, and do not allow resentment to build up. All too often, a couple argue, and then each dwells on the nasty things the other said. Unchecked, the hostilities grow and grow, until a breakup seems inevitable. Don't let this happen. Why terminate a beautiful relationship over a few angry words?

Instead, do the opposite. If your date hurts you, deliberately or not, switch the mood. Dumbfound them. Tell them you respect and value their opinion. Say that you will never forget the magic they have brought to your life. Or agree with them, and turn their hurtful criticism of you into a gigantic and ridiculous caricature of yourself, until they can't help laughing. In short, let them know that you love them for being them, not just for what they say and do. Extend to them the same tolerance and unconditional love you accord your parents.

Honorable endings

With that said, there are times when a breakup is going to be necessary. How do you know when a relationship is "right"? When it makes you feel alive and optimistic for your future together. When it heightens your sensitivity and enjoyment of even the most common experience.

If you no longer look forward to seeing her, if you no longer laugh at his jokes, if she irritates you, if he bores you, then you are in trouble. If you secretly fantasize about her being abducted by space aliens while crossing the road, or hear yourself suggesting to him that he volunteer as a freedom fighter in Bosnia, it is time to end the relationship.

Do not make the mistake of staying with an unsatisfactory relationship out of a sense of guilt. Many women I know are prone to staying with a mean and angry man whom they are "not sure about" even after a lot of time together. Forget about it! "But I love him" is no reason to stay with a louse.

You know when you are in love, and when this ain't it, dump the schlump. Don't stay in an unhappy relationship because you are afraid of hurting his feelings, or, worse, because you fear nothing better will come along. And stop trying to be the Messiah with every guy. Some men are beyond redemption. You are entitled to happiness, so drop the suffering servant posture. If you deny your essential need to feel loved and appreciated for too long, you will either die on the inside or explode on the outside. That is unfair to both of you. By being honest and ending the relationship you will free yourself and your partner to go out and find new dates who are more suitable. You will both be happier.

Above all, you must never remain in a relationship just because you are afraid of upsetting your mother:

> *"I can't believe you broke up with Buster. He was such a nice boy."*
>
> *"But, Mom, he was a drug dealer and an enforcer for the mob."*
>
> *"Why are you suddenly so picky? He made a nice living. Who do you think you are—Marilyn Monroe that you can be so choosy? Now I'll go to my grave seeing you as an old maid."*

Respect your ex

Once you have broken up, treat your former date with dignity, even behind his or her back. Do not disparage him to your friends and ruin his chances of finding another date. Always remember that she was once important to you. There had to be some reason you went out with her in the first place—a spark of interest, curiosity, attraction, a secret trust fund—that made your life that little bit more exciting at the time. Never forget the joy he or she created in your existence, and continue to treat them with courtesy and respect.

Don't make the mistake of resenting your former dates for having "wasted your time." This will only be true if you insist on being bitter and regretful. If you can see your old relationships as having contributed to your personal development, you will emerge a better person. Remember how much he or she taught you to understand and get on with the opposite sex, to anticipate bad moods and duck flying pieces of crockery. Remember all the lessons you learned in patience, tolerance, and the joys of cleaning hair stubble from the bathtub, and take all this good stuff into your next relationship.

This point is especially important to remember if your breakup was acrimonious. Often when you break up from a relationship, you believe that your heart can never mend. This is not so. You should also respect yourself enough to know with complete certainty that you will recover. You can always find happiness and probably even greater happiness than before. The right person is always out there waiting for you. You must believe in your future. The heart can renew itself endlessly and is actually stronger after a minor rupture. Nietzsche said, "What doesn't kill me only makes me stronger."

Stay strong and optimistic, and you will seem even more attractive to the opposite sex. Your love life will become more focused and purposeful, and you will reclaim your joy.

Telling your parents about your date

The Fifth Commandment also places upon us the responsibility of honoring our parents by including them in the major decisions of our lives. It doesn't mean that we have to do what they say. It does mean, however, that we should show them the respect of consulting with them.

Very often parents of my students will telephone and ask me who their children are dating. (Why are they calling me? Because they know that I know everything about people's romantic lives and that, for a respectable fee, I am not averse to sharing my information.)

Most young people do not tell their parents who they are dating. Unless, of course, their parents make it a condition of further funding. Some fear that their parents will disapprove. Especially if your mother fakes a heart attack every time you even bring up the name of your date in conversation:

"Oh no, here it is. Here comes the big one," she says, as she clutches her chest and staggers into the television set.

"Go ahead, keep on dating that Hell's Angel greaseball. Send me to my grave. I'm better off dead anyway. I never thought that any girl could find someone worse than your father. But you have succeeded. After everything I did for you. All those cold nights when I searched through rubbish bins for food for myself, rather than take away the few morsels of food that I saved for my little babies. Now you go and do this to me."

There is, however, sometimes a more significant reason for this exclusion. When entering a relationship, you may feel that you have come to the moment of giving up your dependency on your parents and have moved into a new phase of your life. Thus, the decision not to include your parents at this point is a declaration of independence.

Be that as it may, you would do well not to cut your parents out of your dating decisions completely. Of course, you should not date people just because your parents want you to. But your parents are experienced in life. They are experienced in marriage. And, most important, they know you very well and care about you immensely. As they only want the best for you, they probably have some good ideas about how you should handle your future. Don't obey them blindly, but don't reject their advice altogether either. Isn't it a bit ridiculous that you shouldn't use as a resource the very people who brought you into the world and who objectively desire your happiness?

Don't ever be ashamed to take advice from people older and wiser than you. Don't be arrogant. Hey, schmendrick, are you still listening to me? You're not objective about things when you're dating, especially once the relationship gets physical. So find a mentor, an advisor. If for some reason you feel you really cannot turn to your parents, that's okay. So long as you're still in their will, you're doing fine. Find someone else. Remember the old adage that it takes a whole village to raise a child. Society is the support structure that allows individuals, and individual relationships, to flourish. Have a best friend, who isn't afraid to criticize you when you need it, as someone to whom you can confide.

Bringing your date home to meet your parents

The ancient Rabbis in the Talmud said that if God sees a man who treats his father and mother with respect, then He feels as if He is being honored as well (Kiddushin 30b, 31a). When you bring your date home to meet your family, make a special effort to treat your parents with great respect. Don't be rude and insolent. Your date will realize that you are likely to treat her the same way one day. (When your date goes home, you can lock the old fogies back in the cellar where they belong.)

Complaining about your parents vs. complaining about theirs

Although your parents may not have much of a say in your dating, there's plenty that you'll say about them during your date, isn't there? Very few people remember the Fifth Commandment when they are chatting to their date. This is probably because parents are such a universally fascinating subject. We all have them, and we are all convinced that they could have done a better job.

Get real! This sort of talk about your parents is wrong, and not only because it breaks the Fifth Commandment. Far worse than that—it is *boring.* Of course you hate your parents. Your date knows that already, because they hate their parents too. Surely there is something more original you can complain about? You will come across as a weak individual always wanting to blame others for their mistakes and too fixated on your parents to boot. So, the apple doesn't fall far from the tree.

But if you find your date launching into a harangue about his or her parents, be very careful. An unwritten rule of life is that *only we* are allowed to malign our loved ones. Nobody else is. Even if you don't obey the Fifth Commandment when it comes to your own parents, you *must* do so when it comes to your date's parents. Because by showing them disrespect you are causing offense to your date. She is the product of their loins, after all.

So if your boyfriend curses his father for being an incompetent drunk who drove the family Chevy into the pool, don't chime in with "Yeah, I can see how that bum really messed you up. And he smells too!" When your girlfriend tells you how embarrassing she finds her mother's taste in hats, don't guffaw your agreement. Believe it or not, this will not be well received.

Your date will feel that you have passed judgment on their parents and, indirectly, on them. After all, their parents did create them, so they can't have been *that* bad. Then your date will probably become very defensive and insist that they had the best parents in the world—given the difficult circumstances. They will lift the steak knife and demand that you apologize for what you said, and you will be left looking around for the nearest marked exit.

If your date insists on complaining about their parents, a good idea is to try to defend them a bit. "I know you're angry at your mom and dad, and maybe they did make some mistakes. But after you accidentally drowned Grandma Ethel, your dad was bound to be a little upset and take it out on you subconsciously." "When he said, 'Schmuck, leave this house and never come back!' he was really trying to tell you how much he loves you and wants you close by." "You gotta look underneath all that aggression. When he decapitated your pet turtle, it was his way of telling you that he wants you to spend more time with him."

Your date will feel gratified that you care enough about her to take a sympathetic interest in her family. For the same reason, you must never look uncomfortable when you are in the company of your date's parents. Pretend you don't notice that his father has thirteen fingers. When her mother shows you her "Bobby and

Harry, you gave me a night in Omaha to remember" tattoo, ask no questions, even though her husband's name is Melvin. As far as you're concerned, nothing happened, everything is hunky-dory and you're the happiest person in the world. Even if your date doesn't buy it for a second, they'll be pleased that you made the effort.

Girls will be girls

A natural energy flows between the masculine and feminine poles, and that is why a conversation with your friends is disrupted when a highly attractive member of the opposite sex walks by. A force automatically flows between the masculine and feminine poles and your mind and heart are pulled in that direction just like the needle of a compass. A couple's gravitation toward one another is actually enhanced when their sexual polarity is respected. But when you try and be too much like each other, you become like two magnets whose positive or negative poles are placed next to each other. You will end up repelling each other. Hence, the Bible says (Deu 22:5), "A woman shall not wear a man's apparel, nor shall a man put on a woman's garment; for whoever does such things is abhorrent to the Lord your God."

Too many girls try to behave like one of the boys. It's not a good idea. Any more than a man can impress his woman by breaking into uncontrollable sobs and howling every time you watch *Sense and Sensibility* together. Most women like a man who is strong and confident, albeit sensitively so.

You should value each other's differences, and allow yourself to be enriched by a quality that is different from your own. If a man is rather aggressive, his female partner might teach him to be more nurturing, more loving, and less afraid to show his emotions. A timid woman may learn from her male partner to show greater strength of character and greater discipline in achieving her goals.

That is the beauty of being in a relationship. But for this to happen, we must respect the gender differences. Don't make fun of her or tease her whenever she says something really gushy. Stop cringing inside when she calls you "Pooh-droppings." And buy her gifts that she would appreciate as a woman, not that you would appreciate as a man. Buying her the sweaty jockstrap which Muhammad Ali wore when he floored Sonny Liston may not win her over.

When Debbie and I got engaged, Debbie told me that there were three things I could do that would really make her happy. The first was to wear platform shoes whenever we went out together. The second was that I should try and remember her name, finally, rather than just saying, "Hey, thingamajig." The third thing was for me to bring her flowers every Friday afternoon before the Sabbath.

I ignored the first request as being beneath me. Besides, I felt tall in stature. The second was easy, since I simply convinced her to have her name tattooed on her forehead. But the third was virtually impossible. I was a poor student, and all my traditional sources of income were drying up. The sperm banks were overflowing and needed no donors. Heck, I couldn't even get my normal weekly paycheck for testing experimental drugs. I had already sold one kidney to pay off the Rabbis who gave me my Rabbinical degree, and really needed the other one. My parents, unhappy that I had chosen to be a Rabbi, had long since stopped supporting me, and only sent enough to finance the weekly enema ("This way," they said, "we might actually be able to have a conversation with you").

I thought it was very wrong of Debbie to insist on something like flowers that were a waste of money because they would die within a few days. With the little money I had, I wanted to buy her something that would serve as a permanent memento of my affection for her. So I brought her my laundry to do every Friday afternoon instead. When she showed a total lack of gratitude for my efforts, I bought her a new photograph of me every Friday afternoon (well, it wasn't really a photograph. I pressed my face against the glass of a photocopy machine and got a decent image for only a nickel per week). But even this didn't do the trick.

It then struck me that I was being unfair. As a man, I had no sensitivity to flowers and women's love of the colorful little things. Sure, to me they were a bad investment. But by telling Debbie not to want them, I was rejecting the woman in my wife. I was telling her that only when she thought like a man would I accommodate her requests. What she was saying to me was that she wants my love for her to be like a flower, something delicate and wondrous, which must be renewed and reaffirmed every single day. Otherwise, it will wither and wilt. I corrected my errant ways and started buying Debbie beautiful flowers every Sabbath eve. Thank God, she never discovered that they were silk flowers. To this day, she still comments, "Isn't this amazing? After all these years, they're still alive?"

Don't be afraid to "parent" your date

Never fear taking on a somewhat parental role with your boyfriend or girlfriend. You and your date will each, in a sense, act as each other's surrogate parent. Admit it, you like feeling nurtured, taken care of, and looked after. Especially if you're Jewish. Drink up that chicken soup she makes you when you have flu. Don't hurt her feelings by pointing out that the chicken is still flapping its wings in the broth. And if a girl wants her man to be protective, like a father figure, it is quite natural. No need to go scurrying off to the psychiatrist. One of the real joys of a relationship is the way you can feel that your boyfriend or girlfriend looks after you in almost a parental role. This is a boon and a privilege, and something for which to be grateful. Of course, don't take this *too* far. If your parent *is* your boyfriend or girlfriend, then by all means run to the psychiatrist. And turn off that *Deliverance* video.

Setting boundaries

The Fifth Commandment teaches us that we have to regulate our relationships. While you may always value the support your parents give you, you also have to be able to tell them when you are ready to be independent, free from their judgment and criticism. In short, there must be boundaries to your interaction with them. The Bible commands that you *honor* them, not obey them. You may disagree with them, but do so with the highest respect.

The same thing is true for your date. Very often, what leads to the collapse of a good partnership is that the boundaries and borders were never clearly defined.

If a woman does not desire sex before marriage, or at any rate until she feels ready, she should tell her partner right away. She should not wait until he becomes desperate and alludes to sex every five minutes. If he loses interest in her because of this, then she will know the relationship would never have been worthwhile. She will end it without feeling that she has been unfair toward her boyfriend, because she defined her boundaries clearly.

Some people are very needy and get anxious if they don't spend time with their date every single day. Others need more time to themselves. You must sort out these differences and make allowances if you have different needs in this respect. If you are someone who requires a lot of time on their own, your date will have to understand that it is not because you don't love and need them. It is just how you are. If they can't handle that, perhaps there isn't going to be much future for you together anyway.

Always remember to define your relationships, and to do so first and foremost with the presumption that you are dating someone who may one day become as significant a presence in your life as your parents were, or your children will be. The Fifth Commandment teaches you respect and gratitude for your date, without which your dating will never be anything more than just recreational.

Summary of Gratitude

1. Be grateful for the gift of life.
2. A heavy burden—honoring your parents
3. The power of forgiveness
4. Honoring people who are not perfect
5. Getting along with our parents as a weather vane for how we will get along with our date
6. How to behave on a date: give your date their space, don't interrupt, and disagree deferentially.
7. The three g's: gratitude, generosity, guidance
8. Grateful—but not indebted
9. Never burn your bridges.
10. Honorable endings
11. Respect your ex.
12. Tell your parents about your date.
13. Bringing your date home
14. Always defend your date's parents.
15. Don't be afraid to "parent" your date: be nurturing and protective.
16. Setting boundaries
17. Marriage is one of the chief causes of divorce. Focus on the former and try to avoid the latter.

six

Compliments
Building Up—Not Bringing Down

A compliment is something like a kiss through a veil.
  —Victor Hugo (1802–85), French poet, dramatist, novelist.
  Les Misérables, "Saint Denis"

THE SIXTH COMMANDMENT: Do not murder. (Exodus 20:13)

Never date an ax murderer

O f course, this chapter could be very short. *"Do not murder"* would include not murdering your date. Natch. And it goes without saying: keep clear of serial killers when looking for a soul mate. End of chapter. Next case.

However . . . (Here he goes again.) The Sixth Commandment is about something much more profound and, at least as far as dating is concerned, more important than simply not blowing one another's brains out once you grow too frustrated.

The Ten Commandments were given as divine law to a nation

that already had civil law. The Jews had rules against homicide, so why did God need to reiterate this at Sinai? The reason is that the Sixth Commandment has significance far beyond its literal and merely legal application. The Talmud states that the murder of one person is the same as the murder of an entire universe. And the man who saves one life, saves a whole universe. So what I want you to think about is what the Sixth Commandment teaches us about the essential value of human life.

What are the things that make us feel more alive, and what are the things that make us wonder why we were ever born?

Rabbi Yishmael, a second-century teacher, observed that the Sixth Commandment sits at the head of the second Tablet of the Law, just as the First Commandment heads the first Tablet. He wrote, "If you believe in the First Commandment, which teaches us that there is a God who is revealed in the creation of the human spirit, then the Sixth Commandment goes right along with it. It teaches us: do not destroy the divine spirit, which is in every human being." By asserting the unique value of every human being, the Sixth Commandment teaches us to acknowledge every other person's right to live in dignity. In Jewish thought it is the same as murder to make somebody's life not worth living, i.e., to rob them of their dignity.

A life without dignity is not worth living. The Talmud notes that when a person feels humiliated, he or she goes pale, like a corpse. For this reason, humiliation is perceived in Jewish law as a "living death," and the person who causes it is deemed to have forfeited all chance of heavenly reward. There are similar concepts in Western thought. For example, the word "mortified," which is a synonym for "embarrassed," is derived from the Latin *mors,* meaning death.

The Sixth Commandment now reads: never crush another person's spirit; never undermine their sense of dignity.

Singing their praises

Just as you must never wound a person's spirit, on a date you must also do the opposite, constantly reinforcing their sense of self-confidence and value. A good way to do this is by being effusive with your praise and generous with your compliments.

Feeling that he was getting too old for his work, the aged Jewish matchmaker took on a young apprentice. "Listen to me," he told the apprentice, "the secret of successful matchmaking is to pour it on thick. When discussing a potential girl for a man's son, go to town praising her, and don't worry too much about the reality."

They both went along together for the apprentice's first assignment, at the home of a wealthy banker who was interested in marrying off his son and heir. The old matchmaker began, "Have I got a girl for you!"

And the apprentice chimed in, "Girl? Why, she's an angel!"

"Firstly," said the matchmaker, "she is very beautiful . . ."

"Beautiful?" the apprentice interjected. "Why, Julia Roberts keeps her picture on her vanity mirror, trying to look just like her."

". . . and she is very intelligent," continued the matchmaker.

"Intelligent?" put in the apprentice, "Why! Einstein used to correspond with her by E-mail to verify his equations."

". . . and her father is very rich," went on the matchmaker.

"Rich?" added the apprentice. "Bill Gates went to her father recently to get a mortgage for his new home."

"This all sounds almost too perfect," said the delighted banker. "But tell me, does this girl have no faults at all?"

"Well," said the matchmaker, "to be perfectly honest, she does have a small pimple on her left shoulder . . ."

"Pimple?" exclaimed the apprentice. "That's no pimple, it's a huge hump!"

There is nothing wrong with laying it on a bit thick with your compliments. Don't just tell a woman she looks great—tell her she looks magnificent. Instead of telling a guy that he has a way with words, tell him he is Cyrano de Bergerac. (Of course, stay away from this one if he has a big nose.) If she's pretty, tell her she has an angelic face and is drop-dead gorgeous. Don't just tell him that he's nice, compliment him for his decent heart and generous spirit. If she is large, call her "My Universe." If he doesn't bathe, tell him he's a knockout. If you catch him scratching his nether regions just a bit too often, tell him he makes you all itchy inside. Whatever you do, always make your date feel good about himself or herself. You won't go wrong. It is always better to overpraise than underpraise. Don't worry. Whatever they may say, everyone loves a bit of flattery.

This does not mean lying outright or kissing someone's derriere. But you can usually find something to compliment if you try hard enough. If, for example, your boyfriend writes a poem for you which is nothing but drivel, tell him you're impressed by how wonderfully . . . *legible* it is. And if your young lady gives up on her diet although she still looks like the Michelin Man, then tell her you always wanted a woman of substance.

Do beware, however, of compliments that are heavily laden with sexual innuendo and make you sound like a lecher. Compliments are like gifts—you have to give them appropriately. If the compliment presupposes an intimacy that does not yet exist, then don't say it. You are really overdoing it if on your first date you say something like "Wow, that dress sure highlights your breasts. Why, they're huge!" Your compliment should make her think you're sweet—not a jerk. If you're going to err in complimenting always err on the side of subtlety and modesty. Compliment her large feet instead.

Sometimes there can be a sense of awkwardness about compliments, especially the really lavish ones that might make your date feel shy and wonder how to react. It is always good to follow up a compliment with a question, which allows the person to bounce back with a response. So, for example, you might say, "You have such a phenomenal sense of humor . . . have you always made people laugh?" or "You have such beautiful curly hair, you must have been a really cute baby . . . may I see some of your baby pictures?" The purpose of a compliment is to make a person more receptive, open them up, put them at ease, and make them feel good about themselves and comfortable around you. A compliment should be an invitation to further conversation.

If you are really short of inspiration, here's a tip. You can always use "interesting" as your adjective of choice. "Interesting" sounds complimentary, but in fact it means pretty nearly nothing at all. The NASA space program is interesting. So is trench foot. So keep this word in your cache of compliments and you won't go far wrong.

By encouraging us not to harm our date with criticism, and to give them added life with praise, the Sixth Commandment teaches us an important lesson. In the same way that God created the world with words, we can create each other with words. Praising someone makes him feel intensely joyous. In the same way God created the world effortlessly, we can create people with very little effort—all it takes is a kind word.

A date should be pleasant. Life is painful enough as it is. Your partner spends time with you because you offer encouragement and a refuge from pain. Don't abuse this trust. Never insult or humiliate your date and make them feel like death. Be careful what you say. Hard words are forgiven, but never forgotten.

Never judge

One of my favorite Jewish teachings is that of the ancient Rabbis: "Never judge your fellow man until you are in his shoes." (But if he wears smelly socks, then you may judge him.)

To judge is to assume that you have some divine ability to discern why other people behave the way they do. It is to condemn people without ever knowing the challenges and hardships they face. Judging someone is like killing them. You dismiss them and their pain, as if their struggle doesn't matter.

In the realm of dating, this means that whenever you say something hurtful to your date—whether in anger or in "an honest attempt at constructive criticism"—you may destroy their self-esteem, and it is as if you have killed something inside them.

There are usually two reasons why people criticize each other. The first is to retaliate and inflict injury. The second is to rescue a relationship from a downhill slide. If you are sincerely criticizing to be constructive rather than to cause pain, then you will precede your criticism with a statement of unconditional love:

> *"Gary, you know how much I love you and how I will always be here for you. But that's exactly why I don't understand why you always get so angry with me."*
>
> *"Sue, you know that I'm your little Gobbledy Goose, and don't mean to be cross. But why do you always insist on bringing your Aunt Mildred on our dates? Especially since she has been dead for two years and always has that same expression on her face."*

Do, by all means, criticize in a constructive manner if you are sure your rationale for doing so is the strengthening and furthering of the relationship. But remember, one of the biggest dangers to your future happiness with the person of your dreams may be your own quick temper.

Don't even think about it

Maimonides, perhaps the greatest Jewish thinker of all time, wrote in a discourse on the human temperament that every emotion has its function and should be given expression, albeit in moderation. For example, we should never be too generous and give away all our money, leaving ourselves with nothing to live on. (He did allow giving all of one's money to poor, short Rabbis in an effort to save them from penning treatises on sex.) Of course, neither should we be too careful and not share with the poor. Likewise, as a parent, we should never be hypercritical of our children and undermine their confidence and self-esteem, but neither should we overindulge and spoil them.

But the one exception to this rule, according to Maimonides, is anger. He was adamant that we should go to the opposite extreme and purge anger utterly from our system. To act in anger is to lose our human dignity and betray the divine spark within us. Just look at people when they shout or holler. Don't they look ridiculous? So curb your temper, which, speaking from personal experience, is easier said than done.

When I was courting Debbie, in order to supplement my measly rabbinical student stipend, I worked nights at an adult bar. This was a very difficult existence, especially as I soon contracted pneumonia from having to serve drinks topless. Impoverished and ailing, I decided I would do better to sponge money off my parents.

My father met Debbie at a family get-together one Sabbath. To test her, he asked her where she wanted to live. "Wherever Shmuley wants to live," she responded immediately. My father, a staunch Iranian Sephardi, was delighted by this display of female subservience. Face aglow, he announced that Debbie was a tzaddikka, a righteous woman, and with that he gave us his blessing to marry. He then promptly sent her to the kitchen to do the dishes and iron his shirts.

I moved quickly, taking advantage of my father's elation to hit him for some hard cash. I said I needed a few bucks so that I could take Debbie to better joints than Mario's Italian-Jewish Pizza Bungee-Jumping Palace, which had become our usual haunt. My father responded favorably to my request. "I was always sure that you would turn out to be a loser. But now I am no longer so sure," he told me affectionately.

And with that declaration of confidence, he took out three fresh, crisp hundred-dollar notes and pressed them into the palm of my hand. Wiping the drool from my mouth, I played Oliver Twist and asked for more. My father glared at me, and peeled off two more bills. I was rich. I felt like a Master of the Universe. I was a sponger and proud of it.

I wanted to rush with Debbie to a classy restaurant to celebrate. Unfortunately, even with this small fortune in my pocket, I still couldn't rent a car since I was only twenty-one and in New York you have to have sold Noah the timber for his ark in order for anyone to trust you. So I picked up Debbie using a Brooklyn car service. I knew that God was on my side that night because it took me under an hour to explain to the Jamaican driver where we wanted to go. He dropped us off at the Moshe Peking Kosher Chinese Restaurant.

After the meal, feeling bloated and happy, we wandered outside looking for another car service and met an Israeli driver. Now, for those of you who don't know or who have never been to New York, it is the Israelis who run the city—the restaurants, car services, politicians, Italian Mafia—and they all have the same name, Rafi.

I knew that this man could help us rent a car. I turned to him and said, "Hey, Rafi," to which he replied, "How do you know my name?" I said, "Never mind. Look, I want to rent a car and I think you can help me."

"Chabibi," he said, "boy, did you come to the right place. I have an Israeli friend, his name is Rafi, and he rents cars without a credit card. The price is two hundred dollars for the week and three hundred dollars deposit. Have you got enough, in cash?"

"Do I have enough cash?" I asked sarcastically as I straightened my tie. "Is the Pope Catholic? Do bears do do-do in the woods? Is Bill Clinton heterosexual?"

We jumped into Rafi's seventy-year-old car with trust in our hearts and with hubcaps on our seats. I asked Rafi where we were going and he told me that Rafi, the rental-car man, lived at the other end of Coney Island Avenue.

After driving for three days and nights without stopping, I began to get suspicious. I couldn't pinpoint it—maybe it was the fact that we were now seeing sand dunes and cactuses outside, but something inside told me that things weren't quite right. Rafi, sensing my nervousness, stopped the car and told me that I would have to drive a few blocks to make sure that I wouldn't ruin his friend's car. I proudly drove the car two blocks, thinking, "So there, Rafi, can I drive or what?"

Being as thick as I am, I still did not realize that Rafi was playing me like a fiddle. To further reassure me, Rafi then picked up his mobile phone and called home. "Hello, honey. No, I'm going to be late tonight. I am helping a young, short rabbi who is trying to impress his girl. Kiss Rafi and Rafi good night for me and tell them I'm sorry that I can't tuck them in tonight."

"Wow!" I thought. "Rafi is such a loving father, he couldn't possibly be a rip-off artist." I was too green to notice that Rafi had been speaking into his rearview mirror.

When we finally arrived at our destination it was pitch-dark and all we saw around us was the crater marks of the moon's surface against the soft, night light. We had left civilization behind many weeks ago. In the distance I could hear water running and I suspected that we were just a few hundred feet from where the earth ends and the water falls off.

"Where the hell are we, Rafi?"

Rafi popped out of the car first and ordered us to follow.

"There, just behind the remains of the Apollo lunar landing craft over there, is where my friend Rafi has his car-rental shop."

I could make out nothing in the distance. Rafi continued, "Okay, you give me the five hundred dollars plus your driver's license, and I will be back in a few moments with your car."

By now I had had enough.

"Heh, heh, heh!" I laughed nervously. "What do you take me for—a complete fool? Did you really think you could rip me off?

Did you think I was a British tourist? I am a Talmudic hairsplitter! You can't run one of these fast ones by me. I'm not giving you my money."

But Rafi was quick on the draw. "Hey, Chabibi, why the distrust? Did all the time over the last few weeks we spent driving here together mean nothing? I thought that you and I had become one flesh. Take it easy, man. My own grandfather, Chief Rabbi Rafi of Antarctica, was a pious and holy man, just like you. Here, here are the keys to my car. I can't go anywhere."

Well, that seemed like an okay deal. I was now sitting on $10,000 worth of car as security. I took Rafi's keys and gave him my money.

As we all set off walking, Rafi suddenly said, "Oh, wait for me just a moment. I forgot my sunglasses in the car."

Here perhaps an alarm bell *should* have gone off in my mind. It was three o'clock in the morning on one of the darkest nights of the year. Why did Rafi need his sunglasses? But all Israelis wear sunglasses at all times of the day and night, even sleeping and showering with them. It makes them feel cool.

Rafi leaped into the car behind us. Suddenly, the ignition sounded. Rafi drove off, never to be seen again. Our friendship was over. He had a spare set of keys, and now all I had to show for five hundred dollars was a miserable set of useless car keys.

Debbie looked at me. "Is Rafi coming back?"

"No, something tells me that he probably isn't," I said. "Chances are, we probably have seen the last of Rafi."

At that moment, there was steam coming out of my head. I had never been so angry or so humiliated in my life. Had I got my hands on Rafi at that moment, I would have ripped off his head, pulled out his long and short intestines, and strung him to the nearest cactus. I prayed secretly in my heart that he would get home and in the midst of telling his wife how he had ripped me off, he would choke on a chicken bone. Or at the very least that he would die of the most excruciating bout of constipation.

But I had a problem. Standing next to me was a girl that I really wanted to impress, the girl I wanted to marry. And I was a good Jewish rabbinical student. I just had to control myself and not let any of my anger get out. Debbie looked at me compassionately. "I can't believe this. You mean, he ripped you off? Stole your five hundred dollars?"

I squirmed. "Yes, I suppose so."

"My gosh," she said, "you must be so angry. You probably want to kill him."

"Angry?" I responded, tightening every muscle in my body and making a desperate effort to look calm and relaxed. "I wouldn't say that I was angry. Perhaps ever so slightly . . . perturbed."

By now all the steam emanating from my scalp had incinerated my yarmulke. My beard was singed and standing at an angle of ninety degrees. There was a burning smell all around. Debbie did not appear to notice.

"What I feel now," I began carefully and bravely, "is not anger so much as a profound sense of disappointment. Poor Rafi may have been driven to a life of crime out of sheer desperation, to feed his two little Rafis back at home. What I feel therefore is guilt. I just wish I could have given him more. He needs the money. I just wish that he were here before me now so that I could also give him my watch, even give him the shirt off my back, even pawn some of my vital organs."

"This, this is incredible," Debbie said, radiant with love and admiration. "The average guy would have been quite upset. After all, he lied to you and stole your money. Instead, all you feel is compassion for him and a generosity of spirit. Boy, you are the most special guy in the whole world." There were tears streaming down her cheeks.

"Yes," I said humbly. "I guess you're right. I have never felt average. I must be special. My mother thinks so too." Every nerve in my body was twitching as I tried to compose myself.

We trekked back from the Sahara to Brooklyn, and the next day, capitalizing on my Academy Award-winning performance of the night before, I asked Debbie to marry me. "But I can't," she said. "I don't feel worthy. Even I experience occasional flashes of temper. I have never met anyone with no anger and only love in his heart. But you, you're an angel. Why would you want to marry me?"

"Well," I said, "I take your point. But I don't mind condescending to your level for the next sixty or so years. It gives me more of a chance to practice my generosity." She fell to the ground and kissed my toes and said it would be an honor to be my wife. How could she know that she had just contracted to marry a dangerous psychopath who that very morning had beseeched the benevolent Creator that Rafi should have a 747 jumbo jet land on his apartment tenement?

The fact remains—I controlled my anger and won Debbie's hand.

(Once we were officially engaged, I waited in stealth, one month, two months, three months, until we married in Sydney, Australia. And then, the morning after the wedding, I took the Concorde back to New York. I tracked down Rafi outside the same restaurant and shot him in the back ten times. It was like winning the lottery. I felt great, like a real New Yorker. And it has remained an unsolved mystery in New York until today.)

Anger—the biggest killer of all

We don't get angry with someone unless we have both judged and condemned them simultaneously. So every bout of anger is preceded by an act of judgment. But God didn't create the universe and put us on earth to be judges. When we do judge we are contesting the authority of the ultimate Judge, denying the existence of God, and making ourselves into "gods" in our own right. So not only are we breaking the Sixth Commandment; we are breaking the Second Commandment as well—worshipping false idols.

Every angry impulse involves a fundamental act of judgment.

For example, if you are sitting on an airplane and someone steps on your toe while getting into the window seat, you will only feel angry with them if you think they are insensitive or careless. If you notice that there is no possible way they could have avoided stepping on you, your toe would still hurt but you wouldn't be angry. We lose our temper with those people whom we judge to have hurt us deliberately, or who have behaved selfishly and irresponsibly.

Imagine that a woman is waiting for her date to pick her up and he is twenty minutes late. Unprepared to listen to his very reasonable explanation about the herd of elephants that had escaped across Central Park and held him up, she loses her temper and screams and yells at him as soon as he arrives. She judged him.

Of course, this woman has every right to a reasonable explanation for his tardiness. You are entitled to maintain your standards of what is and what is not due to you. But a display of instant bad temper is destructive, chiefly because it is so utterly narcissistic. It is an infatuation with your own sense of grievance that goes beyond reason, a form of righteous indignation that is unwarranted, an act of self-love that is unacceptable. And even if you don't lose your temper and raise your voice, almost a worse kind of anger is silent anger, where you just sink into yourself, harboring resentment and refusing to talk about it.

Anger is indicative of a deep-seated arrogance. An arrogant person believes he or she has the right to judge other people. They never place themselves in another's shoes, never imagine themselves in another's predicament, never try to understand someone else's pain, and ultimately dismiss their humanity. Devoid of humility and empathy, they cannot possibly sustain a healthy relationship. Hence the Talmud declares that God said of the angry person, "He and I cannot reside in the same universe."

Therefore, a bad-tempered man or woman is a definite no-no on any date, without exception. If your date has done something to upset you, the best advice I can give is to allow the wave of anger swelling up inside you to pass. Don't ride that wave; you'll only end up crashing into the rocks.

Wait until you cool off before you say, in a calm and pleasant voice, that you did not appreciate his bringing his former girlfriend on the date tonight, especially dressed up in a French maid's outfit. If need be, don't go out with him again. But whatever you do, don't rush off into the restaurant kitchen, borrow a hatchet from the chef, and do a Lorena Bobbit on him. He's not worth it. (And he's probably not that well endowed, either. So why bother?)

But never be *too* nice

You should never be too nice to your date, especially in the beginning. If your new boyfriend mentions that his nephew is being Bar Mitzvahed next week, it is probably a mistake to immediately offer to do all the cooking for two hundred guests. If your girlfriend tells you that she must go home early because she's taking her mother for colonic irrigation in the morning, do not offer to bring over a hose and lend a hand yourself. And whatever you do, don't offer to help her younger, more attractive sister find out about New York nightlife. Your date should appreciate you and trust in you, but never take you for granted. The thrill of the chase must always be kept alive. The desire to woo and win over one another is an essential part of dating. Never be a pushover.

One man I know took a girl out who clearly wasn't that excited about him. When he asked her out again, she declined. He then called and told her, "Fine, I understand that you don't want to go out with me. But I like you a lot, and would like to be involved in your life even on the periphery as a friend who is always there for you." Dumb mistake. She took him up on his offer and called him whenever she was between relationships and felt lonely. These meaningless dates, in which she would pour her heart out to him and talk the entire time about other men whom she really liked, just made him feel used. Soon, he resented her greatly, but really it was he who was responsible for the ridicu-

lous behavior of making himself into a doormat. If you behave like a carpet, you can't blame someone for walking all over you. Every doormat says "Welcome" on it.

He ended up shooting her cat and stuffing it into her mailbox.

(Just kidding. I wanted to see if you were still paying attention. But he was one unhappy kitten.)

On giving advice

When listening to your date, try not to give advice too soon. Because we are so eager to please and impress on a date, we tend to try to offer solutions to all their personal and professional problems. But your date probably does not want advice—they are asking for a moment of attention and sympathetic companionship. The way we get through all the petty, needling problems of everyday life is by unburdening ourselves to a sympathetic human listener. Usually the best way to tell your date that you appreciate the way they feel is to use simple statements like "I can't imagine how you put up with it," or "Well, that never happened to me, but I can imagine how painful it must be." I know you are longing to share all that worldly wisdom—but don't. Be a listener before a Mr. Fix-it.

As a child, when you didn't finish your revolting soggy green beans, your mother probably made speeches about the starving children in Africa. Remember how you hated it? Keep that in mind when your date complains about how their boss made them go down the road to the mailbox. Don't say things like "You are such a complainer," or "Man, are you a whiner. I bet if I married you I'd be locked up in the funny farm within a month."

And by all means, don't go into long family histories. "I can't believe how much you complain. You're lucky to have a job at all. Why, my Grandpa Elmer arrived in this country with nothing but a reed covering his genitals."

The important message to give is "You and I are the same. You are not alone. Don't feel despondent or crushed." You are affirming your date's right to feel important, and you are linking his or her life with your own. If, on the other hand, you give advice, you can come across as a know-it-all who is insensitive to their predicament. You can aggravate their sense of isolation and insignificance.

A delay in offering your solution is better than taking the risk of alienating your date. If you have to bite your lip, then so be it. If you can't control yourself, rush out to the car and turn on the radio to discover if the Mir space station has crash-landed in your neighborhood yet. A good general tip for avoiding knee-jerk advice-giving is to ask questions of your date, to be absolutely sure you understand their problems before you offer your advice.

The importance of listening

Never underestimate the importance of being a good listener. Too many married women have told me that often, when speaking to their husbands, they stop talking in mid-sentence because they know they are not being listened to. They feel like a piece of furniture, and this experience of being ignored is a denial of their value. Their spirit is crushed.

So on a date, be attentive to the person you are with when they speak. It will make them feel very much alive. Take note of what they say and commit it to memory. If they tell you they don't like eating fish, or that they are allergic to cats, make sure you don't forget this information. It is important to them, and they will expect it to be important to you. And your cat, Tibbles? Well, he'll be happy to be locked in the closet with the Dover sole.

Avoiding gossip

Jewish law considers gossip a murderous activity. When you talk about a person behind his or her back, they have no way of responding, and if you are believed, their reputation suffers and their credibility dies.

The Sixth Commandment teaches that a person's reputation is as important as life itself. Our reputation dictates how we are received by society, our degree of professional success, and our chances of meeting with members of the opposite sex. When our reputation is ruined, this can be a permanent blow to our way of living and our livelihood. It can be another kind of death, which is why slander is often referred to as "character assassination."

On a date, do not succumb to the temptation of gossiping about someone else. Though your date may enjoy the conversation, they will leave feeling that you are a cruel and callous person. Worse, they will start wondering what you say about them when they are not around. They will also question your integrity and lose respect for you, thinking of you as a small person who takes pleasure in hurting others or achieving things at others' expense. If you find your date gossiping, change the subject. There is, however, no need to say something like "Unlike you, I don't like to gossip. Can we please speak about something else?" Nothing is gained when you put your date down.

In particular, do not gossip about people you have dated. Imagine that there's a great guy out there, who would be perfect for you, but someone says something malicious about him. When you meet him, you turn down his request for a date. Think about how you might have just given up the opportunity for lasting love and passion, all because of someone else's spite. Well, you wouldn't like that. So don't ruin someone else's chances either. Just because your relationship didn't work out with Bobby, that doesn't mean that Cindy down the road won't like him. It could be that she can easily overlook a man who still lives at home with his mother at age fifty-eight, and answers the phone by saying, "Captain's Log, Stardate 8804.1."

Hillel, the great Jewish sage, wrote, "That which you hate, don't do unto others. This is the entire Torah, the rest being but commentary."

Protecting your date

In the Bible, God says to the Jews, "I have borne you on the wings of eagles and brought you unto Me." The commentators state that an eagle carries its young on its back so that its own body will act as a shield against arrows.

You should be similarly protective of your date. In their explanation of the Sixth Commandment, the sages state that a host is responsible for the safety of his guests and has to make suitable provisions for their protection and security. Just so. You should never subject your date to danger, for example by introducing him to your jealous ex-boyfriend, recently released from solitary confinement at the local prison for violent assault.

Guys, if your date does not have a car, always insist on driving her home, no matter how much she protests. And always wait for her until she enters the house. Not only is this very romantic because it shows how much you care, also it is your responsibility to ensure her safety.

If neither of you has a car, perhaps you will be one of those lucky men who have the opportunity to make the ultimate sacrifice for their date and show them their courage and chivalry. You might be walking her home, and suddenly be accosted by a mugger or some other everyday citizen of New York. When held up at gunpoint, never pull your girlfriend in front of you as a shield. She will not be amused. Also, don't fall on the ground at the feet of your mugger and beg and scream for your life like a weasel. Neither should you offer your date as a hostage while you make your escape.

The first thing you should do is get over the urge to panic and flee. Look your attacker in the eye and say with the greatest confidence, "Look here, you miserable, wretched, putrid scum. I worked hard for my money, unlike lazy, twisted dirtbags like yourself. So why don't you go back to having an affair with your mother and producing children with a big eye in the middle of their forehead before I personally do away with you, Mr. Human Refuse."

Very good, you said it. You're her hero. You're a real man. Now, recite your last prayers because you're about to die. After the initial shock of your speech wears off, the mugger will shoot you. Accept the bullet gracefully. Don't be like one of those weaker men who whimpers and moans. Try and die quickly. She is cold and wants to get home. And if you must bleed, try not to do so on her jacket.

Console yourself by thinking that although your life is ending, at least you impressed her and she will never forget you. You took a bullet for her and you will always be in her heart. That is, until she finds her next boyfriend at which time she will flush all pictures of you down the toilet. But who knows, some cute broad at the beach playing in the place where the sewer empties just might find your picture and hang it up on *her* wall. One way or another your immortality is guaranteed.

Oh yes, and if you are mugged, whatever you do, don't say to your attacker, "Lionel, scream louder. You don't look mean enough." Your date will realize that you paid one of your friends to engineer a moment of courage, and she'll be the one to pump a bullet in you, and then she'll never go to heaven.

The difference between a full life and half a life

A person who shies away from relationships is doing more than missing out on one of the great pleasures of life; they are committing a sin. Similarly, someone who gets into relationships but always finds a way to sabotage them and avoid long-term commitment is behaving just as badly. Whether it is done because of a fear of intimacy or of failure and disappointment in love, such self-enforced solitude is wrong.

It is so self-destructive, in fact, that Judaism would equate it with suicide, which is also prohibited by the Sixth Commandment. It is wrong to cause physical harm to your body because it is a holy vessel, given to you by God. Similarly, the Almighty gave you a soul that seeks and needs a companion in order to feel appreciated and whole. All of us need to be needed. Don't kill yourself spiritually by staying single. You will only live half a life. I find it saddening that so many people today have reconciled themselves to unnecessary loneliness.

Judaism views celibacy as a "murder" of sorts. Men and women are obligated to marry and have children. We are all creators. We have been given the physical capacity to procreate, and this must be exercised. Children bring blessings and bills into the world. A person who refuses to date, marry, and have children is rebuked because somewhere out there is a man or woman with whom they were destined to create new life. To do otherwise, to refrain from marriage and reproduction, is viewed as a sin of destruction, because the children who should have been created never were. Of course, having them brings about even more destruction. But this is just one of the many mysteries of life.

Summary of Compliments

1. Build your date up, don't bring them down.
2. Never date an ax murderer.
3. Sing their praises.
4. Never judge.
5. The story of Rafi: never lose your cool.
6. Anger—the biggest killer of all
7. Never be *too* nice—you're not a doormat.

8. Listen without fixing. Hold off on giving advice.
9. The importance of listening
10. Avoid gossip.
11. Protect your date and make them feel safe.
12. Those who forget the pasta are condemned to reheat it.

seven

Mystery
Sexual Focus

It is easier to keep half a dozen lovers guessing than to keep one lover after he has stopped guessing.
—Helen Rowland (1875–1950), U.S. journalist.
A Guide to Men

THE SEVENTH COMMANDMENT: Do not commit adultery. (Exodus 20:14)

An ancient Rabbinical legend tells of the great Reb Yossel the Humble who lived in the Belorussian town of MadameShviabotskasDungeon, who used to confuse the evil inclination by giving in without a struggle.

Ah, adultery, adultery. The violation of the marriage bed. The Seventh Commandment is one of the biggies. It is certainly the most famous and perhaps the most severe of the Ten Commandments. Many people find it hard to observe. Paying taxes seems easy by comparison.

On the face of it, the Seventh Commandment seems a rather premature concern when it comes to dating. After all, isn't adultery by definition a matter for *married* couples to worry about? Surely the priority in dating should be freedom of choice—freedom to make the *right* choice—rather than an obligation to commit oneself to one person and forget about everyone else? Well, yes and no. However . . .

Adultery is really about how we misuse our intimacy, our sexuality, by handing over the most intimate part of ourselves to someone who is neither appropriate nor worthy. It is when a husband or wife takes the most sacred element of their married relationship and gives it away to an outsider, a stranger. In a dating relationship, it is when you give away your sexuality to someone who has no intention of ever being anything other than a stranger. His or her wish is to love you and leave you.

Surrendering sexually too early in a relationship is almost always guaranteed to destroy the budding romance, chiefly because it undermines the sense of mystery. Your body, covered in clothing, is a mysterious treasure which only bonds of commitment can reveal. When you go ahead and remove it all, you are a puzzle that has been solved. Eroticism is lost from the relationship since there are now no obstacles which must be overcome in order for pleasure to be had.

Mystery and revelation

God's revelation to the Jewish people at the foot of Mount Sinai represents a watershed. Until that time, God was only perceived through His actions and through His creation. The vast expanse of starlit heavens, the intense heat of the sun, the wondrous colors of nature, and the infinite variety of living things, all testified to God's existence for those who wished to find Him. God was known by the cloak He wore. His external forms testified to something of His essence, but He remained veiled by nature. This made God intensely mysterious and caused many truth-seeking men and women to embark on a journey to find Him.

All this changed with the revelation of God at Sinai. God made *Himself* known to the assembled nation of Israel—men, women, and children—in one vast display of awesome power. The gathering of the Jewish people at Mount Sinai is unique in the annals of apocalyptic literature in that it is the only work claiming to be divine that speaks of a collective revelation—to an entire nation, rather than to a group of followers or apostles. God courted the Jews through history, beginning with that great knight of faith Abraham, slowly revealing more and more of Himself, until He invited the Jews to know His essence in the great spectacle that was Sinai.

This same brilliant technique should be used in dating. When we first see that beautiful stranger across a crowded room, we can only know their external form. This very thing, the other person's outer veil of mystery, is what produces the attraction in the first place. The last thing you want them to do at that moment is to come over, take off all their clothes, and make you listen to their entire life story. While that might provide an instant of ecstasy, it would burn out as quickly as a candle in a storm.

> *Lucinda came to a lecture I delivered for Jewish singles and was elated when an attractive man asked her out on a date. As they sat eating pasta, he started telling Lucinda about his sexual fetishes and about how he had had sex with three women not only once, but twice. And the second time, he wasn't even related to any of the women. His "grand finale" for the evening was to ask Lucinda if he could take her undergarments home. Believe it or not, this is a true story.*

Being too candid too soon is an appalling display of poor judgment, one that your date will not easily be able to overlook. It is vulgar and ungentlemanly. Don't tell your date narratives that are in very poor taste and compromise your sense of mystery. Stories of how you used to pick your acne pimples as a teenager, or the time when you were constipated for over three months, are best kept to yourself. Talk only about the weather. Ask them if they like rain.

The dreaded 007 complex

Having said this, men should not be too mysterious. In fact, while mystery suits many women just fine, it makes men look like geeks. Don't try to be James Bond. When she asks you your name, say more than just "Cohen, Jack Cohen." Men should talk openly about their emotions. Tell her how you often contemplated murdering your Uncle Mervin, who used to belch at the dinner table and inhale the aroma in order to keep himself awake. There is, however, no need to tell her that were it not for your hernia operation at five, you would have been an international bodybuilder. Women prefer mush to macho. Find the healthy middle ground. Likewise, do not reveal that you are a 24–7 webhead. Even if you don't have a life, invent one.

The Bible describes how the Jewish people, prepared though they were through their long history, still felt almost crushed by God's dramatic revelation at Mount Sinai, and pleaded with Moses that he serve as the medium for the communication. *"When all the people witnessed the thunder and lightning, the sound of the trumpet, and the mountain smoking, they were afraid and trembled and stood at a distance, and said to Moses, 'You speak to us, and we will listen; but do not let God speak to us, or we will die.'"* (Exodus 20:18–19)

We are not all Moses. We are not big enough or strong enough to receive the full impact of another being's self-revelation all in one go. Added to that, there is a great attraction in mystery. Hence the unquenchable human obsession with space exploration. The most beautiful things in life are those which elicit a sense of awe, mystery, and wonder. They attract us and grab us like nothing else. Nothing is more disappointing than being told how a conjuring trick is actually done. Mystery always retains our interest because it is endless. Always keep a part of yourself in reserve for the eventual surprise.

> *A young man goes into a drugstore to buy condoms. The pharmacist says the condoms come in packs of three, nine, or twelve and asks which the young man wants. "Well," he said, "I've been seeing this girl for a while and she's really hot. I want the condoms because I think tonight's THE night. We're having dinner with her parents, and then we're going out. Once she's had me, she'll want me all the time, so you'd better give me the twelve pack." The young man makes his purchase and leaves.*
>
> *Later that evening, he sits down to dinner with his girlfriend and her parents. He asks if he might give the blessing, and they agree. He begins the prayer, but continues praying for several minutes.*
>
> *The girl leans over to him and whispers, "You never told me you were such a religious person."*
>
> *He leans over to her and murmurs, "You never told me your father was a pharmacist."*

Of course, the joke here is that the man is interested in hiding his real intentions from the girl's parents. But notice he does not give a toss what the girl thinks of him. Being spiritual and mysterious rather than purely physical and pleasure-seeking is immensely attractive to your date. And that means delaying sexual intimacy for a time when it will serve the higher interests of knowledge.

Dating the mystery man or woman

So part of the secret for dating contained within the Seventh Commandment is never to lose your mystery or compromise your modesty within a relationship.

Becoming a bore is one of the greatest sins of dating. It is certain to destroy every last hint of love and attraction. The preservation of modesty and mystery is what guarantees that your budding relationship is an ongoing journey rather than an easily reached destination. Many people, especially men, fail to understand this. Rather than thinking of the date as a time for the excavation of the depths of their partner's soul, it is too often used merely for seduction, with the final outcome—sex—being the sole purpose of the enterprise.

I don't altogether go along with the conventional wisdom that says that men are all predators, who love the thrill of the chase, whereas women are far more civilized. It is partly true. For instance, a woman makes a list of things she needs and then goes to the store and buys them. A man waits until the only items left in his fridge are half a lemon with facial hair and something turning green. Then he goes grocery shopping. A woman knows all about her children. She knows about dentist appointments and soccer games and romances and best friends and favorite foods and secret fears and hopes and dreams. A man is vaguely aware of some short people living in the house.

So okay, men aren't perfect. When forced to talk to their girlfriends on the telephone, they can offer nothing more than bodily noises and monosyllabic responses. And they twist every single thing a girl says to have sexual meaning. That is another good reason for neither men nor women to reveal too much about themselves at an early stage—you can easily put each other off.

That being said, I do think the world has changed since the Stone Age, and modern men have their anxieties about dating. They are not all in it for the conquest.

Men today are pussycats

Nowadays, when so many women are professionally successful in their own right and compete with men for the same jobs, it is easy to forget just how emasculated many men feel. Knowing that women have a wide choice, and no longer need them for the traditional reasons of support and protection, many sensitive men have become extraordinarily shy and unassuming.

It is also conventional wisdom that if a man is interested in a woman he will find a way to call or get in touch, and should be left to make all the moves, but in my experience this is not always the case. I know scores of men who are interested in dating a woman but who are fearful of rejection. Sometimes they cannot even summon up the courage to pick up a telephone. Therefore, women should be careful not to be too mysterious and make men do *all* the chasing. *The Rules* got it wrong on this one. In an age in which so many men lack confidence, it could be that the reason he doesn't call is that he's sitting at home with his teeth chattering.

Some handy tips for preserving your ''mystique''

- When you first talk on the phone, don't let the discussion drag on. Face-to-face conversations are much better. More important, when you speak for three hours on the telephone, having not really met, you start to build up enormous expectations of the other person. When you meet them—or when they meet you—it might be a big anticlimax for one of you. Wait for the date!
- So many singles think they will come across as really impressive and cool if they have an incredibly long and exotic answering machine message. Get that idea right out of your head. The best messages are the simple and direct ones that state clearly and briefly that you are not available but will return calls. Not everyone enjoys listening to the entire sound track of *West Side Story* just to leave a message. Stay away from outgoing messages with a *Star Trek* theme. Any guy or girl with even a trace of common sense will hang up as soon as they hear "Star Date 345.98. Phasers have been set to stun.

It is therefore safe to leave a message." Also, those really
cutesy-wootsy, palsy-walsy messages are pathetic. You may lose
a perfectly good date if he calls only to hear "Roses are red,
violets are blue. I'm not in right now, but would love to hear
from you."

- As an American living in England, I was intrigued to discover
how English people are afraid to say "hello" when they answer
the telephone, opting instead to say their telephone number
only: "278364." The prevalent belief in England is that every
third call is a wrong number anyway, so why give away vital
information like the word "hello." After all, saying this word
invites a complete stranger into your inner sanctum. In all
likelihood, the wrong caller is a crazed ax murderer and will
view your politeness as a weakness and come over to
exterminate the entire neighborhood.

- English people also rarely state their names in the outgoing
message of their answering machine. So instead of getting a
nice friendly message that says something like "Hi, this is
Rachel. I'm not in right now, so please leave a message," you
get "584036. The persons represented by this telephone
number and who live here are not in. When we do return,
we'd prefer it if you did not come over and murder us. Please
leave a message instead. Beep."

- The moral is that while your outgoing message should not be
long-winded and silly, neither should it be so brief and
functional that you sound inhuman. Leave a message that is
warm and welcoming, stating your name clearly, and simply
asking that they leave a message and saying that you are sure
to get back to them, especially if they are wealthy and
available.

- It goes without saying that jumping into bed with your date
before you've even exchanged telephone numbers is a big no-
no. By the same token, don't allow yourself to be drawn into
conversations about sex. Neither should you tolerate your date
being "forward." Even if she is penning the sequel to the

Kama Sutra that's no excuse for inquiring about sixty-nine new sexual positions with her on the first date. If he invites you to a threesome with his Swedish friend Inge, or starts unbuttoning his shirt just as he gives you his name for the first time, kick him in the shins, while thanking him for showing you "his item of interest."

- You have to be able to discern and be sensitive to the degree of intimacy you have achieved at the different stages of dating. So, for example, it is perfectly acceptable to tell someone whom you have been seeing for nearly a year that you are on antidepressants. However, if you tell them on the first or second date that your favorite food is Prozac, they will think they are dating a serious misfit who might strangle them in their sleep or jump off a bridge when the Mets don't make it into the World Series.

- Be careful of being too giving too early in the relationship. If she is a student, don't offer to do her revision and take the exams in her place. Don't suggest that he pop around with all his laundry for you to wash and iron the following Friday.

- Dress modestly on dates. Eroticism is about the involvement of the mind, so you have to give a man room to use his imagination. Give him the opportunity to imagine you innocently undressed; don't display cleavage to him and every other man in the restaurant. Once you show him everything he will adopt a nonchalant attitude toward you. You can be sure that the first time you show a lot of cleavage, he will be manufacturing excuses to lean across the table to get a better look. But after a while, he may be eyeing your leftover steak instead and offering you five bucks for it.

- Be especially careful never to have sex at too early a stage. Making our bodies public property utterly destroys mystery and, with it, intimacy. Very, very quickly the sex will become boring and routine. Soon enough you will find that while you are making love to your boyfriend, he actually answers the phone: "Hello? . . . Oh, nothing much. What are you up to?" The next night he tells you, "Let's hurry up, the game's about to start," and ends with "Hold on while I change the channel . . ."

The importance of surprises

What produces the most excitement in life? You go through the endless drudgery of daily existence. You wake up in the morning, shower and dress, grab a piece of toast before rushing off to work. Then you spend the day completing a series of tasks, most of which are pretty routine. Suddenly, a package arrives on your desk. A friend who forgot your birthday last month sends you a book all wrapped up. You are ecstatic.

Does a book really provide such an uncommon thrill? Well, of course, if it's one of mine it does, but I mean an ordinary book. No, it's not the book. It's the fact that it was *unexpected*. Something nice happened—a friend thought of you—when you were least expecting it. In other words, what really causes us the greatest excitement in the world is that one word: surprise! We love surprises. And on dating you must offer up plenty.

In my book *The Jewish Guide to Adultery*, I pointed out that one of the reasons why men and women involved in illicit relationships don't seem to ever get bored is that everything they are doing is covert and secretive. They are constantly applying their imagination and ingenuity to where they should meet next and how they can plan their next rendezvous without getting caught. And there is the constant danger that they may be caught—all the near misses of being seen together in the wrong place at the wrong time. It makes a dull life seem exciting.

We must draw one good lesson from this negative example: one of the first duties of dating is to make life more exciting for each other.

Sex is not a shortcut to intimacy

Within dating, there must be a carefully balanced mixture of growing in intimacy while preserving mystery. Many women capitulate to sex very early in a relationship, even when they know that it's a bad idea, because they think it will be a shortcut to intimacy. They think that by having sex and giving the man what he wants, he will love and appreciate her for it. It will bind him to her. Big mistake.

In reality, women who feel they have to give a man sex, even when he has shown *no* commitment whatsoever, are simply betraying their deep insecurities. They fear that if they don't capitulate, the man will dump them. The opposite is true.

Sex is the most beautiful part of a loving relationship because it brings out our strongest emotions. Nothing is as powerful and nothing has the ability to solidify the love and commitment between a man and a woman like sex. Therefore, if it is abused, misused, or employed for purposes of recreation only, you have squandered the most powerful weapon in your arsenal for achieving intimacy and commitment.

This was the mistake made by Monica Lewinsky. From her testimony in the Starr Report, it is clear that she thought that by giving Bill Clinton sex, she would win over his heart. She became the sexual predator in the relationship, offering her body to him as a sacrifice on the altar of love, so sure that he would eventually give her his heart as well. In the end, it ended in tragedy for both of them. The writing was on the wall after the first sexual encounter when he couldn't even remember her name, calling her "Kiddo" instead.

Death of the female
sexual predator

Indeed, the whole Monica Lewinsky saga has briefly resurrected the ancient image of the female sexual predator. By Lewinsky's own testimony, she pursued Bill voraciously. She would wait for hours on end to see him, however briefly, at public meetings, and pestered Betty Curry for weeks on end just to be admitted to the Oval Office and tell the President (November 12, 1997) how pleasurable oral sex is with Altoid mints. "Ms. Lewinsky was chewing Altoids at the time, but the President replied that he did not have enough time for oral sex. They kissed, and the President rushed off for a State Dinner with President Zedillo." (Starr Report)

Today, of course, it is the men who are perceived primarily as sexual hunters. But in the ancient world it was radically different. Scores of ancient writings portray women as the ones you had to watch out for. Proverbs warns the innocent youth (2:16): "Be saved from the loose woman, from the adulteress with her smooth words . . ." And again in 7:10–12: "Then a woman comes toward him, decked out like a prostitute, wily of heart. She is loud and wayward; her feet do not stay at home; now in the street, now in the squares, and at every corner she lies in wait." Indeed, Judaism has always maintained that women have a far stronger sexual drive than men. Commenting on God's words to Eve, "Your desire shall be for your husband" (Genesis 3:16), Rashi says that this refers to exceedingly intense sexual longing.

Why has this changed? Sexual boredom is today the number one cause of divorce, with more husbands than ever before complaining that their wives are frigid. Indeed, many sexual studies today report the overwhelming majority of women enjoy cuddling and romantic walks much more than sex.

Here is the reason why: Women have a far more mature approach to sex than men. Whereas a man who cheats on his wife deflects the guilt by thinking, "It wasn't love, it was only sex," women have always found it difficult to separate their bodies from their hearts. In a recent study published by *The London Sunday Times,* 84 percent of women said that even if they had a night of fantastic sex with a guy but he didn't call them back later, the memory remained one of pain rather than pleasure. Unlike men, women have always treated sex as an act of love, a consummation of intimacy. This is also why their sex drive is so much stronger than a male's, because it is not as superficial. It springs from an intense and deep desire to connect and become one flesh with the object of their affection.

But the sexual revolution changed all that. Encouraged as they were to liberate themselves and their bodies from the stodgy, conservative mores of their parents, women were persuaded to engage in premarital sexual encounters with virtual strangers. This in turn led directly to the unhealthy separation of emotions from the mind. Aside from the mountain of data which supports the self-evident fact that women much prefer sex with a man they love and find it difficult to enjoy making love to a man who is a stranger, there are simple physiological factors which support this conclusion as well. For a man, sex is almost an out-of-body experience. His genitals are on the outside. Thus, he treats sex as doing something to someone else. He therefore finds it easy to divorce his emotions from the act. For men, while sex can be meaningful, it can also be something as mundane as hammering a nail into the wall. Far too many men treat sex as an everyday, mundane activity. And this is their great shortcoming. But a woman's genitals are on the inside. For her, sex is about inviting someone into her most private space, her inner sanctum. Since it is an inner experience, it becomes impossible to separate the flesh from the emotions, the body from the heart. Nobody feels comfortable with a stranger in their home. Having sex with a man she does not love may be experienced by a woman as a form of trespassing, a violation of her private space. Thus, women find it most difficult to separate love from sex. They want to feel intimate and familiar with the man that shares their bed and invades their body. They want to trust and love him. The partition of love and sex is irregular and strange. This unnatural compartmentalization is why so many women who have engaged in commitment-free sex later tell their husbands that they are far more interested in romance than sex, in hugging and holding each other, to sexual intercourse. They no longer see sex as an act of love or an emotional act of consecration. Rather, sex is about pleasure. The great sex they had in their youth, rather than liberating them, made them instead feel used and exploited. So when they want to feel loved, they allow themselves to shut off sexually and prefer to hug and talk.

Case in point, studies show that women who have been sexually abused at an early age develop a characteristically male approach to sex, separating mind from body when dealing with sexual relationships. Many women who have been abused are as sexually promiscuous as men. They find it easier to have sex without love. This is how they coped with being taken advantage of against their will. They locked their emotions into a box and told the offender, "I am powerless to stop you from using my body, but you will never have my heart." The result is that they experience terrible problems of intimacy later on in relationships because they find it difficult to reconnect that which has been severed.

The same is true, albeit to a more limited extent, of men and women who have sex with someone they do not love. Today both men and women make sex an independently pleasurable experience of the senses, instead of a passionate act of soul fusion. They have sex, but while they involve their bodies in the act, they do not engage their personalities. Because so many people practice this deception, *they forget how to share intimacy.* Later, when they want to use sex to achieve intimacy, it doesn't work. Once you cut off your mind from your heart, how do you know it can ever be reattached? We all take intimacy for granted, as if it can be produced simply by flicking on a light switch. In truth, the sharing of intimacy is one of life's most noble but also most difficult goals. For it to be successful, trust, attraction, affection, and security must all be present.

If none of these are there, then sex will be a purely physical experience that will leave you empty and disillusioned. While Woody Allen has said, "Sex without love is an empty experience. But as empty experiences go, it is one of the best," this humorous comment does not take into account how damaging a purely sexual relationship can be.

The monumental study *Sex in America* showed that young people no longer believe sex to be a central component of a relationship. Rather, communication, shared values, and common interests are the strongest criteria for long-term relationships. Hence, 94 percent of American college graduates will only marry someone of similar education. This kind of superficial nonsense is a direct product of the contemporary debasement of the sanctity of sex. No amount of political conversation or mutual dedication to saving the whales has the power to bring forth our strongest, most deep-seated emotions, making us feel intensely good about ourselves and our partners, the way sex does. And when things don't work well in the bedroom, they're not going to work well in the living room either. Hence, it is imperative that we respect our sexuality and develop its potency to maximize the intimacy and closeness that we feel within a relationship. If you have the forbearance to wait until you're married, your reward will be a sex life through which you come to know each other in the deepest possible way.

Sexual compatibility is a myth invented by a bunch of impatient and lazy men

Many people tell me that they have to have sex before marriage in order to ensure that they are sexually compatible. But "sexual compatibility" is a myth. All men and women are extremely sexual. If a man and a woman are deeply attracted to one another, if they care about the relationship and are willing to invest the time and effort required to make each other happy, then the sex will be great. Men complain of sexual incompatibility in order to excuse poor performance. It's that simple. Unlike men, women usually need to be warmed up in order to have steamy, hot sex. But when the men have not even taken the time to heat up the oven, how can they complain that the sex was half-baked? While a man's sexual drive is immediately manifest, a woman's is more latent. It must be drawn out with care and consideration. A woman's libido is like the fire that lurks in a hot coal. You can't see it, but it's there all right, and it's a lot hotter than the male fire. But it needs to be fanned into a flame through a man's patience and attention to a woman's sexual needs.

This, ultimately, is the reason that Judaism condemns sex outside the commitment of marriage. When you have sex with someone you don't love, you ignore the power of the emotions. You have sex with half your personality tied behind your back. You're firing on only one cylinder. The result is boring sex which later leads husbands and wives to enjoy watching television together far more than making love.

Don't fool around
with someone else

You are dating in order to find a partner for life and get married. And when you do finally stand at the altar or under the wedding canopy, you will undertake to be faithful to that person until the day you die. You will mean it sincerely, and you will try to maintain that vow. But it will be difficult. Throughout your life you will have to exercise self-control and avoid temptations to commit adultery. In overcoming these challenges, you will discover new strength in yourself and reap the rewards of a satisfying and completely monogamous marriage.

With this in mind, why, oh why would you want to be unfaithful and fool around while dating? Remind yourself that the person you are dating could one day be your spouse. Do you think he or she will take kindly to you cheating at this early stage of the relationship? Absolutely not! The fact that the two of you are not yet married will mean nothing at all. You will have betrayed the fact that you are not worth staying with for another five minutes, let alone a whole lifetime.

By learning to control our "natural" sexuality, we are actually becoming more human. The Ten Commandments require us to reorient ourselves, enhancing and focusing our nature and raising it to a higher level, to the plane of civilized humanity. The difference between an animal and a human is that while an animal can only behave instinctually, a human has an inner will to dedicate his impulses and desires to a higher cause. Therefore, we must use sexuality to enhance and define committed relationships, rather than just unleash ourselves in a series of meaningless flings.

So get a grip on yourself, be tough, take a cold shower, hang up a picture of Richard Nixon making a "V" sign in your bedroom, throw out the Viagra, and remember what's really important. By setting your priorities straight while dating you stand only to gain in the future.

"It's only natural"

Is sexual infidelity really such a big deal? Many argue that, from the example of the animal world, it is unfair to expect men and women (especially men) to adhere to monogamous relationships. Surely it is better to turn a blind eye to occasional indiscretions rather than risk ruining the relationship with unreasonable demands?

This reasoning is specious and silly. The belief that we are somehow helpless to disregard our hormones, that when our body calls we must obey, is just plain irresponsible. Sure, the temptation to sleep around is quite natural. But then, so is laziness and selfishness. Would anyone tolerate it if you insisted on never working for your living or never sharing your belongings with friends and relatives? Would *you* tolerate this sort of thing in yourself? Of course not! So why indulge in the silly belief that you have some sort of natural right to cheat on your boyfriend or girlfriend?

> *While appearing on a television talk show in Australia, I took a call from a twenty-five-year-old man named Brian. Though he loved his girlfriend very much, he said that he was frustrated by her lack of sympathy for a condition that he suffered from. He called his condition "sex addiction." Brian felt that he "must" sleep with other women, but his girlfriend would not tolerate it.*
>
> *I asked Brian if he ever felt the desire to have sex with his mother or sister. Of course, he responded that he did not. Then I told Brian to imagine that he was in a pub, making eyes at a beautiful woman across the room. Suddenly, her boyfriend appeared—a big, mean-looking rugby player holding a machete. Would he still go over and try to make time with her? After a pause, Brian admitted that he would probably not take the risk.*
>
> *"Lord Almighty!" I exclaimed. "It's a miracle! You're cured of your addiction!" I said to him. "Congratulations. Now go home to your girlfriend, if she'll still have you."*

Dangerous dualism

The idea that sexual indiscretion, particularly but not exclusively by men, is to be tolerated as something unavoidable is far too prevalent. Increasingly both men and women subscribe to a belief that sex can and should be somehow divorced from love. This is a huge obstacle to monogamy, as more people underestimate how sexual fidelity can truly be important for a relationship.

Sex is popularly perceived as something naughty, carnal, and dirty. Or if not something that is actually bad, then at least something that is only about sensual pleasure. And since sex is seen as essentially illicit, any underhanded tactic used to acquire it is thought acceptable.

Contrast this with popular views of romantic love. Love is idealized as something sublime. It is almost better, and more beautiful, when unrequited. It is glorious and it is marvelous . . . but not especially sexy. It is seen to transcend sex. Society seems to have embraced the idea of nonphysical, platonic love as the highest ideal. So is it any surprise that 87 percent of men who cheat on their wives still claim that they love them? They honestly feel that their married lives and their sex lives can exist in separate spheres, and that the illicit sex of their extramarital affairs has absolutely no bearing on their loving marriages.

The Jewish view

Judaism has always rejected this idea of a sexual-emotional dualism. Jewish wisdom, being profoundly monotheistic, maintains that there is only one God and no devil, that darkness is merely the absence of light, and that what we perceive as evil is the absence of God's presence rather than a separate, wicked power at work.

Similarly, Judaism insists on a holistic approach to human love and sexuality whereby they are one and the same and cannot be separated. Carnal love must be accompanied by heartfelt love, and attraction to the body must engender attraction to the soul. This is what the Seventh Commandment is all about: the preservation of sexual focus so that sex is a function of both body and soul.

The Bible says that only in sex do two people disrobe fully. That is, they shed not only their clothes but, more important, their emotional and spiritual defenses as well. Within a loving relationship, sex allows us to lose our inhibitions and reveal our innermost essence. We become completely honest—innocent—with one another. However, when sex is separated from love, all the barriers remain. Sex becomes a performance rather than a soul-stirring event. You can't make love with your clothes on. And neither can you fall in love when the clothing of inhibition and insincerity is left on either. So don't be afraid to commit—to get naked. Only then can you have passionate sex with the man or woman who is your other half.

The seed of adultery is sown by confusion

The essence of adultery is to misunderstand what we really desire. It occurs when a married man or woman puts the excitement of illicit sex before the deeper excitements and pleasure of a committed and loving relationship.

The proof that sex is not what we really want can be seen when you compare how you feel during the sexual act with how you feel as soon as it is over. When there is true love, sex is a satisfying act that brings you closer. You fall asleep all tangled up in each other. But when there is no love, and no commitment, you are often left feeling incredibly empty and let down after the act, almost as if you had done something wrong or illegal. You wake up next to a face which is essentially a stranger and immediately condemn yourself for not exerting greater self-control. You will look at your accomplice and despise them. They gave you what you said you wanted—but deep down you know that it wasn't what you really, really wanted.

Sex is the most beautiful act a man and woman in love can do together. So why do many people feel so rotten after having it? Because the longing for sex, which builds up inside, is really a longing for intimacy. Trying to have sex before you have achieved spiritual and emotional cohesion is putting the cart before the horse, and gets you nowhere.

Dating a married person

For those of you who are single, it is still possible to commit adultery—by dating a married person. Unfortunately, this happens all too often and leads to much heartache.

> *Neil came to me and said he needed advice because he was involved with a married woman.*
>
> *It had all started quite innocently, he claimed. They worked in the same company. She was unhappy because of problems she was having with her husband and the impact this was having on their children.*
>
> *Initially Neil had given her a shoulder to cry on, but this had turned into an intense mutual attraction. Before long, they went from exchanging confidences to sleeping together. Now, at twenty-one, Neil was having an illicit affair with a married, older woman.*
>
> *He knew that he had nothing to gain other than a lot of guilt and pain. The pain was much more intense for Neil, however, because he was an observant Jew, and he could not believe the situation in which he now found himself. The woman was calling him nightly saying that she wanted to leave her husband for him and would stop at nothing until they could be together.*

According to Jewish law, adultery is a sin committed by two parties. The single man or woman who has an affair with a married person is *just as guilty* of adultery. Always remember that there is no such thing as a marriage that is "open" or "effectively terminated." Until the divorce papers are signed, that man or woman you have your eye on is as married as the day they stood at the altar. They are untouchable. So stay away.

Putting the moral issue aside for a minute, adultery is just plain stupid. Look, your love life will be complicated enough, so why complicate it further by getting into a dead-end extramarital affair?

Don't believe the man who says he'll leave his wife for you.

Surveys prove that 92 percent of men who make this promise eventually break their word. In any event, do you really want a relationship with a person who betrays their spouse? What if they betray you one day? And, honestly, can you live with yourself knowing that you were party to the breakup of a marriage and a family?

> *I told Neil to break off all contact with his lover. I even recommended that he quit his job, to avoid seeing her in the office. Neil said that even if he did this, he would still be concerned for her happiness.*
>
> *"If that's the case," I responded, "then you should refer her to a good professional counselor."*
>
> *Neil's attempt to "console" the woman had only worsened her marital problems and messed up his own life.*

Note how confused Neil felt in this situation. Having committed himself to a sexual relationship, he had lost sight of reason and responsibility. That is because sex is the most potent and defining factor in a romantic relationship. And when this power of sex is channeled in the wrong direction, there's trouble. It retards our ability to think straight. This is the message of the Seventh Commandment: the need for sexual focus in relationships.

Why do people with integrity still date those who are married?

For a moment, let's look at why a person who is honest in every other area of life, who would never contemplate stealing or cheating people in financial matters, will still date and have a relationship with someone who is married. If you are an honest person and value your integrity, why would you allow yourself to become a home wrecker and serve as the instrument by which a person breaks their marital vows and causes deep and perhaps irreversible pain to their spouse?

The overwhelming response given by those who are in extra-marital relationships goes like this: When a man finds you so desirable that he is prepared to risk losing his spouse, children, job, career, home, friends, social standing, and entire social circle—that fact is so seductive and makes you feel so powerful and irresistible that you can't turn it down.

All of us want to be wanted and need to be needed. And when a woman is made to feel that a man will sacrifice anything to have her, it is incredibly flattering. So flattering that it can cause a person to give up all their values just to be with someone who is passionate about them.

There is a positive lesson here, even though it is garnered from something negative. Do you see what the power of desire can achieve?

Redefining adultery for singles

"Adulteration" is an act of *dilution* or *debasement*. When you adulterate something, you always harm it. If you lay the twin tablets of the Ten Commandments side by side, the Seventh Commandment falls exactly opposite the Second Commandment, which deals with the need for exclusivity in relationships. The Seventh Commandment roots this idea in a specific area. With its emphasis on the very carnal act of adultery, the Seventh Commandment teaches us the need for *physical* exclusivity and sexual focus in our dating.

While sleeping around behind your date's back may not be an act of marital infidelity, it is still an adulteration, a weakening of your relationship. You are deceiving your partner and showing utter disregard for the trust and time they have dedicated to you. Worse, since your emotional and physical needs are being met by a stranger, it lessens your dependency on your partner. And when you don't *need* someone badly, you tend to take them for granted. Once they discover what you have done, their affection will curdle into contempt and even hatred. You will have debased and cheapened the relationship, and lost forever what might have been a worthwhile romance or friendship. Flirting and joking with members of the opposite sex is one thing, but when you go to bed with someone behind your date's back you have crossed a boundary into conduct, which is totally unacceptable.

Some telltale signs of an unfaithful date

- He suddenly becomes overprotective of his privacy. If you ask about his schedule and day-to-day conduct, he becomes defensive and accuses you of spying.
- She spends more time than usual in deep, secretive conversations with her best girlfriend.
- He is less patient with you, and more likely to find fault with your dress or behavior.
- You walk into his bedroom and catch him in flagrante delicto with your best friend. (Yes it *is* what it appears to be. Don't believe him when he says he was just helping her discover if she has an irregular heartbeat.)
- He receives phone calls from a woman named Mary Christiansen claiming to be his grandmother. Yet he's Jewish. And you also remember that he told you that his grandmother was killed when a bread shelf at the grocery store fell on her three decades earlier.
- She spends far more time on her appearance and dress, even when she's not supposed to be seeing you that day.
- She is always busy on weekends and tries to convince you it's because she is a volunteer for the Symbionese Liberation Army.
- He gets hot and sweaty whenever you drive by a farm.

Communicating through body language

Now that I've mentioned to you exactly what gives your infidelity away, as a brief digression I'll teach you body language that can be used to convey extra-special attention to your date and make them trust, instead of suspect, you. And don't make the mistake of thinking that body language is a negligible form of communication. Remember that, at Sinai, God first caught the attention of the Jewish people through His use of visual spectacle—lightning, clouds, legions of angels—and only then used the spoken word in order to communicate.

On a date, make sure that the way you handle your body accurately represents your personality. Fingers, hands, limbs, and face will all reveal what kind of person you are, whether or not you can express your emotions, and whether you are expressing *true* emotions. Keep the following things in mind:

Eyes

A person with shifty eyes reveals dishonesty. Afraid that you will look right through him, he looks away and tries to avoid confrontation. Also, shifty eyes betray a lack of confidence. If you want to impress someone, you have to believe in yourself. If you don't, why should your date believe in you? Therefore, always look intently at your date. Do not fear direct eye contact. Don't stare at your groin as you tell her you love her.

Hands and limbs

To show confidence, you must speak with conviction. When doing so, I hope you will find yourself getting so animated that you use your hands. I'm not saying that you have to flail about as if you're Leonardo DiCaprio drowning in the Atlantic. But you do have to give the impression that you are totally involved in and enthusiastic about what you are saying. When you tell him you love him, say, "I love you this much," and extend your hands fully.

Rabbis especially are masters at using their hands while they speak, and if you ever want to silence a Rabbi, don't gag his mouth, but tie his hands.

When using your hands in conversation, never clench your fists. Don't slug her either. Extend your hands and fingers fully. This is a gesture of acceptance and openness. You are an open book. You have nothing to hide. You say what you mean and mean what you say. When you speak or listen, don't move your hands in front of your mouth or face. This makes you look guarded, as if you don't mean what you say. Don't let your extremities become your screen. Words are powerful, and they need an uninterrupted medium in order to maximize their potency. For the same reason, don't cross your legs or arms. It will look like you're defending yourself, like you're afraid that your date is about to take you prisoner. Of course, for women, crossing your legs is a natural movement, especially around some of these perverts you have been dating. Mace him if he gets too close, but do it in a spirit of love and acceptance.

If you are talking to your date while standing, never ever place your hands in your pockets. You will look awkward and wooden. This is also a classic sign of nervousness. Neither should you simply stand with your hands at your sides, unless you want to look like a cadaver. You are at your best and most attractive when you demonstrate intense life.

Don't fidget either, as this will betray unsettled nerves. No one likes a nervous date. They get enough anxiety at work. A date should be a haven, a time of solace, soothing, and comfort. Don't touch your nose, rub your eyes, or scratch your ears. All these nervous twitches will make your date think that you are either deceitful or suffering from mange. It will also make you look as though you are not especially interested in what your date is saying. Never reach for your briefs either, even if you put your wallet there for safekeeping.

Head

Hold your head up. No matter how tired you are, don't let it slip from side to side, and certainly do not slump forward into your entrée. You cannot afford to make your date feel that they bore you and that you are not excited to be with them. If you can't keep your eyes open, overdose on No Doz.

Politely excusing yourself for being tired just isn't good enough. If you are really excited about your date, adrenaline should kick in and you should feel distinctly alive. So, no matter how fatigued you are, find a way to perk yourself up. Do whatever it takes. Pretend your date is Homer Simpson. Connect a steady electric current to your temples. Down a tablespoon full of Tabasco sauce.

Whatever it takes, keep your chin up. If you do fall asleep listening to your date and fall faceflat into the soup, make like nothing happened. Borrow their handkerchief, clean yourself up, and calmly say, "Now, where were we?" Since they're just as bored as you, they probably didn't even notice. Your head should be mostly upright and perpendicular to your neck. As your date speaks, nod a little here and there. Not too much. You don't want to look as though your head is on a bungee spring.

Posture

Lean forward whenever you make an emotional or sentimental point. Do the same when your date is saying something important. This gesture shows that you feel close to them and want to draw nearer to them. After a while you should be so close that you can hear her heart beating. (Now you're too close and she has just slugged you. Draw back a little.) Don't slouch or lean back too much. When you do, you look tired, uninterested, disrespectful, and unanimated. Living things are attractive. Dead things are not. The more life you show, the more attractive and interesting you become.

Smile

Keep a smile on your face at all times. Show that you are enjoying yourself and are easy to please, easy to be with. But ladies, if you don't feel this way, then just remember that he is paying. Let him at least get the satisfaction of thinking that you like him. You can always lie at the end of the date and say that for the next two years you will be working undercover as a man for a *Vanity Fair* exposé, but that you will get in touch with him when the assignment is over.

When your date tells a joke that truly isn't funny, there is no need to break into uncontrollable peals of laughter. Most people who aren't funny know they aren't funny. They'll know that you are patronizing them. Conversely, don't just smile politely, barely baring your teeth. This kind of smile always looks condescending and false. The half-smile conveys the thought, "Boy, are you one sorry loser. I can't believe your mother brought her pregnancy to term."

Instead, smile fully at your date's joke, to show that you found it delightful, even though it didn't plunge you into hysterical fits of laughter. You're showing them that you appreciate the effort that they made to make you laugh, notwithstanding how pathetic it was. You may ask yourself, "What if he/she is never funny? How can I marry them? I'll end up spending my life pretending to be amused." Don't worry about this, as every time you see your spouse in underwear, it will be so funny that you'll have to force yourself not to laugh.

Mouth

Your lips should be moving when you speak. Don't try to seem really mysterious by having your voice sound like it's coming from the restaurant china. And always chew with your mouth closed. Displaying your masticated food and digestive tract to your date, although intimate, is unappealing.

Tongue

Keep it in your mouth. Even if you are lusting after your date and are trying to follow my advice to wait for marriage to have sex, do your best to control that mighty muscle. If it has a mind of its own and simply won't stay put, nail a tack to it just before the date. Don't lick your lips repeatedly. Your date will think that you are a lecher or are too cheap to buy lip gloss.

Cheats are bad lovers

The special joy of being in a relationship is the refuge it offers from the outside world, where so often you must behave in a calculated, premeditated manner in order to make "the right impression." With your partner you can be transparent and candid, always knowing that you will be accepted and loved. You delight in the fact that you have nothing to hide, and this enhances your sense of intimacy.

This unique pleasure is destroyed once you cheat. Now you must cover up for your indiscretion. Your innocence is gone, and so is your ability to release yourself entirely to your loved one. Where once you shared everything with your girlfriend or boyfriend, now you shield yourself from them. You have imported the dishonesty of the outside world into your love life. It is a shame. Like Adam and Eve after their sin of eating from the forbidden fruit, you can no longer be "naked" or innocent—totally open and honest—around your date. You now feel the need to cover up.

What's worse, by cheating you will have debased your sexual performance. Regardless of all that "practice" on the side, you will have actually become a worse lover. How so? By depriving yourself of the most important ingredient of truly great sex—utter honesty. When you come together with your lover feeling that you can disrobe emotionally and spiritually as well as physically, that you can unleash the deepest, most instinctual passion in your soul, then the sex will be fantastic. This is impossible after sleeping with someone else. At that point your lovemaking will be self-conscious and guarded. You'll be bad in bed since you are making love with half your personality tied behind your back.

Cheating as "therapy"

There are those relationships "experts" who claim that adultery can actually be good for marriage. An extramarital fling, they maintain, can rebuild a person's confidence, make them feel more attractive, and allow them to return to their husband or wife all the more enthusiastic about being married to them. It is tempting to apply this theory to dating, as well, for isn't that just one step away from marriage?

This notion of beneficial infidelity is utter nonsense. Whatever improved self-confidence a man or woman gains by cheating on their partner is paltry when weighed against the permanent damage caused to primacy, exclusivity, gratitude, mystery—and all the other things we have discovered about the secret of happiness in dating. We must debunk the myth that "falling in love"—in other words, sexual infatuation—should take precedence over the love that is built up with time and trust between man and woman.

Anyone who feels dissatisfied should examine their own relationship anew. If you are feeling used, or taken for granted, and in need of a confidence boost, then the first thing to do is to confront your date with it. Perhaps you have both slipped into too comfortable a routine and you may need to discover new passion in the union.

If all this fails, then the relationship should be brought to an end at once, rather than resorting to a slow death via infidelity.

Dealing with temptation

While you should never submit to the temptation to cheat on your girlfriend or boyfriend, you shouldn't become too worried about *feeling* temptation. These thoughts are natural. You should acknowledge them and then forget about them. The Baal Shem-Tov, the founder of the Jewish Hasidic tradition, was once asked how he could tell a true religious leader from a charlatan. "Ask him if he knows a way to prevent impure thoughts. If he says he does, then he is a charlatan."

Of course, there is truth to the axiom that "he who sins with his eyes is also an adulterer" (Job 24:15). First of all, to fantasize about a person other than your partner may well bring you one step closer to actually cheating. Even if it does not, the fact that you are thinking about someone else reflects a lack of sexual focus on your partner. But no Jewish teacher would go as far as the former U.S. President Jimmy Carter, who confessed in a *Playboy* magazine interview that by "lusting in his heart" he felt that he had actually committed adultery.

Your guilty feelings are unfair—to yourself. It is almost impossible to control your thoughts, especially in this day and age when tempting images of beautiful people are everywhere to be found in the media. Chances are that your fantasy came up spontaneously in your mind and will pass fleetingly if you ignore it, like nothing more than a sort of "mental hiccup."

If anything, by stressing the illicitness of the thought and your own feelings of guilt over it, you will merely strengthen its hold on your imagination. The best way to deal with tempting but illicit thoughts is to pay scant attention to them and simply move on.

If that doesn't work, try flagellation. If that only gets you more excited, drop the ultimate nuclear bomb on your libido—put on some country music. All your desires will reverse themselves from lust to wanting to go coon huntin' and spit tobacco. And in moments of dire emergency, dust off that old photo of Liberace and stare for ten minutes until everything simmers down.

The point is, you are going to find other people attractive from time to time. But there's no need to rub your partner's or your own nose in it.

I met Jillian and Max coming out of a cinema. They had just seen The Ice Storm *and Max had obviously very much enjoyed it. "Shmuley, it's about wife-swapping in the seventies," he marveled. "What a decade! I wouldn't have minded some of that . . ."*

Jillian looked unhappy at this joke. Her face was swollen with seasonal allergies, and I guessed that she might be feeling a little insecure about her looks.

Max also noticed Jillian's reaction and became a little defensive. "Come on, Jill," he teased, "you know polygamy's the way to go!" When she did not respond, he looked at me with a sour little smile and said, "Lucky for her I'm too much of a coward to do anything about it."

If you must entertain silly ideas about cheating, then keep them to yourself. No one will be impressed by jokes about adultery, polygamy, ménages à trois, or any of that naughty stuff. By raising the subject you will merely draw attention to the fact that you are, indeed, tempted. You will cause a lot of unnecessary pain and find yourself subject to much unwanted scrutiny and distrust from your partner.

After the fact— forgiving adultery

When the Jews at Sinai built the Golden Calf, their idolatry was tantamount to an act of adultery. Moses, infuriated by this betrayal, smashed the two Tablets of the Law with the Ten Commandments etched upon them. Rabbinical commentators observe that this was a metaphor for the way in which a bond of trust and devotion within marriage is also destroyed by sexual infidelity.

With this said, it is significant that God forgave the people for their sin, and wrote a second set of commandments. Admittedly, these were not as powerfully supernatural as the first. Whereas the original tablets were written by God Himself, the second tablets were carved into the stone by Moses as God dictated them. Nevertheless, the fact that the covenant between God and the Jews was renewed is extremely important, as it shows that a deep relationship can recover from the traumatic effects of adultery.

Couples should not immediately break up because of an act of infidelity. A number of factors must be taken into consideration first. Was the betrayal a one-time fling or part of an ongoing pattern of behavior? Was it the result of stupidity and poor judgment, perhaps as a result of drink, or was it a more serious expression of unhappiness? Most important, is the guilty party willing to apologize sincerely and even undergo counseling or therapy if necessary to avoid doing the same thing in the future?

While adultery is a sin that is *committed,* it is often made worse by the sin of *omission.* Men and women who cheat worsen the situation by treating their partners with indifference or hostility. It is as if they have withdrawn all their affection, in order to devote it to their illicit lover. They will have effectively killed the relationship by this act of neglect. If they refuse to give up the "other," it is completely unforgivable, and the relationship should be ended summarily.

In fact, the reason a woman will leave a man who has cheated on her often has far more to do with this neglect of her than with his actual infidelity. All of us can forgive someone whom we love with all our hearts. After all, we forgive our children the most heinous actions, like accidentally hitting Grandma Lilly on their first time out with the car and denting it. But we don't forgive strangers for hurting us. When a man cheats in a relationship, and gives all his affection to another woman, his relationship with his girlfriend is starved of affection and he becomes a stranger to her. And that is why she leaves him.

However, if the adultery is discovered more or less by accident, probably the dating relationship is still strong and the cheating partner has continued to be loving and supportive. While the sin is grave and damaging, the relationship may not be completely beyond repair.

In short, if you feel hurt by your partner's infidelity, this shows that you care about the relationship. Don't hurry to throw it all away. If your boyfriend or girlfriend asks you for forgiveness, then it is worth pausing to consider if the situation can be salvaged. Whatever you do, do not act in haste. Even if your partner is willing to change, they may not want to if you become infuriated and refuse to listen to explanations, apologies, and reason.

In the final analysis, however, judge them by their actions rather than by promises or words. The adulterer must break off all contact with his or her illicit lover and redouble their efforts to invest their original relationship with new life, love, and vigor. If they are not prepared to sever the connection entirely and never stray again, then they should be abandoned immediately.

Deepening your attraction to your date

This is the role of the Seventh Commandment. In instructing you not to commit adultery, it also requires that you redirect all that sexual energy into the relationship itself, to deepen and enrich the erotic bond rather than letting it be weakened by boredom and complacency.

God is challenging you to find within your dating "vertical" renewal rather than "horizontal" renewal. So many of us today only pursue a horizontal renewal. We get bored at work, so we move to another job. We buy a beautiful new set of clothes and then go shopping for more. We get into a relationship which seems to be getting nowhere, so we move to someone else's bed.

God teaches us that the deepest kind of fulfillment and the greatest new discoveries come about vertically, by looking down into our own souls rather than across to a new partner. If we reach deeper within the same relationship, into the recesses of our own and our partner's soul, we will come upon amazing new discoveries and richness. You have to learn to tap into this—the spring of new life inside yourself. Love is infinite and we must plumb its depths. Those who do obtain the deepest experience and understanding of this life's greatest blessing and treasure, whereas those who do not never attain more than a superficial knowledge of it.

The hot tip

In the 1970s, Henry Kissinger was voted "Sexiest Man Alive," because women were fascinated by his inscrutable, enigmatic charm—and not necessarily his physique. (Let's be diplomatic here.) This just goes to show that looks aren't everything.

Need a hot tip for attracting the opposite sex? There is a tremendous fascination and mystery about a God that is all-powerful, but invisible. In a date, too, these qualities are enormously attractive. Forget pheromones and NLP—try cultivating a little personal mystery, some mystique. God is mysterious and you should be too.

Summary of Mystery
1. The importance of sexual focus
2. Mystery and revelation
3. The dreaded 007 complex
4. Dating the mystery man or woman
5. Men today are pussycats—If he doesn't call, it could be because he lacks the confidence to do so.
6. Some handy tips for preserving your "mystique"
7. The importance of surprises
8. Sex is not a shortcut to intimacy.
9. Death of the female sexual predator
10. Sexual compatibility is a myth invented by a bunch of lazy and impatient men.
11. Don't fool around with someone else.
12. "It's only natural."

13. Dangerous dualism
14. The Jewish view
15. The seed of adultery is sown by confusion.
16. Dating a married person
17. People with integrity still date those who are married because they make them feel desirable.
18. Redefining adultery for singles
19. Some telltale signs of an unfaithful date
20. Communicating through body language
21. Cheats are bad lovers.
22. Cheating as "therapy" is balderdash
23. Dealing with temptation
24. After the fact—forgiving adultery
25. Deepening your attraction to your date
26. The hot tip
27. Taxation *with* representation isn't so hot either.

eight

Sincerity

Respect for Others—The Real Importance of Not Stealing

Sincerity: if you can fake it, you've got it made.
— Daniel Schorr, U.S. journalist, broadcaster. *International Herald Tribune*

THE EIGHTH COMMANDMENT: Do not steal. (Exodus 20:15)

Once again, you have to ask yourself why God would bother to reiterate as a holy commandment a rule that the Jews, a civilized nation, must have already had on their statute books. No society permits its members to rob from one another—and what in the world has it got to do with dating anyway? Well, I'll tell you. It all has to do with respect.

Respect can be best defined as acknowledging someone else's humanity and the rights that follow from their being your equal. The way to show respect for another person is by being sincere and honest in all your dealings with them. That is why I sum up this Eighth Commandment with the word "sincerity."

From the moment you first meet your new date to the time when you are ready to commit, you will find yourself in situations where you will be tempted to be insincere and disrespectful. This can happen in all sorts of ways, as I am about to show, and it amounts to theft. You must not do it. In fact, if you always do the opposite, you will come out the winner, I guarantee. You do that by showing you understand the importance of respecting others, because *everyone* wants to be in a relationship with someone who respects them.

Stick to your principles

Never underestimate the power of honesty to attract the opposite sex. By showing yourself to be principled you are displaying immense strength of character. After all, one of the hardest things to do in life is resist the urge to get ahead, even if it means you have to cheat a little. It is so tempting to think, "Well, everyone else is doing it!" and allow yourself a little indiscretion. But if you manage to overcome this urge, you will have something to be very proud of. And you'll be perceived as a *real* "hot date"!

> *Until recently my friend Jerry was earning $500,000 a year in investment banking, but then suddenly he quit. His reason? He was tired of advising clients to invest in ventures that might or might not be profitable for them, just so his company could make more money. He felt it was immoral and tantamount to stealing.*
>
> *Ironically, as soon as word of Jerry's decision got out, his telephone started ringing off the hook. The "buzz" around town was that he was a very eligible bachelor. The women heard about his "gentlemanly" action and they couldn't wait to meet a real life hero. Jerry, bemused by all this attention, has nonetheless made time for all of these women. He says he's looking forward to finding a new job in the city, as a work regimen will be "less exhausting" than his social life!*

Sure, rogues can be attractive people. Hollywood has given us all sorts of villain heroes, but they have to have a sincere heart and an ethical spirit, and end up behaving very morally and nobly for the sake of a good woman. Take Robin Hood, for example. Had he stolen from the rich in order to bankroll a villa in Saint-Tropez rather than to feed the poor, no one would have asked Errol Flynn to play him in a movie.

Many women claim to find "dangerous" men attractive. However, by this they really mean a man who has a romantic sense of mystery and spontaneity about him, someone who excites them by being unpredictable and independent. Perhaps he is a little wild— but he will definitely be tamable in the hands of a good woman (by which they mean themselves). In fact, this is *the* reason that so many women are attracted to flawed men. They feel that their ability to reform them is the ultimate testament to how much he loves them. He is prepared to change for her sake. They certainly don't mean men who abuse other people's property and break the law. That is just stupid. No one wants to date across the bars of a jail cell, and no woman wants to bring home a man whom Mama turns in for the reward.

Stealing hearts

Of course, you wouldn't dream of stealing somebody's wallet, but you might try to steal their heart. This Eighth Commandment is a stern prohibition against engendering false emotions in your date merely in order to get something from them. Stealing someone's emotions, manipulating people and creating a false sense of intimacy by saying things we don't mean, is a grave sin. Once found out, it will never be forgotten. Always be sincere.

A relationship is principally about love. If you are building an orphanage, it makes no difference whether you are doing it purely to save the children's lives or because you want your name on the front of a building—the outcome will probably still be good. But when it comes to love and relationships it makes all the difference in the world what your motives are.

Everything you do must be motivated by a genuine desire to make your partner happy. Don't tell a woman you love her just to get her into bed. She will know she has been robbed when you never call her again. Don't mislead a guy into thinking you're interested in him, when the truth is you're on the rebound from a failed relationship and are just looking for someone to give you back your confidence. Don't steal or break people's hearts.

Why? Aside from the fact that you will have hurt another human being, you yourself will be compromised in the process. Once you become a master of manipulation, you will be too much in love with yourself and your own desires to have anything left to give anyone else. And one day you will run out of people who are interested in wasting their time being conned by you.

Larry is a friend of mine from Australia who brags about his success as a Lothario. He tells me that the most reliable method he employs to get women into bed is to tell them at the very beginning of the date that he doesn't have sex because he wants to save himself for the woman he marries.

"Even women who normally would never contemplate going to bed with any man, let alone me, suddenly can't keep their hands off me. They see me as this romantic kind of guy who they want to be with in a relationship."

Unfortunately for these women, Larry is simply using their love of sincerity and honesty against them, but at least you get the point of how much women value those last few romantics out there who are more interested in love than sex. Five hundred years ago, the greatest Jewish mystic (Cabbalist) of all time, Rabbi Isaac Luria, taught, "The Messiah will not come until men learn to listen to their wives." In other words, a perfect world will come about when men learn to nurture their more feminine and less aggressive and competitive instincts.

Women today want men who are much more open about their

feelings and aren't afraid to cry. The man who seeks to understand women rather than conquer them on a date is the one who will ultimately triumph. Oddly enough, it is this more sensitive man, interested in caring over conquest, who has become the modern-day sex symbol. The John Wayne types are out. The Leonardo DiCaprios are the new sex symbols. Women want nurturing, emotional men who aren't afraid to open up.

Greeting people

The ancient sages declared that it is forbidden to "steal" a person's greeting. The Talmud requires that whenever someone greets you, be it friend or stranger, you must always return or at the very least acknowledge the gesture. To withhold a response is, effectively, an act of theft, because you rob them of their dignity. The Bible, always sensitive to human dignity, cannot allow this to happen.

In the dating scene, everyone knows that a good first impression is crucial. However, sometimes you will be approached by someone who doesn't stand a chance with you. Maybe it's his BO or the strange way her eyes roll back into her head that makes you want to turn and flee before they utter the first word. But you must not. They have made the effort to introduce themselves, and you cannot steal their self-respect by ignoring them.

Be nice. Who knows, maybe he or she will become a great new friend. You can judge very little from appearances. Be generous with your time, and this will only reflect well on you. (If you do find the person truly odious, however, and are certain that they will not be satisfied by your politely declining the all-night game of Scrabble, then you can try more devious tactics. Pretend you don't speak English. Send yourself a telegram demanding your immediate return to HQ. Fake a heart attack and hope the paramedics whisk you away in time. Or just say that you are now so much happier as a woman than you were as a man.)

Women are especially inclined to reject unwelcome advances

coldly. This is because of a common belief that men are "only after one thing," so they think it best to get the message across to save the guy from his testosterone-induced delusion that he stands a chance. While men are indeed sex maniacs, women should still take pity on them. He's already going home alone, so why deprive him of his pride as well? Be nice but firm and find a way to end the conversation courteously. If you find that all the men who approach you are just too persistent for your liking, then go to a more respectable place to look for a date. Quit the singles bar and try the local old-age home or monastery, perhaps.

But seriously, don't be rude to people who introduce themselves to you, even if you know you are not interested in them. If you humiliate them, they will be very reluctant to introduce themselves to someone else. Imagine if you yourself end up never meeting the person of your dreams because he or she was too shy to approach you—all because of the way they were treated at the previous party. What goes around comes around. There is a strange karma always at work in dating, and if we're nice to people in general, it makes for an all-round more compassionate dating scene.

Try always to be the first to greet your date. Offer a warm, inviting smile the minute you see them come into the room. It will make them feel great. If your girlfriend or boyfriend says hello in a way that is less than rosy, don't get defensive and refuse to answer. Don't let the date get off to a bad start. Respond cheerfully, and later on you can chide them for being a sullen sap.

The importance of sincerity in introductions

Whereas you must be polite when other people approach you, you need to be exactingly honest with yourself before you approach others. This is especially important when you introduce yourself to a member of the opposite sex in whom you are interested. What are your real motivations? Because it is only when your approach is genuine that you will appear confident and attractive.

If you are approaching a girl simply because you'd like to get her into bed, at the very least admit it to yourself. And if you want to be a decent person, leave her alone. If you decide to go and talk to a guy just because he looks rich and you want to impress your mom, then do yourself a favor, and stop. There are better ways to prove her wrong for telling you that you'd marry someone like the repairman who comes to the house with his jeans worn on his hips and the crack in his behind always showing.

The rule is this: always approach someone in dating with the highest possible motivation. You can fool some of the people some of the time, but you will eventually be found out. People aren't idiots, and they will see through you. Not only will you gain a reputation for superficiality, but you will also cease being effective because you will not be sincere, and after a while you may lose the ability to *be* sincere.

Wise King Solomon declared in Proverbs (27:19): *"Just as water reflects the face, so one human heart reflects another."* What you show people will be reflected back. Artificial people make an artificial impression. Approach them with ulterior motives, and they will respond with the same level of manipulation. Use them and they will end up using you. You have no time to waste with these silly games. If you have nothing to hide, this will come across as charm and candor, and your encounter will be successful.

With the exception of the promise of a long life for honoring your parents, God offers no reward for the observance of the Ten Commandments. He never said to the Jews, "And if you make me your God and destroy all the false idols, then I will get you on MTV and reward you with a harem full of White House interns."

In order for the Jews to enter into a loving relationship with God at Mount Sinai, they had to have the right motivation. When Moses told them that they were about to receive the Ten Commandments, they responded affirmatively with "We will do and we will try to understand." They didn't quibble. Descendants of

Abraham, they had an inborn instinct and need to connect with God. They were committed to the relationship and did not make conditions. Had they been interested in God for what He could provide for them, had their readiness to live by His commands been predicated on His ability to punish and reward, to give them riches and deliver them from their enemies, then the relationship could not have worked. God never offers a prize for the devotion of the people. He simply insists that the Jews love Him for what He is, and not for what He can provide. For us, in our relationships, this defines the difference between looking for a partner and finding your soul mate.

Returning affection, measure for measure

The prohibition on stealing teaches us that there must be give-and-take in all our dealings. If we take something, then we must give equally in return, otherwise we are stealing. In your love life, make yourself open to receiving love and giving back love.

Guys, this is an especially important rule for you. In general, men tend to be more naturally selfish than women. A man's idea of doing something for his girlfriend is giving her a wedgie before she goes to work. They think that the honor of picking up their smelly socks should be enough to please a lady for life. Men have to be especially wary of becoming complacent and taking their girlfriends' affections for granted.

So, all you men out there, be creative and resourceful, and always try to think of ways to show your girlfriend that you appreciate her. Shower once a week, whether you need it or not. Fill her car with M&M's. Sing loud love songs under her bedroom window in the middle of the night. Buy her a copy of my book. No one likes a miser. Be generous in everything you do for her. Even if you go over the top, she'll appreciate the gesture.

But, girls, if your man does express his affection, you should not abuse his generosity. If he takes you out to an expensive restaurant, don't order forty main dishes and pack thirty-eight into a doggy bag to take home for your immediate relatives and distant cousins. Your date will think you are greedy and difficult to please. By not being appreciative of his generosity, you have actually stolen his trust and affection.

Instead, be modest and express wonder and gratitude for everything he does. If his idea of a romantic dinner is ravioli straight out of a can, say this is the best meal you've had since your stint in that Turkish women's prison. Don't worry, once he marries you, then you can make him *really* earn your affection.

Say what you mean, and mean what you say

Men and women often have a problem communicating in a relationship. For her, the problem is that he doesn't communicate at all, especially with regard to anything pertaining to the relationship. She'll say, "Honey, do you love me?" And he, staring squarely at the television, will offer a grunt designed to allay her fears. Curiously, he offers the same grunt when she wakes him in the middle of the night and tells him that the house is burning down. Men are amazingly versatile and can use a single monosyllabic response to convey a whole range of meanings.

For his part, he complains that no matter what she says, she really means something else. Here is a chart I found to translate a woman's words:

She says:	*She means:*
Do what you want.	You'll pay for this later.
I'm not upset.	Of course I'm upset, you moron.
You're certainly attentive tonight.	Is sex all you ever think about?

I heard a noise.	I noticed you were almost asleep.
Do you love me?	I'm about to ask for something expensive.
I'll be ready in a minute.	By the time you've read *War and Peace*.
Yes.	No.
No.	No.
Maybe.	No.
I'm sorry.	You'll be sorry.
Do you like this recipe?	It's easy to fix, so you'd better get used to it.
I don't want to talk about it.	I'm still building up evidence against you.

As for him, things are a lot simpler.

He says:	*He means:*
It's just tomato juice, try it.	Three more shots, and I'll take you to my place.
I really want to get to know you better.	. . . so I can tell my friends about it.
I miss you so much.	I'm so horny my roommate is starting to look good.
Let's give the relationship a few more days.	I want to have sex a few more times.

While this chart is undoubtedly useful, it is impossible for me to provide words for every scenario. So be aware of what you say and make sure it reflects your true feelings.

Stealing sex

The Eighth Commandment prohibits stealing someone's sexual innocence. In Exodus 22:16 we read about a man who seduces a virgin. Jewish law demands that he marry her, if she will still have him. This is because he must compensate her for the theft of her trust and affection.

I've said it before and I'll say it again, you may be tempted to fake affection for your boyfriend or girlfriend just to get them into bed. "Why not?" you may think. "Everyone knows that sex is what it's all about anyway." But this deception is wrong. It is a form of stealing. And what if your boyfriend or girlfriend is genuinely attached to you, and construes sex as a sign of your true affection? When they find out the truth they will feel utterly betrayed. You have robbed this person of their most prized possession, their heart. Now, you're the kind of guy who would never steal someone's watch or wallet. So why would you take something which is so much more valuable?

Compliments and other romantic gestures

While I have talked about the important role of compliments in dating, even including stretching the truth just a little bit, *false* flattery is prohibited by the Eighth Commandment. This means when it is done for the wrong reason. If you find yourself buttering up your date in order to further your own ends, then you are in the wrong and you should back off immediately. If you compliment the woman you are with on her great beauty in the hope that she will feel flattered and jump into bed with you, you will have stolen her trust and her body. You will have taken something that is not rightfully yours. You stole.

If, however, the woman you care about is having a bad hair day and is annoyed, you are right to assure her that she is still beautiful. While this may not be completely honest, neither is it a lie. Because you love her, *to you* she is beautiful, in all circumstances and times. The whole beauty of love is that it makes rational evaluation impossible.

(Consider the fact that there are a billion parents on this planet and each is convinced that their kid is the cutest. They can't all be right. They're delusional. But love makes you delusional. The exception, of course, is my mother. As a boy, I once asked her if she loved me, and she responded that she liked me as a friend.)

Even if you don't think she really is beautiful, there is *someone* out there to whom she is attractive and beautiful. Also, within her there are many beautiful things. You can love things about her. Your act of flattery is not false because it is not self-serving. You intend only to make her feel better and bring more joy to the relationship. You are not manipulating her for your own purposes.

The definition of a romantic gesture is that it is completely devoid of self-interest. A romantic gesture is one undertaken with the sole intent of making your date feel cherished and special. Any ulterior motive destroys the romance.

While compliments are important romantic gestures, there are plenty of other things you can do to show your date you care. When you are buying a present or planning some great surprise, you can double-check whether it is truly romantic by honestly thinking about whether you stand to gain anything from giving it. If you do, then choose something else.

So, for example, if your girlfriend is a terrible housekeeper, she won't feel flattered by your giving her a vacuum cleaner. Rather than telling her with this gesture that she's special and beautiful, you're telling her, "Do a better job of cleaning your apartment. And by the way, if you have some extra time, come and do mine as well." She'll feel used. And if your boyfriend snores, then a gift of nose braces may well seem insulting. Spend the money on earplugs for yourself. Always go for something that serves no other purpose than to please your date. Buy her flowers, and watch her light up. Flowers can't clean a coffee stain or do the laundry; they can only express your affection for her. Similarly, you might want to try writing him a poem. He'll feel moved, because poetry is such a private and selfless offering. Also, if you put something in about "all those sleepless nights with you," he may get the hint about his snoring.

If you are given a gift on a date and you hate it, should you lie? If Mr. Squeaktight bought you plastic roses instead of the real thing, should you say that you love plastic flowers even more than real flowers? Of course not. There is no need to compromise your integrity in order to flatter your date.

You could say, "This is the most beautiful gift I have ever received" when really you're thinking, "You cheap so and so, you should be shot, although you'd probably recycle the metal if you were." Or you could say instead, "Thank you so much for thinking of me. I am touched that wherever you go I am on your mind. When I marry Jerome, I'll be thinking of you too."

In short, always make your date feel cherished, special, and remembered.

Stealing time

The Talmud is especially emphatic about the prohibition against deceiving people in business. This is true even in relatively minor situations such as asking a salesperson in a store to show you a product that you have no intention of buying. The salesperson is being paid to make money for his company. You know he won't get anything from the time he spends with you. Effectively, therefore, you have stolen his time. Similarly, a boss who delays payment for his employees is stealing their time by not abiding by the agreed-upon payment schedule.

Why all this emphasis on time as a commodity? Because it is, indeed, the most precious resource that we have. Time is the measure of our lives. Once lost, it is irretrievable and irreplaceable. Nowhere is this more true than in dating, when we devote our free time to other people, again and again, in the hope of finding that one person to whom we want to give all of our time—our lives.

Therefore, you must never make your date feel you have stolen their time. Try not to arrive late, as this is especially infuriating. If you are unavoidably delayed, then punch yourself in the face once or twice and pretend you were mugged. Don't bother your date too much with unnecessary telephone calls at work, or by demanding too much attention. You will make them feel that you do not respect their need for time on their own. And ensure that your dates are all enjoyable, happy, and memorable. You must make your date feel the time he or she spent with you was worthwhile.

Be sincere about your intentions

It is important not to cheat your date by being dishonest about your intentions for the relationship. If your boyfriend says he would like to settle down by the end of the year, don't tell him you'll think about it, when in fact you have no intention of committing to any relationship until you have slept with a different guy in every one of the fifty states. If your girlfriend says she's an old-fashioned girl who is looking to get married, don't nod your head solemnly while thinking that you'll change her mind once you've introduced her to the joys of casual, meaningless sex.

Be honest about your intentions always. If you make a commitment to your boyfriend or girlfriend, you must be willing to make good on it. Otherwise shut up. Even if your partner gets fed up and leaves, it is better than to have deceived them. So what if the only company you can expect in the near future is from Harry the Hamster? At least you have your moral integrity.

Being possessive

While Debbie and I were engaged to be married, I took it for granted that she would always be available to meet with me. One

Friday afternoon I called to tell her that I would pick her up the following night after the Sabbath to go out for pizza. She told me that she could not, because she had already arranged to meet with her cousin who was in town for a visit.

I was devastated. I felt that I was engaged to the most insensitive and cruel woman in the world. How could she possibly make arrangements to go out with anyone other than me? Surely I should come first? I put the phone down in an angry huff.

Of course, twenty minutes later, once I had thought it over, I realized what a jerk I had been. But I did have some excuse. As the child of divorced parents, I always felt insecure. This insecurity was compounded by my parents charging me room and board up to the age of my Bar Mitzvah. (At my Bar Mitzvah, they confiscated all my cash presents, saying it was compensation for putting up with me. I then was broke and went to my dad, the world's greatest haggler, to borrow some money. "Hey, Dad," I said, "can I borrow five bucks?" "What, four bucks? What do you want two bucks for?" he asked me.)

Debbie's decision to spend the following evening with someone else had touched a nerve. However, she was not responsible for my feelings of rejection—I was. I called her up to apologize for my behavior and resolved to direct my energies at my own insecurities rather than expect her to cope with them.

Remember always that a relationship is about two individuals coalescing together to become one. It is not about one individual totally subsuming the other's identity. Give your partner breathing space, room in which to develop on their own. Let them be who they are without trying to dominate them. They will feel all the more happy to share themselves with you, and you will have the privilege of being in a relationship with a strong, independent-minded person. All this is symbolized by a hug, wherein you create a circle with your arms, thus establishing a space within yourself where your loved one can exist as they are rather than having to become you.

Don't steal your date away from their family

The sages concluded that the Eighth Commandment against stealing also prohibits kidnapping. Exodus 21:16: *"He who kidnaps a man, whether he has sold him or is still holding him, shall be put to death."* Two of the rabbinical commentators, Rashi and Rabbi Samson Raphael Hirsch, maintain that while theft of a person's physical freedom is obviously forbidden, so is theft of their spiritual and emotional freedom.

Today, this prohibition would include the mind control exercised by religious cults over their members. It is also a warning against the more insidious threat of abusive relationships. We've all heard of jealous men who mistreat their women because they believe they are "thinking" about being unfaithful. Or jilted women who stalk their ex-boyfriends, simply because they cannot accept the fact that he has moved on. Remember *Fatal Attraction*?

Don't be a bastard or a bunny-boiler. Don't try to take over your partner's life. If you find yourself becoming demanding and dictatorial with your boyfriend or girlfriend, take a step back and analyze what you are really feeling. Keep in mind that even within a relationship, your date is still an individual with the need for individual freedom. Don't kidnap them or unreasonably restrict this freedom.

In addition, as tempting as it might be, do not try to steal your boyfriend or girlfriend away from their family. Don't be so insecure that you feel jealous and unhappy with how close they are to their families. A romantic relationship should be something that adds to one's family life, rather than detracting from it.

(However, if you happen to be a woman dating a Jewish man, you should disregard this advice completely. Unless you put your foot down right away, he'll end up wanting to live with Mother after he marries and just visit you and the kids on weekends.)

Many men feel upset when they date a woman who is extremely

close with her parents, and many women feel threatened by a potential mother-in-law who is too controlling of her son. (A man told his Rabbi that his mother-in-law had just died, and asked if it was permitted to bury her, embalm her, or cremate her. The Rabbi responded, "Take no chances. Do all three.") They feel that the purpose of a relationship is to experience independence, and they cannot do this when the person they are dating remains so fixated on their family. The man then begins trying to slowly pry his date away from her family, or she makes him feel guilty when he spends too much time with them. He pouts like a little puppy dog and says, "You don't love me," every time she is expected to be home with her parents on weekends. She accuses him of making her feel like she is not the most important person in his life and that he puts everybody before her.

This is not fair. Instead of the dating experience being something pleasant, it now becomes strenuous and anxiety-ridden. Get a grip on yourself. Clean your apartment or get the wax out of your ears as a distraction.

In fact, one of the best ways to endear yourself to your date is to show an interest in his or her family. Although everyone complains about their families, deep down they love them dearly. Tell them that you love them too. Lie if you have to. Tell him that his mother is beautiful and kind, even if you think that she is the Wicked Witch of the West.

In Jewish households, one of the best ways to get around the "choose between me and your family" dilemma is to invite your date to participate in your family's weekly Friday night Sabbath meal. Let them feel that they are a part of your family instead of being in competition with them.

. . . or their friends

In the same way, don't be jealous of the time your boyfriend or girlfriend spends with their friends. Don't worry about them having a better time with them than they do with you. They wouldn't be with you if they didn't enjoy the relationship. Probably, after he's done stripping naked, painting himself blue, and running through the forest with the guys on one of those Iron John, head-butting weekends, he'll quite look forward to your feminine charms. And how much talk of nail polish and perfume can she really handle? She'll start missing the virile bouquet of your underwear and the solid stench of beer. So rest assured that after the break they had with the pals, your boyfriend or girlfriend will come back to you all the more appreciative of your company.

Stealing someone's lover

This has been more or less covered by the previous commandment, but it is worth reinforcing it here. According to Jewish law, if you buy goods that are stolen you are considered partially culpable for the theft yourself. And pleading ignorance is of no use. The Bible insists that it is incumbent upon you to discover whether or not the goods are stolen before you make the purchase.

All too often, I come across young men and women who are having affairs with married people. They claim that they never knew he or she was married until late in the relationship. Never mind the fact that they always had to meet in roadside motel rooms, that home phone numbers were never exchanged, and every sound made her jump out of bed screaming, "He's here to kill us both." My young friends insist that they were ignorant of this deplorable fact.

I argue that their ignorance is just too convenient to be believed. They are at fault for not making sure everything was kosher about their partner before they jumped in the sack. Amazingly, I usually discover that they never asked the simple question, "Are you married?" and instead just blithely carried on the relationship, hoping for the best.

If you are romantically involved with a person who is married, or who is in a serious relationship already, you have stolen them away from their partner. If you never paused to verify that they were unattached, you are guilty of negligence. It's that simple.

Returning "lost" partners to each other

Among the laws regarding theft, the Bible commands us to return lost property: *"You shall not watch your neighbor's ox or sheep straying away and ignore them; you shall take them back to their owner . . . You shall do the same with a neighbor's donkey; you shall do the same with a neighbor's garment; and you shall do the same with anything else that your neighbor loses and you find. You may not withhold your help"* (Deuteronomy 22:1–3). The same principle would apply to people who have been lost from their relationship.

If someone comes to you on the rebound—they have broken up with someone but their heart is still in the relationship—send them gently back. Don't take advantage of their current state of vulnerability to keep them for yourself. For example, a woman who is your platonic friend has a fight with her boyfriend and comes to you for advice. You might feel tempted to take advantage of the situation, to win her for yourself. But this is someone who has lost her possessions. Her heart belongs to someone else, so you cannot steal it from him. You must restore it. Do the right thing. Be a good person. Always seek to rebuild other people's relationships.

In general, you should always try to strengthen the relationships of the men and women you know. Rather than stealing away their affection from one another, you should always try to reinforce it. Isn't that what you would want a friend to do for you? If you see two of your good friends fighting, offer to mediate. Don't fall back on the weak excuse "it's not my business." Remind them of how much they mean to each other. And then at the wedding ceremony, take pride and pleasure in the part you played.

If you came across an expensive piece of jewelry in the street, would you not try to return it to its owner? Of course you would. Right? Okay, don't answer that question. The point is, when you are witness to a troubled relationship, you must do what you can to help.

The penalty for stealing: how to make up for it

The penalty for stealing recommended by the Bible is full compensation of the amount stolen and an equal amount paid as a fine. Why is this required instead of spending time in prison? Because Judaism maintains that there is little chance of a thief being rehabilitated by spending years in the company of other criminals. By stealing, the thief has betrayed his fundamental lack of empathy with his victim. Had he known what it feels like to be robbed, he would not steal. In being forced to pay a fine, the thief can be made to understand how such a drastic loss of property is hurtful. He is less likely to steal again.

There is a lesson here for healing wounds in your relationships. All too often, you will find yourself causing pain and offense to your date. You will say things you do not mean. You will lose your temper and display the worst aspects of your nature. You will allow yourself to act maliciously because, for a few moments, you forget how hurtful this is to your date.

There is one sure way to make amends for this carelessness. See yourself as having stolen love from your relationship and apply the biblical penalty to yourself. For every measure of pain you caused your date, now bring him or her two measures of joy. For every neglectful incident, be twice as attentive the next time you meet. Redouble your efforts to make your boyfriend or girlfriend glad to have you in their lives.

Confession is good for the soul mate

The Bible mitigates the penalty exacted on a thief if he feels genuinely remorseful for what he did and confesses. Numbers 5:5–7 requires: *"If he admits guilt himself, then he is fined only a 20 percent penalty in addition to the terms in principle, instead of 100 percent."* By confessing, the thief has not only saved the community an expensive legal process but has also shown himself to be repentant and less deserving of full punishment.

If you wrong your date and don't admit it, then when he or she finds you out they will exact a 100 percent penalty. They will not forgive you. But if you make a mistake, admit it, and promise humbly not to do it again, they will find it easier to forgive you. Learning to say you're sorry is one of the most important things you can do within a relationship. So go on. Apologize. And next time, make sure you don't get caught.

Men who won't commit steal from their women

Perhaps the best way for you to compensate for your unforgivable act of insensitivity and insincerity is to take the plunge into commitment. The greatest form of stealing in a relationship is to date people endlessly, lead them to believe that you will marry them, and then either dump them or continue stringing them along. Many men steal women's hearts by leading them to believe that now that she loves you and wishes to spend the rest of her life with you—you will reciprocate and pop the question. Raising someone's expectations, only to drop them and shatter their heart in the process, is stealing.

Why is it that men find it so hard to commit? Why do men date so many different women, shower them with affection and attention, even agree to move in together, but never go the extra step and commit to marriage?

Why? Because they *can,* of course!

Let's face it, women are much more keen on the institution of marriage than men. To them, marriage is a simple, logical outcome of a loving relationship. They love their man and are happy to pledge that they will go on loving him forever. And the whole business of weddings will occupy a woman's imagination from the day she first starts playing with dolls. Women talk and fantasize endlessly about how beautiful the ceremony will be, and how they can't wait to wear the pristine white dress in a big white church with their father walking them down the aisle. It is no surprise that the bride magazine industry is so huge and lucrative.

But notice that there are no bride*groom* magazines. No guy ever sits with his friend in a pub, chugging pints of Fosters and saying, "Johnny, I can't wait for that big day when I walk down the aisle wearing a dark suit with a beautiful bow tie in a big white church." Any man who said that would be beaten up by his mates and called a fairy. On the contrary, men focus on the *negative* side of marriage. To them, it means confinement and imprisonment even. Committing to one woman, to the exclusion of all others, does not make any sense to them.

When it comes to marriage, the natural female temperament is to think about all the good things that will follow, all the things she will gain by being married. To be sure, she could also focus on the negative if she wished. Instead of focusing on the beauty of sharing one's life with a warm human being, to nurture, care, and look after her, she can instead focus on all the odors he is sure to bring into the house, how he will leave his hair all over the couch and toilet, how his gut will double in size, and how he'll never pay attention to anything she ever says while football is on the tube. Yet, women choose to be positive about marriage. They focus on everything they will be gaining rather than giving up.

With men, however, it's the exact opposite. Rather than focus on what they will gain in the marriage, they focus only on what they will lose, namely, their freedom. For him, commitment means *to be committed*. And the institution of marriage means to be institutionalized. Men have a knack for seeing only the negative things in a marriage.

So while a woman thinks about all the beautiful bridesmaids that will grace her wedding, her boyfriend thinks about it too. Only he focuses on the fact that he will never be able to touch any one of them ever again. And even if he so much as flirts with one of them, he will end up in a full body cast. Men realize that by marrying they will never be able to have sex with any of those beautiful bridesmaids ever again, and they run a mile.

How men think

I asked a good friend of mine, Derek, why he thinks men are so reluctant to commit. He is a successful entrepreneur, in his late thirties, attractive, very wealthy, and he spends his time dating one beautiful model after another. You might say he knows something about the subject. He put it to me this way:

> *Men are businessmen. They are, therefore, always looking for the next deal. The idea of focusing on one thing and getting hooked on it, opening one branch of a business and not moving on to another one, is not something they can fathom. They thrive on the thrill of the chase, of conquering something, and cannot accept that there should be one big conquest. Men enjoy "conquering" a woman sexually, and like to think that they could go on conquering others—if they so chose. Marriage, to a man, is nothing short of a bad deal, a bad business enterprise.*

Cynical, but often true. It is sad that men take such a commercial approach to relationships. If anything, they should view dating as a series of job interviews, in which they are looking for the right profession to which to commit their lives. They should see marriage as the chance to orchestrate all aspects of their personality and focus them on one rewarding "career path."

The special role of sex

The real question should not be "Why do men have such a tough time with commitment?" but "Why do some men commit to a woman at all?" Surely, the answer is that there are certain things that can only be acquired by paying a price. The old adage—"marriage is the price which men pay for sex, and sex is the price which women pay for marriage"—while exaggerated, is also partly true.

Let's say a man is dating a woman and he really wants to have sex with her but she won't because she wants to wait until she is married. Now, by getting married, there is suddenly a very positive benefit for him. What he gains is the greatest thing of all, YOU! You will move in with him, agree to spend your days and nights with him, agree to travel with him, maybe even cook him dinner occasionally. So now he looks forward to being married. But, if you've moved in, and are acting like his wife, then all he can think about is how marriage is a really bad deal. He gives up so much and receives nothing in return. He has it all already. So if a woman really wants to get a man to commit to marriage, she has to show him that there are certain benefits that are going to come about only by marrying. Now he will focus on the positive side of marriage, what he will be gaining, rather than what he will be giving up.

Demanding marriage before sex is not blackmail or prostitution. It is just the natural, exclusive setting which sex requires in order to be an act of intimacy.

Some may accuse me of overemphasizing the importance of sex in the decision to make a commitment. Others might even go so far as to say that I am advocating a form of prostitution. A prostitute gives her body away and gets money in return. It might seem that a woman who withholds sex in order to secure a marriage proposal is not much different. But this sort of choice is not prostitution. Rather, it accords with the very nature of what sex is.

After all, what is sex? Surely, it is the ultimate form of intimacy, the highest form of knowledge. Whereas a man intrinsically feels sex to be something compulsive or hormonal, a woman feels the desire to bond with a man as the highest form of communication. She wants him to want her, to want to know her. For her, sex is about exclusivity. It's about sharing the most intimate knowledge, the most intimate secret, which can only be shared with one person, and cannot be diluted with many. Therefore, unlike the prostitute who asks for money—something totally unrelated to sex— thereby demonstrating her superficiality and her demeaning approach to sex, the wife asks for marriage before sex because that is the natural and normal precondition. What she is saying is this: *First tell me that this secret I am about to share with you will only be between us.*

When a woman goes to bed with a man who has not committed, it is the height of irrationality

The simple fact is that women today are so submissive, and so undemanding in relationships, that it is no surprise that men don't commit in marriage. They're having a party out there. Who would want to spoil it? Men have even invented all kinds of names for pain-in-the-neck women who actually have the nerve to demand some level of commitment. A woman today who pesters a man to get serious is either a bunny-boiler (inspired by the movie *Fatal Attraction*) or a commitment-crawler or a party-pooper. "Get everything you want and put no money down—sounds like a damned good deal to me!" they're thinking gleefully to themselves. But you're smarter than that. Don't let them get away with it! Marriage dictates that no relationship flourishes or prospers without exclusivity. There are rules to a relationship. Override them at your own peril. So to women who say to me, "I refuse to play games with men and withhold sex just in order to get him to marry me," my response is, "You're not playing games. You're living by certain mandatory rules, without which there can be no relationship."

"Not ready for commitment"

Remember that it is better to marry the right person at the wrong time than the wrong person at the right time. Often I am approached by couples who feel committed to one another but fear that they are too young or too financially insecure to get married right away. I always assure them that they should go ahead and tie the knot, that this will only strengthen them and make it easier for their relationship to succeed.

It is for the same reason that I do not believe in indulging male fantasies of "not being ready" for marriage. If a man is ready to have sex, to allow a woman to become emotionally dependent on him, and if he is financially stable and not criminally insane, then he is ready to get married. It's that simple.

Women should know that when a man says he is not ready for commitment, what he means is that he is not ready for commitment with *you*. Don't believe the garbage that you are wonderful but he is not ready. He's not interested in you for anything more than a fling. Thank him for his passing interest and move on.

When I was twenty years old and engaged to marry Debbie, I found myself fearing that when we married, she would bore me. She wasn't willing to be especially adventurous on our dates; when we went on a helicopter ride, she got sick, and even when I drove the car fast, she would grab the rosary beads and scream "Hail Mary" until I would remind her that she was not Catholic. Once married, I thought, the situation would just get worse. Every time I would suggest we do something exciting, she would find some excuse not to. If I suggested going bungee-jumping, kayaking on the Norwegian fjords, or skydiving from a commercial airliner at 30,000 feet, she would find a way to beg off.

So I said to her the now famous lines "I think I'm too young for a commitment." I knew in my heart that I was really saying, "I think I'm too young for a commitment with you." Debbie then told me that, in that case, she wasn't interested either and she would have to think about whether we should continue seeing each other at all. My pride was wounded. I couldn't believe her response. To risk losing the perfect masculine specimen? But it was particularly her act of defiance and show of courage that inspired me to continue the relationship until we actually got married. Now this is a bit of an incoherent story, I know, with no real point. But I just suddenly felt the urge to talk about myself again. Let's now get back to the real point.

As a result of this experience, I now know exactly what it means when a man says he is not ready. He is directing it specifically at you and it is an insult. Don't take it from him. Preserve your dignity and break off the relationship. If he wants a plaything, he can buy a life-size blow-up Barbie doll.

Men and intimacy

I totally disagree with those people who say that men's refusal to commit is due entirely to fear of intimacy. That's nonsense. It is not because of their humility and their fear and their sense of inadequacy that they don't want to commit; it is precisely the opposite. Most often, they foster the secret, arrogant belief that they are a prize catch and could have an even "better" woman than the one they are with. Men want all the benefits of a relationship without the commitment. It has nothing to do with fear of intimacy and everything to do with arrogance.

> *A woman once came to me for advice, saying that for four years her boyfriend had been pushing her to marry, but she had put off deciding one way or another. When I asked her why, she said that her boyfriend "has a problem with intimacy." I asked her to explain what she meant. She said that although now he was a perfect gentleman, she was afraid that after marriage he would become too chauvinistic and would not help around the house anymore.*
>
> *I told her that her boyfriend was not suffering from a problem with intimacy, but rather with balancing two opposite modes of behavior: chivalry and chauvinism. What she must do is be honest with the guy and say, "Look, I need to know that you are not going to take advantage of me once I am your wife. I need you to show me the extra effort in order to win me over." Tell him to be more chivalrous.*

There are occasionally well-intentioned men who think they are afraid of intimacy when in fact they are mistakenly afraid of hurting the woman they love. The more this type of man feels for his woman, the more he refrains from getting serious because he is afraid that he may not be able to commit to her and will therefore end up hurting her.

This is a fear that men have to overcome. There are strange paradoxes in relationships. You like a girl and you don't date her seriously because you are afraid of abandoning her. What you have to do is not fear commitment. Fear of commitment undermines any possibility of long-lasting love and condemns your love life to be of a temporary nature. Not only because you're not prepared to be committed but because you are going to alienate the people you are closest to.

One of the things a woman can do, when she sees in a man that he is holding back and she suspects that he is afraid of commitment, is to make it clear to him that she won't be hurt. She should say to him, "Let's just let the relationship go and wherever it goes, it goes. If it doesn't work out, it doesn't work out, but don't be nervous about the future."

Dealing with him

Ladies, don't be afraid to be a little tough in the way you deal with your man's commitment phobia.

In a recent television discussion about men who cannot commit, a woman named Louise called up and said she had been dating a man for eight years, they live together and have a child but her boyfriend will never commit to the relationship. She doesn't know what to do, she loves him and doesn't want to leave him.

I told her to tell him that she has made an arrangement to go to Bournemouth or Las Vegas or Bali on a set date, to be married by a justice of the peace, or a priest, at a set time. That's it. I told her to let him know in no uncertain terms that she is going, and if he does not want to turn up at the appointed time, then she will just find whoever is available and marry them. But there is nothing wrong with forcing the issue.

Ladies, when confronting your man on this issue, remind yourself that you are not desperate. You are an attractive woman who could find plenty of other men. Be resolute, because nothing is more attractive to a man than a self-confident woman. Women who respect themselves are determined and resolute, purposeful— and therefore successful.

The soft touch

Many women don't understand how hard it is for a man to commit himself. Be understanding and talk him through it, it will make things much easier. If he feels as though he is giving everything up, you can show him that things will be better.

Another method, however, is for women to be compassionate about a man's struggle to commit. Don't judge him, instead just establish facts.

There is nothing wrong with a woman who has been dating a man for a long time suggesting that maybe they should get married. If he says that he is not sure, then tell him fine, you understand that he is not sure. Then simply ask him, "Shall we get married in July or August?" When he says, I don't know if I want to get married, then just say, "Of course, I understand. Now, will the ceremony be in your hometown or mine?" The best way to get a guy to commit is not by discussing marriage, but by creating facts. Don't be offended that he is not sweeping you off your feet and getting down on one knee. Don't make a big deal out of the fact that it is you who are taking the lead. Getting married is like any other significant decision: we are not happy about doing it, but once it's done, we are very happy. You don't need a guy to get down on his knee. As long as he gives you the ring, his last name, and his laundry, he has committed himself.

The rewards of marriage

A woman must always show a man what he will gain by getting married rather than what he will lose. Make him understand that marriage is a godsend because it brings focus and the complete orchestration of all his bodily senses and every aspect of his personality. Imagine what a curse it would be for men if they didn't marry. I see men like this all the time who enter their middle thirties and forties still wondering which woman is right for them. They are dating, looking, permanently distracted, and can't really focus their energy. They live in a state of permanent vacillation and end up appearing highly unimpressive.

A woman roots a man. She grounds him and brings him focus and he is able to get on with other important things in life. One woman is all he requires to satisfy all of his needs.

Summary of Sincerity

1. Respect for others
2. Stick to your principles
3. Never steal a heart
4. Greeting people with a smile
5. Importance of sincerity in your introductions
6. Returning affection, measure for measure
7. Say what you mean, and mean what you say
8. Dont' steal sex. Pay for it with marriage
9. Compliments and other romantic gestures
10. Stealing time
11. Be sincere about your intentions
12. Being possessive
13. Don't steal your date away from their family
14. . . . or their friends
15. Stealing someone's lover
16. Returning "lost" partners to each other
17. The penalty for stealing is compensating doubly
18. Confession is good for the soul mate
19. Men who won't commit steal from their women
20. There is no "groom" magazine
21. The special role of sex
22. When a woman goes to bed with a man who has not committed, it is the height of irrationality
23. "Not ready for commitment" is another way of saying "I don't want to marry you"

24. Men and intimacy
25. Dealing with him
26. Use the soft touch
27. The rewards of marriage
28. Cole's law: thinly sliced cabbage

nine

Trust

A Good Name

Real love is a pilgrimage. It happens when there is no strategy,
but it is very rare because most people are strategists.
  —Anita Brookner (b. 1938), British novelist, art historian.
  Interview in *Women Writers Talk*

THE NINTH COMMANDMENT: Do not bear false witness
against your fellow. (Exodus 20:16)

Getting Naked

My friend Colin came to me with a problem. "I date and
date different women, but I can never seem to fall in
love." Sharona told me the very same thing. "I like guys
and I enjoy going out on dates. But I just don't seem to connect
with any of them." It's a complaint that I hear with increasing
frequency.

Time was when a man and woman would date and they would
"fall" for each other. The initial process of objectively evaluating

one another would slowly meld into an emotional entanglement. They would lose their footing and fall in love. They would slowly become orchestrated into a single unit incapable of existing without the other. Men and women began dating but ended up missing each other. Commitment and exclusivity quickly follow. But whereas once men and women were made of Velcro, today they are made of Teflon. Men and women go out time and again and no trace remains.

One of the main reasons for this development is lack of trust. If you don't open up to your date, then you can't grow dependent on them. Trust is the soil without which the seeds of love have no place to grow. If you want to make love, you have to take your clothes off (unless you're especially creative). But the same is true if you want to *fall* in love. You have to remove your clothes, dismantle the ramparts, lower your defenses. A closed heart leaves no room to be touched.

This is a generation which lacks trust. With a 50 percent divorce rate and so many broken hearts, we all want to date but are afraid to really bare our souls. People are not falling in love today because they lack nakedness. If you don't share your heart with your date, if you are afraid of revealing too much and therefore end up having banal and perfunctory conversations, all those imposed layers on your heart will ensure that you never fall in love. They will serve as barriers to intimacy.

There is a normal progression which is meant to be followed on a date. Physical attraction is meant to lead to emotional connection, which is meant to lead to commitment, and which is finally meant to culminate in physical union. But today it's all out of sync. Ironically, we have no problem opening up our bodies, so long as we forever seal our souls.

The main thing you are trying to achieve on a date is to cease being strangers to each other. Nobody trusts a stranger. You can't become lovers until you first stop being strangers. And you can't stop being strangers until you learn to trust each other. You learn to trust each other by opening up. By revealing parts of yourself that would normally be concealed. And that's what the Ninth Commandment is all about. It is an instruction to refrain from action that undermines trust, and to undertake action that establishes trust.

Janet was dating Bob for four months. It started out well enough, but their dating quickly set into an uninspiring routine. Janet told me that she felt that rather than growing closer in their dating, she and Bob were just growing further and further apart. "Have you ever taken Bob into your confidence," I asked her. "Sure I have," she responded.

"Oh really," I continued, "what have you shared with him?" "Well, I've told him about how I like work, and my favorite vacations as a child, and my favorite films."

I was disappointed. "Why haven't you shared with him your greatest fears, your deepest anxieties, your nagging insecurities. Why haven't you invited him to be your soul mate and companion."

"Because I barely know him," she continued.

"But how can you get to know him when you don't share anything substantive with him?" I countered.

Janet took my advice and decided to gamble. Few people knew about the fact that she was adopted and that, having tracked down her real mother at age twenty, her biological mother told her she didn't want to ever see her again and to go away. Janet shared this with Bob.

"It was like a miracle, Shmuley. Whereas before he seemed cold and standoffish, he leaned over and kissed me on the cheek and thanked me for reposing trust in him. He then began to share his own fears, of how, amid having a successful business, he walks around with the constant fear of failure, and that people only like him because of his money. He told me he feels condemned to a life of name-dropping just so that people would like him. I comforted him and told him how special he was. We have never had such an intimate conversation before."

Isn't it a shame that so many young people today are only

interested in getting physically naked with their date, and couldn't give a toss about being emotionally naked. If you don't take risks, you will never fall in love. Early on in your dating, when you have determined that the person you're with could indeed be the right one, open up to them. Speak to them from the depths of your heart. Build trust in your relationship. Reveal what you know about yourself and what you would still like to find out. Tell them your secrets. Show that you have humility. Don't be afraid to be naked. So you're not macho man. So you're not Mr. Cool. So you do have deep fears. This doesn't show that you're weak. It demonstrates your strength. You are mature and wise enough to reach out to a stranger and invite them to become your lover.

Don't harm your own reputation

The prohibition against bearing false witness is also a warning against harming anyone's reputation—*including our own.* So many of us say we don't care what other people think about us, but deep down we do.

God says that it is not enough to be a nice guy, you actually *have to come across* as a nice guy. Let your deeds bear witness to your integrity and character. On a date, above all, you are going to have to witness to the truth about your real self. (Unless, for instance, you're someone who hasn't had a date in a decade, in which case you should lie about it and say that you were just released from a Vietnam prisoner-of-war camp.)

Essentially, the Ninth Commandment sets out to help us improve our character as well as our reputation. Aren't these one and the same? Ideally, yes. In reality, rarely. Though you may have a thoroughly decent character, if you do not demonstrate this with good deeds, you could easily earn a bad reputation without even realizing what people are thinking and saying about you. However false it is, however unfair, however much you think you don't care, it can do you immeasurable harm. It is that simple.

There is a further point. One of the biggest dating mistakes is to focus on personality at the expense of character. Personality is the external part of ourselves. It is all about how we project ourselves to the world, how we cause other people to react to us. To be sure, how a person portrays himself or herself and how you feel toward them is of great significance in a relationship, but character is even more important. What happens if the skin on the orange looks shiny and healthy, but underneath it all is a worm-infested fruit? Over the years I have heard endless stories, particularly from women, of how they were swept off their feet by a man's electric personality, only to discover that he was financially dishonest, lazy, a womanizer, or just plain mean and nasty. Character is not the part of a man or a woman that you can immediately see. Like God Himself, it is initially invisible. But it is the most important part of the person. Subsumed within the rubric of character are our core beliefs, our values, long-term goals, and the degree of our sensitivity to others. On a date, learn to look beneath the surface. Try to discern whether or not in ten years' time, even if he can still make you laugh, you will respect him still. Or will you be so unimpressed with the contrast of his character and his personality that all you'll want is out? Most guys want to undertake penetrating activities on a date. Turn this to your advantage. Discuss penetrating subjects instead. Find out about his inner self. Is he manipulative? Is he concerned with morality, decency, and honesty? Is he empathetic to human suffering and pain? Or does he want to go into politics?

The Ninth Commandment tells us to work on our character, and have our reputation match our character, and vice versa. By being trustworthy, reliable, and straightforward on your date, you will be protecting your own good name, demonstrating your good character. Even if the two of you do not end up together, your date will always feel that you are a good person, even if not exactly right for them, and will spread the word.

The power of gossip

When the Ninth Commandment is repeated in Deuteronomy, the wording is slightly different from Exodus, because it prohibits "testifying in vain," as opposed to "bearing false witness." "In vain" probably means outside a court of law, so your testimony has no legal weight. Because of this distinction in the text, the Talmud concludes that the Ninth Commandment prohibits not only perjury but also any form of gossip. "In vain" comes to mean destroying somebody's reputation just for your own entertainment.

There is no more effective way to ruin another person's reputation than by gossiping about them, particularly if it is done cleverly, with wit and just a grain of truth. They are not there to defend themselves, so your words can carry enormous weight. What is especially tragic about gossip is that its damage is irreversible. It is a sin for which you cannot really atone. You can never take your words back, or know how far they may have spread.

> *A Rabbi was approached by a man, who fell on his knees and begged him for forgiveness. He confessed to having disparaged the Rabbi behind his back and harmed his reputation. He now asked him to forgive him and to tell him how to make amends.*
>
> *The Rabbi told the man first of all to take a feather pillow to the tallest tower in the city and to shake out all the feathers. The man did so, and returned. Now the Rabbi told him that he must go back and retrieve all the feathers.*
>
> *"But that's impossible!" said the man. "They are blown to the four winds."*
>
> *"Then how will it be possible for you to collect all the words that you have spread about me?"*

Gossip is cruel and a weapon of aggression. It is marginally better than taking an ax to somebody, but it scores zero in life enhancement, either for you or for your victim. There is nothing positive to be gained by it, except a bit of cheap entertainment at someone else's expense. It exists only to highlight human failings, and you end up feeling depressed for having indulged in it. It goes against every single one of the Ten Commandments, and above all the Ninth.

There is one possible exception. If in the past you have dated someone with a violent temper, or who is a proven liar or cheat, and you are asked by someone who wants to go out with them what they are really like, you are permitted to tell them the bare minimum. This is in order to protect your friend from harm. But don't dress it up or make it sound worse than it was, and be very honest with yourself about your motives. Are you really doing it to protect somebody else, or is your real purpose to get revenge?

A benevolent eye

Do make an effort to bring up any virtues a person has. Don't forget to mention their party trick of firing bottle rockets out of their nostrils. Try to balance out any bad news with something good. The Rabbis of the Talmud said that one of the greatest merits a person can have is a benevolent eye. A benevolent eye sees the good in all people. So look kindly on the poor guy. Let's face it, no one's perfect. Maybe your friend will manage to bring out all the good things in the chump that you missed.

This is an important point. If you dated someone and it failed, that doesn't mean that the next person won't be able to see and bring out their good qualities. Remember how much Sylvester Stallone changed Talia Shire in the very first *Rocky* movie? And this despite his inability to speak English.

Akiva, one of the great Rabbis, was once a poor, illiterate shepherd boy, whom the daughter of the wealthiest man in Judea, Rachel, took a liking to. She promised him that if he began to study she would give up all her riches and marry him. He accepted the challenge. She was disinherited by her father, but he went on to become the greatest Rabbi of his generation, with more than 24,000 students.

How to deal with your date's "reputation"

We have already seen from early commandments that if you break up with your date, you should not begin to gossip about them. Not only will this seem immature and petulant, but it may also ruin their chances of finding another date.

You will discover just how bad this feels when *you* hear rumors about your date spread by his or her ex. Now, of course, being a sensitive sort, you will refuse to believe any of it. *At first.* But, trust me, as time goes by, your curiosity will get the better of you, and those unexplained rumors will begin to nag at you.

Defuse the situation by talking it through with your date. However false you are sure the gossip is, it is worth getting it out into the open between you, for your own peace of mind. So if her name and telephone number are on the walls of every public toilet in town, or if her mobile phone continually rings with guys calling for a good time, don't ignore it. Ask her about this strange fact—there is probably a very good explanation.

And don't get distressed when you hear that his nickname during all those years he spent in juvenile penitentiaries was "The Beast." He can probably explain that he was a young, idealist animal-rights activist, cruelly persecuted for his beliefs.

Avoid repeating friendly hearsay

It is worth noting that the literal meaning of the Ninth Commandment is *not* merely "Do not *bear* false witness," but even more, "Do not *answer or repeat* false witness." Maimonides, the medieval codifier of Jewish law, rules that this is a prohibition against hearsay. In Jewish law a witness may not repeat what someone else has told him, but can only testify about what he or she has experienced directly.

So do not pay too much attention to hearsay about your date. If your family and friends voice their opinions about your boyfriend or girlfriend that does not seem to be born out by the facts, do not take it to heart. People—even good people—have all kinds of motives for saying things. Don't blindly adopt their views as your own. If you hear something negative about your date, do not give it a high priority in your mind. Judge them by their actions, not by someone else's opinion. Once the relationship has developed to the point where there is great confidence and trust between you, then discuss it openly, if it still interests you.

That is the beauty of trust. Where there is trust, sensitive issues can be discussed without fear. Where there is no trust, all the sensitive issues must be swept under the carpet for fear of hearing what you dread.

Bearing false witness against yourself

Everyone knows it's wrong to lie. And yet, in dating, you may find yourself slipping into the habit quite unintentionally. You'll start by trying to make a good impression and before you know it, your long nose will poke out your date's eye.

I attended the birthday party of a close friend from Oxford University. There were plenty of other former students there, including David. David had studied business management at Oxford Polytechnic, which didn't have quite the same prestige as the university. David felt insecure about it.

He started chatting with a girl at the party and pretended that he had graduated from Oxford University. He didn't get very far. "Since when do they have a business school?" she asked him, baffled. David turned red and rushed out. Because of a silly fib, he had blown his chances. He should have known that the girl would have been far more impressed with his honesty than his pedigree.

Don't let your insecurities overtake you when you date. Be comfortable with yourself and be clear about who you really are. Don't exaggerate your achievements, job, earning power, only to have to backtrack later. Be accurate. Better to be honest and not all that impressive than to lie and be exposed later.

However, just occasionally you might get away with it.

When I was a little boy, my elder brother Chaim, who was a pet freak, took a perverse delight in beating me to a pulp. We shared a room and he tried his best to get me out, once going so far as to stage a garage sale where he disposed of my bed and all my clothing. I retaliated by shaving the hair off his pet tarantula. Bad idea. He was much bigger than me.

He stormed out of the bedroom and grabbed me by my hair. He dragged me to the toilet bowl, where he proceeded to pummel my head against its rim, causing a huge gash just over my eye and permanent damage to my brain.

It was terrible. Blood was gushing everywhere. My IQ went down from 248 to 240. I could no longer instantly calculate the square root of 35,392,641. I now needed a few seconds. My brother felt terrible about what he had done and ran to get some glue. He sawed away the piece of skull that was sticking out, and then stuck the skin back together. A few minutes later, my mother came home. She turned pale as she saw me sitting in a pool of blood. "Oh my God," she cried. "My carpets, my carpets."

Many years later, on a date with Debbie, she asked me what the gash above my eye was. I didn't think I was going to sound very courageous by telling her that it came from a toilet bowl, so I did what came naturally. I lied through my teeth. I told her that it had happened only that morning. "I dreamed that you didn't love me," I said. "I woke up and didn't realize that it was only a dream, and I felt that I didn't want to live anymore. So I stuck my head into my own laundry basket to end it all. But then I thought that there were less painful ways of dying. So I smashed my head against the wall. When I did that, it dawned upon me, as I lay dying, that it was only a dream. And suddenly, I wanted to live. I wanted to live and make you happy. I ran and kissed a picture of you and felt instantly better."

When I finished my story, there were rivers of tears streaming down Debbie's cheeks, and she was gently wiping my gash with the handkerchief she had just used to blow her nose. She told me how lucky she was to be with the most romantic guy in the whole world.

I got away with it—but can you imagine how awful my life is going to be when Debbie reads this? Luckily, she doesn't understand how I ever got published and never reads a word I write.

Life is unpredictable. We are all part of the rat race; we have to work, we have to look good, and until we find our soul mate, we have to be part of the singles cattle market. Complete strangers are constantly criticizing everything we do.

When we come home we want an anchor, a rock. We want a place where we can be ourselves, where we always feel that we are good enough. We don't always want to perform. We don't always want to act. The moment we have to question the truth about ourselves or about our date, our peace of mind is destroyed. When people lie, trust is lost and our feeling of security disappears.

I had a close friend who was married with four children and provided for his family in every way. But because he was going through a life crisis after watching his younger brother get a fabulous new promotion, he started to tell his wife lies. At first it was about little things, like why he was late getting home. He wasn't having an affair with anyone else but would go to a bar to drown his sorrows. Then his lies escalated into big things, about investing money in the stock market, until his wife discovered that everything he had told her was untrue. He had wanted to make himself sound more important.

She felt she had to leave him, even though I tried to persuade her not to. "How can I live with a man who lies?" she said. "Not only do I not trust him, I no longer respect him either. And I cannot spend the rest of my life with a man for whom I have contempt."

Respect is the bedrock into which all love must be anchored. It is important not to tell even the smallest lie in a relationship. Learn to be who you really are. Even if you are always late for everything because you are so disorganized and not because you are needed at important meetings, your date will have to learn to live with it if they love you. But don't lie about it. Don't make a person believe you are something that you are not. Don't forfeit their trust.

Sharing yourself

Many of us feel the need to be in control and are afraid to express our emotions or admit to weaknesses, because we feel people will take advantage of us. There is a big difference, however, between not showing your emotions and being cold. You can learn to express your feelings, while still remaining resolute about what you want from your relationship.

If you ever feel tempted to misrepresent yourself to your date for any reason, go to the other extreme. Tell them some of the true stories and anecdotes about your life, even funny ones against yourself. You will create a sympathetic bond. Don't be afraid to disclose personal experiences, even your deepest pain, with the person you're dating. Be open and honest. Your trust will breed their trust, your openness will create a mirror reflection, and you will bring them out of their shell, thereby creating intimacy.

But don't be *too* critical about yourself

It's a good thing to be open, to talk about your feelings, even your fears. It is even okay to tell funny stories against yourself. But another rule derived from the Ninth Commandment is never to give damning testimony against yourself.

In other words, don't be too hard on yourself. Ours is a generation that suffers from an unreasonable sense of low self-esteem. We are in reality a whole lot better than we think. Therefore, don't be too hard on yourself. Your date may end up believing you are as hopeless a sap as you make yourself out to be.

Don't go on and on about what a bad person you are, how you are always late for everything, always disorganized, always losing your temper. Never say how unattractive you feel. Don't say things like "I can't believe I'm on a date with you. I know I don't deserve you. Why, you're the first woman I've ever dated I didn't pick up in a retirement home." Nor "My last boyfriend was a nice guy. Unfortunately, we had to break up after I gave him the detailed version of my early childhood. He simply never woke up again." Don't say that you don't think you're pretty or that you were always jealous of the really popular girls at school. If you show how much you doubt yourself, your poor date is bound to start doubting you too. Show them that you have self-confidence.

Friends, enemies, and strangers

Being a child means that everybody apart from your parents hates you. The neighbors, the postman, the bus driver, and your teachers at school are all equally convinced that you are the devil incarnate, ill-mannered, destructive, and raised in a barn by a pack of sheepdogs. But there are two delusional grown-ups back at home who not only do not share everyone else's opinion, but actually find you cute and even let you live with them.

Halloween is a child's most cherished holiday. Once a year, at Halloween, not only do the neighbors *not* set their dogs on you or use you for target practice with their machine guns, they actually allow you to walk all the way up to their front porch, knock on the door, and say, "Trick or treat." And some of them actually do then give you candy.

What crazy transformation has overtaken them? The answer, according to your parents, is none whatsoever. Whereas children absolutely adore Halloween, it is a parent's worst nightmare. Like a colonel warning his paratroopers about the treacherous enemy terrain just before they jump from the airplane, your parents sit you down and warn you about all the low-life human scum you are about to encounter. Every old man in a raincoat you meet will want to show you his little friend whom he has named Herbie, and every elderly woman could be a secret witch who wants to turn you into a wart-covered toad.

They tell you horror stories about the little boy who was given an apple and then cut his mouth on a razor blade that had been put inside. It took his mother a month to sew his tongue back on. They tell you how all the nonkosher M&M's they give you will have been injected with poison that will make your foreskin grow back, necessitating a second circumcision. And most of all, they tell you never to accept any invitation to "come inside," because once they get you, they'll tie you down, pour gravy all over you, and serve you for supper to their giant hound, Bratkiller.

And why all the suspicion against your otherwise civil neighbors? Because they are that dreaded word . . . "strangers." From our earliest years, our parents instill us with the belief that you must never, ever trust strangers.

A stranger is, almost by definition, someone whom you don't trust. You question their motives and suspect their actions. The saddest moment is when someone you love becomes a stranger. A woman can be married to a man for twenty years and then discover that for the past five years he has been keeping a mistress. At that moment, he becomes a stranger to her. She no longer trusts him. And the essence of every relationship is trust. A relationship is about making yourself vulnerable to someone, lowering your defenses, trusting them absolutely.

In dating we are trying to stop being strangers

The essence of a date is that two people, who begin as strangers, want to find out more about each other, so that they can become lovers.

Why would some guy or girl who is a stranger want to become intimate with you, give themselves to you? Because they are going to learn to trust you.

Here are a few basic guidelines by which to engender trust in your relationship:

Always keep your promises.

Never exaggerate about yourself. If she asks about the scar on your arm, don't say that you got that while "taking out" the head of Libyan intelligence during your time with the SAS. She'll soon discover that you slipped in the shower while doing the macarena.

Be honest about your emotions. Try to express what you are feeling. (Unless you're feeling constipated. Keep that to yourself.)

Don't force your date to do anything that they don't feel comfortable with. Stop pressuring them to enter the Budweiser World Belching Contest.

Demonstrate that you have standards, both moral and spiritual, and never ask your date to compromise their own. If she normally gives a 20 percent tip to the waiting staff, then you should do so as well. (I know it hurts.) If he observes the Jewish Sabbath and doesn't drive or go to movies, then don't try to push him into picking you up from work, or to watch television with you. If she goes to church on Sundays, then don't pressure her to go to the beach instead.

Summary of Trust
1. Learn to open your heart and express your nakedness
2. The power of gossip
3. A benevolent eye
4. Dealing with your date's "reputation"
5. Avoid repeating friendly hearsay
6. Bearing false witness against yourself
7. Sharing yourself
8. Don't be *too* critical of yourself
9. Friends, enemies, and strangers
10. In dating we are trying to stop being strangers
11. To let a fool kiss you is stupid. To let a kiss fool you is worse.

ten

Contentment

Being Happy with What You Have

True contentment is a thing as active as agriculture. It is the power of getting out of any situation all that there is in it. It is arduous and it is rare.
—G. K. Chesterton (1874–1936), British author.
A Miscellany of Men, "The Contented Man"

THE TENTH COMMANDMENT: Do not covet your fellow's house. Do not covet your fellow's wife, his manservant, his maidservant, his ox, his donkey, nor every thing that belongs to your fellow. (Exodus 20:17)

A t first sight, the Tenth Commandment is a bit of a letdown. We might expect the last of them to have a little oomph. Perhaps a prohibition on some really heinous sin like double parking or bringing a crying baby on a plane. But what does the Tenth Commandment forbid instead? Coveting!

The first question is: How can coveting be forbidden? Coveting—like its naughty cousins jealousy, envy, and lust—is an emotion, not an action. A person covets secretly, in his heart, and may never reveal it. Unlike stealing or murder, coveting cannot be perceived by outsiders, and is therefore impossible to police. *However . . .*

The cosmic guide to contentment

As we have seen, the Ten Commandments are not simply a bunch of legal edicts. They have universal and eternal significance. The Tenth Commandment brings us around full circle to the First Commandment, which is also pretty unusual in what it demands. What do these two commandments have in common? They both aim to ingrain in us peace of mind and a sense of contentment.

The importance of contentment in your dating

"Who is a rich man?" goes a famous rabbinical teaching. Answer: "He who has lots of money." (Just kidding.) No, the real answer is "He who is content with everything he has." The wealthy man who still wants more is a poor man. Nothing is ever good enough for him—he must always be looking for more and better. He has no inner contentment, and without contentment there can be no joy.

The First Commandment teaches that by subordinating ourselves to the One God and giving Him primacy, we can trust that everything that happens to us is for the best. There is a plan to Creation. Nothing is arbitrary and everything has a higher purpose. The Tenth Commandment reinforces this by telling us not to yearn for what we do not have, because what we do have is enough.

Only if we are free of worries and strain can we devote ourselves to God and to each other. When you feel at peace with the world, you are able to treat others well. But when you are frustrated and miserable, you treat others miserably. When you date, a sense of contentment will allow you to connect to your boyfriend or girlfriend on the deepest possible level. Your mind will be unencumbered by trivial concerns, and you will come to them with a clear conscience and a pure heart.

And if that doesn't float their boat, then nothing will.

Covetousness is just not cool

A covetous man sees some guy driving a nice car, and suddenly feels that he wants one too. And then a primitive mechanism kicks in and convinces him that no two cars like that exist, or at least that no other car will be quite as good as that one. Our man believes that he can only be happy if he takes the car away from the other guy and keeps it for himself. The result? He's unhappy.

To covet is to be a prisoner of desire. It is to be shackled in a cage of discontent. What you want and what will make you happy is always outside you. It is forever calling out to you, tempting you from the distance, mocking your weakness and inability to rise above it.

Someone who covets always breaks two commandments—the First and the Tenth. Coveting is a denial of God's abundance. Instead of seeing how God provides everything for everyone, a person who covets believes that the world is made up of a very small pie, and anything that others have deprives him of his rights, his share. He has a "scarcity mentality." There is only so much money, so much happiness. When someone else is happy, he feels miserable because they have taken his smile. It is what my corporate friends call a "win/lose" mentality.

Having a win/win mentality

There is no place for this kind of thinking in God's world. "Survival of the fittest" is for the jungle. No one has to lose just so you can win. Think of yourself as being like a candle. One candle can light ten thousand other candles without losing any of the intensity of its own light. Think "win/win" and the world becomes a better place. Believe in God and in His infinite blessing.

Once you have purged yourself of covetousness, you are now ready to love because rather than feeling deprived, you now know you are blessed.

If your sense of pride depends on your ability to outdo others, then you have nothing to be proud of. Human glory is only worth something when everyone involved in the achievement, in however small a way, shares it equally. Cut the unhealthy competitive streak.

Don't be the Darwin of dating

Nowhere is this truer than in dating. No one wants to go out with a person who is on some sort of romantic power trip, who thinks a relationship should be as competitive as the workplace or the sports field. If you find yourself wondering whether you have more influence over your date than he or she has over you, then you will make your partner into your adversary rather than helpmate. If the thought "What am I getting out of this?" pops into your head, pop it right out again. You are building a beautiful relationship *together* that will bring joy to both of you equally. This is the ultimate "win/win" situation.

> Sam had a real problem in his dating. On the one hand, he only wanted to date intelligent "career" girls who were as interesting and ambitious as he was himself. On the other hand, whenever he got serious with any of these girls, he found himself feeling very insecure.
>
> It was only when he and I discussed this that the truth behind this came out. His father had gone bankrupt and his mother had been the family's main supporter ever since. Sam looked down on his father as a failure, and for not being the traditional breadwinner, and he assumed that his mother felt the same.

I said to him, "You are looking at your parents as though they were competitors. But they are married to each other, they are equal partners in everything that they do. They love each other and see themselves as one organic unit. It makes no difference to them who brings the money in. When you marry, you will feel the same.

To succeed in dating, you must feel and believe that you were created to make someone else happy and the love they give you is a gift from God. Don't keep looking around to see if other people are getting a better deal, and don't put your date through endless battles of wits to see which of you is top dog. Happiness is something that everyone is entitled to, it is a birthright, and you can give it to the one you love.

Everything is predestined—especially dating

We all sometimes love to marvel about things like "Had I never gone to the Pizza Hut that day, I would never have met her . . ." or "It all began when I spotted him in the police lineup." This is fine, so long as you understand it as a deep mystery—the romantic beginning of the story of how your fates have been intertwined—not as a simple accident.

To say that anything happened by sheer luck can ultimately be a threat to your relationship. When we believe that we gained something merely by chance, that it was not preordained, we are adopting a dangerously cavalier attitude toward it. Just look at the way lottery winners spend money, compared with those who have to earn it through hard work. Rewards which come about arbitrarily are always taken for granted by their recipients.

So if we believe that we bumped into the person we are dating only by accident, we may be far less committed to making the relationship work when things begin to go wrong. We adopt the mind-set that what began by chance could end by chance. We think, "Heck, it's a shame that after all these dates this thing ain't working out. But had I not rescheduled my appointment at the proctologist that day, we never would have met anyway."

Judaism maintains that nothing happens by accident. According to Jewish thought, the Almighty has a soul mate intended for each and every one of us. And when a couple that was meant to be together separates, we are told that God *weeps* for this disruption of His plans.

A belief that God brought us together inspires us to try much harder. This is the reason that the Tenth Commandment closes the circle originally opened by the First Commandment, "I am the Lord your God." Someone who believes in God will be satisfied that what he has is a blessing from God, and will never covet anything belonging to another man. Armed with a firm belief in the Almighty, he will accept life as guided by Providence. He will exert every effort to make God's blessings work, rather than always looking over his neighbor's fence to see what he is missing.

> *Moishe the tailor came to the Rabbi to complain. "Rabbi, I had a wonderful business until that wretched cheat Shalom the tailor opened next door to me. He has taken all my business. And do you know what? I put in six stitches per inch, where Shalom only puts in four. I use one hundred percent wool, while he uses a polyester wool blend. And I put double stitching in all the seams. Shalom puts only single stitching."*
>
> *The Rabbi looked at Moishe and said, "My dear Moishele, it seems to me that if you concentrated half as much on your own business as you do on Shalom's, you would probably have as many customers as him."*

Your life is *your* life. There is no need to focus on what you *don't* have. Work with what you *do* have.

Contentment = self-confidence

I have said repeatedly that one of the most attractive features you can develop in dating is your self-confidence. And contentment is key to this development. When you are content, you feel you lack for nothing. Not self-worth, not self-esteem. In short, you are firm in your convictions, proud of who you are, comfortable inside your own skin, and consequently very, very sexy to your date.

By feeling envious of another person's property or achievements, you will merely distract from the rich qualities you already possess. You won't seem confident—in fact, you will begin to appear deeply insecure. Unless your date is a professional therapist, they aren't going to want to hang around. Only by refusing to covet will you remember everything you have to offer and feel secure in your capacity to give and contribute to someone else's happiness.

Imagine that you are on a date and your companion tells you about some great achievement of a mutual acquaintance, someone in the same profession as you. If you immediately look down and mutter, "Wonderful," simultaneously offering up a prayer that the Almighty strike him down with an unspeakably cruel death, your date will know that you are not such a good person and that you are very insecure. But if you can say, and mean, "Wow! That's wonderful. I'm so happy for them!" your date will see in you your great and generous spirit that never feels jealous or deprived by someone else's triumph.

I introduced Helena to my friend Derek. Although Helena was spiritually oriented and Derek was secular, I thought that they could be a good match for each other because they shared an interest in medical research. Neither of them was in the first bloom of youth. Derek had been a doctor for several years before retiring because of failing health. Helena was a nurse.

After the date, Helena told me that she had no intention of seeing Derek again. During the date, he had told her that he expected to die in his fifties of cancer, as had his father and uncle. He was cynical about everything. They had gone to a restaurant with a live band, and Helena had suggested they dance together. Derek had declined and pointed at the young people dancing, saying, "I wish I could be like them—blissfully ignorant and happy. They don't have to worry about dropping dead from a heart attack . . ."

"Shmuley, it was a nightmare," Helena said. "I want to date a man who is a happy, whole human being who makes me feel glad to be alive. Derek's a decent man, but he's got one foot in the grave!"

Hungrier than any stomach, a relationship needs constant nourishment. It needs regular deposits of love, joy, attentiveness, romance, physical embrace, spontaneity, and time spent together. Don't waste time moaning about what you lack: "He doesn't pay me enough attention," "She puts her mother ahead of me," "We can never afford to go anywhere nice," or "I wish he sent me flowers, like my friend's date does." Overlooking all the good things life does bring you, and coveting that which you don't have, is a surefire way to destroy your self-esteem and your relationship.

Count your blessings

Even if you are not overtly religious, you should make an effort to trust in Providence and believe that you already have everything you need. By showing that you have a deep faith that your life is going in the right direction, you will be irresistible to your date.

Your date will know that whatever happens, you will turn even the saddest experience into something good, rather than feeling sorry for yourself or coveting someone else's life. They will know that you will devote yourself to maximizing your own potential. They will know you are interested in making something of your life rather than blaming someone else for your failings, or being jealous of other people's happiness. They will want to be part of such a rich and satisfying journey.

> *On his deathbed, Rabbi Zusya of Anipoli cried inconsolably. His students were baffled and troubled. "Rebbe," they asked him, "despite poverty and persecution you were joyous throughout your lifetime. So why do you weep now?"*
>
> *"Because I am about to die and come before the Heavenly Throne," he said through his tears, "and the Almighty will ask me, 'Zusya, why weren't you as great as Abraham?' and I will say, 'Because, God, You did not make me Abraham.'*
>
> *"He will ask me, 'Why weren't you as great as Moses?' and I will say, 'Because You did not make me Moses.'*
>
> *"He will say, 'Why weren't you at least as great as King David?' and I will tell Him, 'Because, God, You didn't make me King David.'*
>
> *"But when He asks me why I was not as great as Zusya, then what will I answer?"*

Is it ever okay to covet?

Covetousness is a feeling, and all our emotions, being God-given, have a good purpose as well as the possibility of misuse. It is the misuse that we are warned against. If there were no good purpose at all in covetousness, God would not have created us with the capacity for it. The Tenth Commandment does not forbid coveting per se, but rather coveting something that already belongs to someone else. As long as we don't deprive someone else through our desires, the urge to covet can be channeled to good ends.

Covetousness is part of our impulse toward self-advancement, the drive to expand and develop our inborn gifts and talents. God has implanted this aspiration into all His creatures, animals and humans alike. Every being, in serving itself, improving its own lot, finds its place in the divine universal order and thus serves the entire world.

It is vital that we see humankind as part of the whole circle of God's servants, part of the divine plan for the whole earth. When we want things solely for our own ends, this tears up the charter of divinity in man, and there is no sin, great or small, that it will not bring about. We end up destroying the happiness of everything around us, and are dissatisfied with everything we gain. What we have seems valueless, and only what is not yet ours holds any attraction for us, only to lose its appeal the minute it has been acquired.

How does this apply to dating? Use the good side of covetousness—the desire to expand your horizons and improve your lot—as something to be shared, not something to feed your own ego. Never be selfish, thinking that what you achieve should serve only you. Let your desire to be something special—a somebody—define itself by your capacity to make someone *else* feel special.

Coveting a good character

The items that the Tenth Commandment forbids us to covet are all valuable material objects. While it is wrong to covet another person's material wealth, it is permitted, even encouraged, to yearn for another man's spiritual virtue. We should be inspired by the goodness of other people and strive to emulate them. We should save our greed for the spiritual riches of life.

So when you see someone who has something you want, whether it is a material possession or a social success, whether they dress in beautiful clothes or have an interesting job, try to think about what they may have done to deserve this. You may well find that the other person, who at first seemed no better than you, actually has qualities of character that you would do well to emulate. Perhaps he or she is especially hardworking and saves hard for their nice things. Perhaps they are popular socially because they are very generous or sympathetic and people like being around them.

Perhaps they are unusually charming, and win people over to their cause. Perhaps they have worked hard to develop their minds so that they can contribute a lot to their interesting job.

And perhaps you could do just as well as they if you put your mind to it. So don't covet what they have in terms of possessions—envy instead their good qualities and develop your own. Not only are you more likely to succeed but you will be far more attractive to the opposite sex.

Getting your date to covet

Don't expect any less of your boyfriend or girlfriend. While it is improper to goad a date into making more money, faulting them for not driving a more expensive car, or beating them over the head to be more ambitious, it is absolutely correct to subtly and diplomatically inspire them to stretch themselves and to achieve what they can spiritually. A relationship in which neither party grows, and neither one inspires the other to grow, will lead to boredom and a feeling that things just aren't right. People will always feel more satisfied within a relationship that brings out the best in them. Both a man and a woman need to feel enriched and uplifted within the relationship.

While you should not covet your best friend's date, you have every right to covet the chivalry, patience, humility, and spirituality he shows her. Be careful how you phrase your covetousness to your own date, however. You should never tell your boyfriend, "Josh, I wish you were more like Ken." That will merely raise their defenses.

The best thing to do, if you want your Josh to grow spiritually, is to appeal to his sense of ambition. Perhaps you could put it like this: "Josh, I am concerned that people don't know what a nice guy you are, the way that I do. When you call your lawyer a rat scumbag, your colleagues at work may get a false impression of you as having a bad temper. I want everyone to know how kind you can be. Do you think that the next time you get upset, you can wait a few minutes before you shout at people, so that you can calm down and talk to them in the constructive and positive way that I'm accustomed to?"

The chaotic quest for "the best"

They say that when women first start dating, their fantasy perfect man is tall, dark, and handsome. At age twenty-five, they change it to tall, dark, and handsome with money. At age thirty-five, they change it again to a man with a brain. At age forty-eight, it's any man with hair. And at age sixty-six, a man.

Because they date so much, men are becoming experts in women, and women are becoming experts in men. An expert is someone who can spot the flaws and point out the imperfections. Even within a loving, long-term relationship, people often feel they are being compared and evaluated as though they were an acquisition, rather than an equal. And far too many people have become so fussy, they end up as permanent singles, never able to settle for anybody.

The problem is that everyone wants to feel sure that they are dating the "right" person. Everyone today wants the best. We are a prosperous generation, capable of purchasing the best clothes, the best microwave oven, the best television and video player, and the best politicians. So why shouldn't your date be the best member of the opposite sex as well? Isn't that simply logical? And isn't it something that you deserve? This reasoning accounts for why so many men and women will date without committing. They think that just as they tie the knot, somebody better will come along.

There is an important flaw in this argument. It is relatively easy to assess the best stereo system, since all we want from it is to get the best-sounding music. And we can easily make an objective evaluation of the best sound by measuring tangible things like decibel level, wattage per speaker, whether we can get it into our van, and whether or not it can make the Spice Girls sound tempting. The same is true of a car. We can objectively evaluate which car can accelerate from zero to sixty in as few seconds as possible, without being pushed off a cliff.

But when it comes to love and human needs, the evaluation is totally subjective. Coveting objective traits is pointless. No one can seriously believe that a tall man is "superior" to a short man, or that a woman with blond hair will be a superior soul mate to a woman with brown hair.

(I say this because I have always been vertically challenged, or in my case, vertically at war. When my mother asked what gift I wanted for my Bar Mitzvah, I responded that I wanted to grow. "You mean you want to grow as a person, to grow spiritually?"

"No, Mom, grow *literally,*" I said as I pulled myself out from under the orange peel she had just discarded. She took me to a growth hormone specialist, who at first offered to hire me as a full-time paperweight and then showed us a pill the size of two horses, costing hundreds of dollars, and told me I'd have to take one of these each day.

"We can't afford this, Mom," I said.

"Don't worry. I can always start working nights again. It'll be worth it for me to spend time away from you."

And never in the history of parental endeavor has so great a sacrifice produced so little for one so small.)

You date for so many different things about the other person, their looks, their personality, their sense of humor, their rich daddy . . . not just for one particular quality. No one dates someone *just* because they have nice hair. Everyone dates out of an inner human need for company, and it is the man or woman who assuages your loneliness who is best suited for you. Therefore, dating endlessly in the pursuit of something slightly better, far from producing an even better companion, will prevent you from ever finding any real companionship at all.

I stress this point because I have met too many men and women who have given up good, happy relationships for no other reason than they thought they might have found something slightly better. This is especially true of the more successful men and women that I meet. They think that because they are successful in their other endeavors they are entitled to the very best human being that God created. Of course, no matter how often they change their date, they are never satisfied because they worry they could someday find someone better. What a paradox: success in business means failure in love?

Money should bring freedom, not enslavement

It is axiomatic that money doesn't buy you happiness. So what does it buy? Only one important thing: freedom. If you have money, you can choose where you want to work, how much you want to work, or even whether you want to work. You can pop over to another country for the weekend, or buy a beautiful country retreat. You can spend your money on clothes, fancy restaurants, or your favorite pastime. You are free to choose. How sad it is, then, when successful men and women become enslaved rather than liberated by their money (although I pray daily that such enslavement will overtake me rapidly), slaves to their desire to possess the best human being. Finally, feeling their biological clock ticking, they end up marrying in haste, often to the man or woman least suited to their needs.

In dating, you should only look for the guy or girl who meets your needs, or in other words, who brings out the best in you. No one will ever be perfect. But there will come a time in your dating life when you will just feel attracted, comfortable, and happy with one man or woman. They will offer you that one thing that is the very essence of every romantic relationship—namely, they will make you feel special and cherished. Even if, objectively speaking, there are other guys or girls out there who are taller, prettier, richer, thinner, or even more loving, this does not change the fact that you have found everything you need. I am not advocating that you lower your standards in dating. On the contrary, I am advocating that you raise your appreciation and sense of thankfulness that you have found someone who uniquely suits you.

Dealing with "date envy"

Every day you will see storybook couples, infuriatingly happy with one another. Everything looks good about them—their smiles, their hair, even their fashion sense seems flawless. They look completely absorbed in love. Their sex life is great, you don't doubt, and each and every second they spend together must be as hot as a bonfire night.

Then you'll look at your date. You'll see his or her flaws, and then you will feel troubled by the *fact* that you are seeing the flaws. You will think that the people around you are much more attracted to each other than you are to your date. You may well become convinced that because you have your doubts about the relationship this is proof positive that you are not truly happy. And then you will remember all those "perfect" couples out there, and envy their "happiness." They say that getting married is very much like going to a restaurant with friends. You order what you want, and when you see what the other fellow has, you wish you had ordered that.

Coveting another person's happiness is just as wrong as coveting their property. What's worse, it is very stupid, as you cannot possibly know *how* happy they really are—if at all. You are merely projecting your standards of happiness onto them, and then envying that illusion.

> *A woman with a broken heart came to her Rabbi to lament the difficult times she was having with her husband. "We fight a lot and I look around and see how happy all my friends are with their husbands and I feel even more miserable."*

The Rabbi said to her, "How could you possibly know what goes on behind closed doors? You don't, but I do. Because when people have problems in their relationship, they come to people like me, not to you."

He then encouraged her to take a more realistic approach to the effort which every marriage needs in order to succeed.

Do not covet your neighbor's wife . . . or every *thing*

Note that the Tenth Commandment emphatically uses the term "every thing" in prescribing the act of coveting. There is a profound lesson attached to this, as it points to the fact that we tend to covet selectively, rather than perceiving the entire picture when it comes to the object of our desire.

In this commandment, it is as though God says to us, "Really, you covet your neighbor's house? You want to have what he has? You want to be him? Okay, we can arrange this. But you can't covet selectively. If you want to be him, it's got to come with everything. Sure, you'll get his Ferrari. But you'll also get the abuse he takes from his boss and his customers, the internal pressures he feels to succeed, the irrational fears he has of failing, and all the misery that accompanies that inner turmoil."

You may see a young couple kissing passionately in an airport and envy them—but think for a moment. Perhaps they are kissing because he is her lover, and she is trapped in a loveless marriage and they will never meet again, and he will die a sad old bachelor. Or maybe she has something stuck in her teeth, and he is helping her get it out. Or perhaps they are starring in a really mushy long-distance phone call commercial and can't stand each other. Or maybe they are both drug smugglers and she is passing sixteen kilos of cocaine into his mouth to bring into the country. These are all very real and likely scenarios.

Do you still envy them? No. You were only coveting the image of happiness. You don't know if there is any real happiness there.

An old Jewish folktale relates how the few inhabitants of a small village all gathered around in a circle, each carrying his "peckel," his package representing his life's troubles and personal sorrows. They all threw their sacks into the middle and were instructed that they could pick up anyone else's. They could give up all their problems and take on someone else's peckel.

After a short deliberation, each of the villagers chose their own sacks once again and made their way home with a renewed confidence.

It is crucial that you apply the moral of this story to your relationship. The guy and the girl who swoon over each other at the racetrack and whom you envy have their own peckel of trouble. You are not privy to "every thing" about their relationship—they may have troubles you couldn't begin to handle. Your own problems are part of your life and God never gives us anything in life that we can't deal with. Never grow despondent or be defeated by your worries. Rise to the challenge of life and focus on reducing the size of your peckel instead of wishing to switch with someone else.

The importance of jealousy

In case you skipped this bit in an early chapter, it is worth repeating here. Jealousy within a relationship is not only allowed, it is healthy and even mandatory. The Tenth Commandment prohibits coveting another man's wife. But it allows you to covet your own wife.

So often a couple begins to date, but then the spark is lost. Their mutual sexual attraction tapers off and the intense feelings fade. It seems in so many relationships that this sad phenomenon is unavoidable. For sexual attraction to thrive, the sexual relationship has to seem new. However, as novelty cannot last forever, monogamous relationships are bound to lose their spark. Men especially have a very short sexual attention span.

Therefore, to remind a man of just how desirable his woman is, she must always remain just slightly outside his grasp. When the two of you go to a party together, no woman should hang around on her man's arm the entire time, as if to say, "Don't worry, I'm not going anywhere. I'm yours. You're now free to let your eyes roam and see who is available." He should always be concerned about whom *you* are speaking to, and who is drawn to *you*. When he sees how other men are interested in you, he is reminded—via a totally new pair of eyes—just how beautiful and desirable you are. You show him that you need to be wooed at all times, and that you are an attractive and sexy creature who other people find appealing. Jealousy is the key to keeping sexual attraction alive. It is our most intense emotion, and rather than burying it, we should employ it for beneficial use within our relationship.

Coveting yourself: the perils of materialism and greed

Although the Tenth Commandment specifically forbids coveting someone else's property, the prohibition applies equally to coveting your *own* property.

In other words, don't be materialistic. Becoming too attached to your material possessions virtually ensures that you will have less time for your relationships with people. Once you begin to define your happiness and security by what you have, you begin to find human beings dispensable, and your inherent ability to love and be loved will become stifled. You will come across to your date as too independent, too self-absorbed, incapable of giving and sacrificing yourself for another. Worse, you will begin to think that what makes you attractive to the opposite sex is your possessions rather than your person.

A man is driving his BMW sports car at very high speed down the highway and gets into a terrible accident. He emerges dazed, looks at his car, and starts yelling, "My BMW! My

BMW!" A policeman runs up to him and says, "Forget your car, sir. I don't know how to tell you this. But your arm was torn off and is lost somewhere on the highway." The man looks at his empty arm socket and begins to yell, "My Rolex! My Rolex!"

Love vs. livelihood: striking the balance

Too many men and women place their financial situation ahead of their need to find a good relationship. They will put off marriage, or even dating, until they have secured the house, the car, or the commission. They place career prospects before everything, including health and hobbies. Although people may claim that this is "responsible" thinking, it is really just a veiled version of materialism.

The Tenth Commandment lists the items that you must not covet in a very specific and important order. First, it says that you should not covet your neighbor's house, then his wife, then his manservant, then his maidservant, then his ox, etc. This is a lesson in the proper order of priorities.

The "house" represents basic financial independence. A man must make sure he has some security to offer a woman. His work enables him to have the necessary home for them to live in, and then he is ready to seek a partner for life. After he marries he can work on getting the other things.

So you get the house, then the wife, and only then should you worry about servants and pets, etc. But make sure you don't reverse the order. There are plenty of people who put the pet before the partner. So many people fall so much for their cat, they don't have enough love left over to give to their date. He goes out and buys a goldfish to talk to because he's lonely. On St. Valentine's Day, he gives it little heart-shaped bits of food. His romantic drive is satisfied. He loses his longing and need for a date. Don't do it. Place the search for a soul mate first, before all other things.

Such is the importance of finding a spouse before worrying

about more petty material concerns that in the second version of the Tenth Commandment, in Deuteronomy 5:21, it puts not coveting your neighbor's wife *even before* not coveting his house. Here the Bible puts the search for a spouse before everything else.

Go for broke in your love life. Find the man or woman of your dreams, commit to them, and you will grow wealthy together—both in love and in livelihood.

The importance of charity and generosity

Don't let greed reduce you to a tightfisted moral invalid. In order to reach a healthy distance from coveting your own wealth, try to err on the side of being too generous. Indeed, the Talmudic sages suggest that by placing the prohibition on coveting in the *Tenth* Commandment, the Bible is reminding us that we must *tithe*—that is, give 10 percent of our earnings to charity.

Generosity is very attractive in a partner. Generous people attract others to them, while misers are a turnoff.

If you take a girl out, always make sure to show her your generous heart. If you're walking down the street together and you see a beggar, don't say, "Go and get a job," and kick them in the groin. Give them some money to buy food. A charitable man is a caring man, and it will impress her. Give the waiter a good tip. When the check arrives, for goodness' sake don't pull out a calculator and work out what 15 percent is precisely. And if you are without a calculator, don't turn to her and ask her what 15 percent of two dollars is. And whatever you do, don't ask her to work out her half.

If you don't own a car, there is nothing wrong with asking your date to take the subway or a bus home with you. But if it is freezing cold outside, then call a cab. If you can't afford it, sell a nonvital organ. Kidneys can fetch up to $80,000, and unused kidneys can get even more, so limit all liquid intake throughout your dinner.

The most important thing when choosing gifts for your date is the frequency with which you give, and the imagination you invest in choosing each item. *Not the cost.* The mere fact that you regularly choose to part with your money in order to make your loved one happy will show them that you are generous in spirit as well as in pocket. Don't worry if it's only something small. When she removes the three layers of wrapping paper, and finds the paper clip you bought her, she will smile and appreciate all the effort you went to lift it off your desk and put it in a box. To make it extra special, twist it a bit before you wrap it, to show her that your loving handiwork went into it as well.

But don't be flashy

With that said, don't go to the extreme of becoming extravagant in the generosity you lavish on your date. While there is something to be said for allowing your good traits to attract the opposite sex, you should be wary of trying to lure your boyfriend or girlfriend to you just by flashing your assets.

There are those who always show off their possessions on a date, what they own and what they wear. They think that what makes them really attractive is their job or the kind of car they drive. They are wrong. And they are doing themselves a disservice. Their relationships will be built on such shaky foundations that collapse and heartache will be inevitable.

Harold was a friend of mine from a wealthy family. As his parents had divorced when he was six, he grew up with much insecurity. Stout and large, he was thrilled that a girl as gorgeous as Monica agreed to date him.

He immediately proceeded to lavish upon her every beautiful gift in the world. She would arrive at airports to discover stretch limousines awaiting her arrival. On their third date she received a gold watch, on the sixth date a pearl necklace. After four weeks' dating, he bought her round-trip airfare on the Concorde. And so it went. She was swept off her feet, and eagerly accepted his proposal for marriage after only three months of dating.

Two weeks into the engagement, it all started to unravel. Harold, who had a strong spiritual streak, was surprised and upset at the amount of time Monica devoted to the practical details of the wedding, without almost any thought to the religious aspect. Matters came to a head when Monica insisted that Harold's mother wear a pink-and-blue outfit, to match the colors of the bridesmaids' dresses. But things really exploded when Monica insisted that Harold's father dye his hair pink and blue so that he would match as well.

Harold came to me to complain. "How materialistic can she be? I'm losing all respect for her."

I responded, "Dr. Frankenstein can hardly complain about the monster he has created. You never believed in the power of your soul to win her heart, only the power of your checkbook. This is your mess and you have to clean it up."

Unfortunately, after confronting her with her obsession with materialism, Monica replied, "You're one to talk!" and canceled the engagement.

By relying overly on your possessions to attract your date, you will betray yourself as an insecure, shallow person with little to offer from the inside. This insecurity will only grow with time.

So don't take the easy way out and use lavish gifts and other material gestures of affection as substitutes for yourself. You will lose a lot of money, a lot of pride, and, ultimately, the relationship itself. Be brave, and rely on your personality to win his or her heart. (If you have no personality, then memorize any funny lines in this book and win their hearts. If they don't laugh, then they obviously have no sense of humor and you are better off without them.)

If you find yourself on the receiving end of too much generosity from your date, be careful how you tread. Always express your gratitude without seeming materialistic. If she buys you some expensive cuff links for your birthday when you've only been dating for a week, accept them only if you are absolutely sure you want to go on seeing her. If he takes you to the most expensive restaurant in the city, show how surprised you are to be there for the first time. Make a point of not ordering the most expensive item on the menu. Ask him if you can take home the difference in cash instead.

Most important, do not encourage them to continue being so profligate. Steer them clear of expensive escapades and introduce them to some of your own low-life haunts. Make sure that you have dates where you can meet on equal terms—not just a series of expensive adventures that they have to pay for. Otherwise you may never get to know one another.

How to use coveting to your advantage

However, there are times when you may feel you have no alternative but to use a person's covetousness to your advantage. This is especially true for you guys out there who are just hopeless when it comes to meeting women.

If, despite every humiliation you have received in the past, you are desperate to meet women, then I suggest that you accessorize. Have something in hand that you know will draw the females to you. The following are good ideas:

A Dog

As opposed to iguanas or lice, dogs are pets that are guaranteed to enhance your social life. Borrow or steal one if you have to, and take it for long walks in the local park. It will be well worth it. You will stop and chat with every dog owner of the opposite sex and compare notes about the lovable beasts.

If you're really lucky, then your dog and hers will be of opposite sexes and will feel a natural attraction. Being far less inhibited than humans, they will express this interest in no uncertain terms. This will be a fantastic intro for you to ask for her phone number. Alternatively, if your dogs don't get along and yours takes a big bite out of hers, you can meet up with her in court when she sues you over the loss of poor little Pumpkin.

Children

Okay, so you're not a parent. But still, your married sister can lend you her children. She'll even pay you for keeping them, although she may stop speaking to you once you bring them back. If you're a guy, go walking through a park with a child and women are very likely to come over to you to talk and play with the kid.

Do, however, make sure the women walking by know that the little monster is not actually yours. First, if she thinks he's yours she'll stay away. She doesn't want to be the one raising him. Second, the fact that he isn't yours and you're still out there with him will identify you as the kind of soft, emotional guy that women love. Never mind that you haven't fed the kid all weekend and you've made him wear the same underwear for three nights running. She doesn't know that. And she doesn't need to know. As she draws closer, tell the kid a stupid joke. Pinch him really hard and force him to laugh. While he laughs his socks off you can meet her eye and invite her into the charmed circle you've created.

All children are God's agents to punish adults for all their past sins. Therefore, you may as well get some mileage out of them. Use them to your advantage and then dump 'em back with their parents.

A good book

As you sit there on the bus or the subway riding home from work, face it, you look pretty boring. With the exception of one woman, nobody, but nobody, could ever possibly be interested in you—and your mother is already married. What you need therefore is something that blares like a neon sign that you are incredibly misunderstood. As a person, you are really interesting.

Pull out a great, controversial, avant-garde book, like *The Real Truth: Jackie Shot JFK,* or *True Stories of Cannibalistic Siamese Twins Who Devour Their Doubles Alive,* or a self-help book like *The Alien Inside You* that will show her you are interested in personal growth. Display your love of history by reading aloud from *Ten Famous Belgians.* Make sure the book you're reading shouts out loud, "Hey, I'm different. I'm interesting." This is also the reason that a great place to meet people is at a book store or library. You can just walk up to people and ask them what they are reading. And the subject of the book can provide for instant conversation.

Coveting and coercion

Rabbi Yonah says that even if you are honest and open about coveting something, it can still have destructive consequences. For example, if you desire to buy an object that belongs to your friend, and you know that once you ask him for it he will find it difficult to say no, it is forbidden to make the request. Your covetousness has become coercive and therefore very unfair.

This is a very important lesson in dating. Don't even use subtle means to make your date do something they don't want to do. If you know they can't say no to you about something important, then do the right thing and don't ask for it in the first place. If you know that she or he must work over a weekend or risk losing their job, then don't insist they come away with you. Don't be childish and say, "I don't think you love me." They may be so reluctant to disappoint you that they will consider agreeing, but the consequences of this action will be harmful to them.

And, gentlemen, if your girlfriend is not ready for sex, but you know that she won't refuse your advances because she is afraid of offending you or losing your trust, then do the right thing and don't ask her. Even though she gives in, resentment will build up and she'll be upset that you pushed her to do something she wasn't comfortable with.

A final word on coveting and contentment

After he had conquered the entire known world, Alexander the Great left instructions that he should be buried with his hands left outside the coffin so that all could see that although he had conquered the world, he could carry nothing with him out of it.

When all is said and done, many of the measures listed above will not be necessary, once you have properly internalized and understood the central message of the Tenth Commandment that you must be content in your relationship for it to succeed. An inner sense of satisfaction will prevent covetous feelings from occurring in the first place. The real value of human life is derived from the joy of acknowledging all blessings. And the most important of these is love.

Adam and Eve, the first man and woman, were naked. They had nothing to hide. They had no need to put on clothing because they didn't feel inadequate. They didn't need external accessories to lend them dignity. Nor did they need to put on clothing with a designer label because their own name wasn't good enough. They were naked and innocent, confident and proud.

Every man and woman is born like Adam and Eve, born innocent. It is not a virtue you have to acquire, but it is something you can lose.

Go back to the beginning of this book, read, mark, learn, and inwardly digest the lessons of the Ten Commandments, understand their secrets, and, unlike Adam and Eve, you may never have to leave paradise. You can live forever in the Eden of a long and happy marriage.

Summary of Contentment

1. Being happy with what you have
2. The cosmic guide to contentment
3. The importance of contentment in your dating
4. Covetousness is just not cool
5. Having a win/win mentality
6. Don't be the Darwin of dating
7. Everything is predestined—especially dating
8. Contentment = self-confidence
9. Count your blessings
10. The times when it is okay to covet.
11. Coveting a good character
12. Getting your date to covet you
13. The chaotic quest for "the best"
14. Money should bring freedom, not enslavement
15. Dealing with "date envy"
16. People only covet selectively—don't go after someone else's peckel
17. The importance of jealousy
18. Coveting yourself: the perils of materialism and greed
19. Love vs. livelihood: striking the balance
20. The importance of charity and generosity
21. But don't be flashy
22. How to use coveting to your advantage
23. Don't ask for something you know your date can't refuse
24. A final word on coveting and contentment

Last Word
Take the Two Tablets and Find
Your Soul Mate

One of the most interesting things about the giving of the Ten Commandments is the place where it was given. Where is Mount Sinai? Nobody knows. Hard to believe, isn't it? It's the most famous place in Jewish history, the place where Moses went up and got the Torah, where all the Jews assembled after the exodus from Egypt to hear God speak to the entire nation for the only time ever, the place where the Ten Commandments were carved onto two stone tablets. And nobody knows where it is.

Certainly, there are some speculations and theories, and there is the monastery of Santa Katerina built on one of these putative locations. Yet the fact remains that the mountain cannot be located with utter certainty, as the knowledge of its locale was never passed down by tradition. This is because Mount Sinai has retained no special place in Jewish history. It is not considered holy in itself, and is certainly not a place of pilgrimage.

There was a good reason for this. God wanted the people to focus on *what was given* at Sinai, and not on Sinai itself. The mountain was only a conduit to this most important of messages, the Holy Torah. God feared that the Jews would get so caught up in the experience and thrill of receiving the Torah that they would never get beyond it. They would forever tell their kids about how

exciting it was to see the thunder and lightning, to hear the deafen-
ing sound of the Shofar, and to witness the splendor of the divine
revelation. In so doing, what God *said* at Sinai might lose impact
by comparison.

We all make mistakes of this kind, glorifying form at the expense of substance. I see this frequently within the Jewish community. A Jewish boy becomes a man, responsible for his own
behavior, at the age of thirteen. A special celebration known as a
Bar Mitzvah is held to emphasize to the boy the importance of the
occasion. But for many Jewish families, the Bar Mitzvah becomes
an end in itself, its spiritual message entirely subordinated to fancy
parties and impressing the parents' guests.

I remember growing up in affluent Miami Beach and watching
the ridiculous extremes to which some parents took the Bar Mitzvah. While they barely provided their child with a Jewish education, they would all compete to outshine each other in ever more
elaborate Bar Mitzvahs. One friend of mine had a *Star Wars* Bar
Mitzvah, in which Darth Vader greeted all the guests as they en-
tered the hall with a deeply intoned "mazel tov," and R2D2 was
seen running around the hall with a little tallis (prayer shawl)
attached to his metal chassis. And Chewbaka was dispensing big
bowls of chicken soup from a pot made in the shape of Java the
Hutt.

Even more absurd was the Bar Mitzvah of my friend Morrie. As
you walked into the hall, there was the head of the Bar Mitzvah
boy, carved out of fresh chopped liver.

Another very wealthy friend had a Miami Dolphins Bar Mitzvah in which some of the leading players on the team turned up in
their uniforms. The Bar Mitzvah was held at the Orange Bowl and
the invitation came in the form of a game ticket. Even the Bar
Mitzvah boy arrived at the reception in helmet and shoulder pads
with the team. He was so small and puny that the other members
of the team had to keep from stepping on him and squashing him.

But zaniest of all was the Bar Mitzvah of Josh, modeled on the
Wizard of Oz, in which the Rabbi came dressed as the Cowardly

Lion, and Josh's mother forced her mother-in-law to dress as the Wicked Witch of the West.

While I enjoyed these extravagant occasions, I knew deep down that there was something wrong about them. Bar Mitzvahs are meant to be sublime *religious* celebrations, yet these became farces, cheap—or, rather, very expensive—empty spectacles. This is not at all in keeping with what the Almighty meant when He gave the Ten Commandments to the Jewish people. (Of course, this doesn't mean to say that I wasn't jealous as hell that these Bar Mitzvahs had so much more flash than mine, which naturally took place in Uncle Barney's Bargain Basement.)

But now it's your turn. Don't live for the thrill of the chase or the excitement of the date. Rather, date in order to find your soul mate. Don't promote the journey to the exclusion of the destination. Remember the ten secrets contained in the Ten Commandments. Read, mark, learn, and inwardly digest them:

Primacy	Compliments
Exclusivity	Mystery
Confidence	Sincerity
Sacred moments	Trust
Gratitude	Contentment

And one day, I know it, you'll meet your soul mate and fulfill your heart's desire.

And if you are fortunate enough to already be married, please remember how the lessons in this book apply to you as well. Only if you continue to date in marriage will you prevent monotony and boredom from setting in. Married people are extremely important. They increase the potential readership of this book many times over. Indeed, I never sought to alienate the married people at any point in this book. I don't do that kind of thing. I don't believe in burning bridges. I will never forget the dying words of my pious and saintly great-grandfather. His life was ebbing away quickly, and before he expired I begged him to leave me his parting words of wisdom, a maxim by which I could lead my life. He looked up at me, coughed up a few pints of phlegm over my shoes, and then said, "My son, never fall out with any person. You never know when you might need to use them again." And with that, his eyes closed, and we thought he was gone. The good news, however, was that he wasn't ebbing away nearly as quickly as any of us supposed, or indeed hoped. No, it turned out that the stubborn old mule lasted another forty years, coughing up phlegm and calling for pretty nurses with big, shall we say, features, until the very last moment. When the end really did come, I said to him, "Grand Old Goat, please, before you go, just one last pearl of wisdom. Sum up life for me." He tried hard to give his trademark cough, but only managed a few unimpressive choking sounds, and then said, "Life, well, life is like a spring." And his eyes closed as his candle flickered away. "No, Grandpa, don't go yet. Tell me, tell me what it means. What does it mean that life is like a spring?" He gathered his last remaining bits of strength. Courageously and heroically, he raised himself to his full height of two foot five inches, and then uttered his very last words in this life, "Okay, so it's not like a spring." And with those beautiful words on his very holy lips, he spat one last time, and he was gone.

But I will leave you with my own aphorism by which to live. Marriage is about finding someone who makes you feel special. It is enjoyed and prospers specifically among those who believe, deep in their hearts, that they were created primarily to make someone else happy. That human greatness is achieved particularly in the giving rather than the taking. Therefore, always remember, *you are unique, just like everyone else.*

Love,

Shmuley

Join *LoveProphet.com*—
The World's Wisest Web
Dating Community

www.loveProphet.com

Rabbi Shmuley has launched a unique and exciting matchmaking Internet site which guarantees to find your perfect soul mate. *LoveProphet.com* offers creative and exciting technology allowing men and women to meet each other online with real-time audio and video. But more than a mere dating service, the Love Prophet will remove the obstacles that stand between you and a successful relationship and help you identify exactly what it is you're looking for. Rabbi Shmuley, the Love Prophet, also helps develop relationships from their embryonic stages by offering advice to subscribers who write in with summaries of their dates as well as help disentangle them from problems in their relationships.

Colorful and humorous, challenging and insightful, *LoveProphet.com* is the most unique dating site you will ever experience.

You can register now by going to the *www.loveProphet.com* and filling in the form. First 100 registrants receive a copy of Rabbi Boteach's bestselling book *Kosher Sex* plus a free six-month membership.

The L'Chaim Society

Rabbi Shmuley Boteach is the Founder and Dean of The L'Chaim Society (Hebrew for "To Life"), an organization dedicated to the creation of values-based leadership with branches in Oxford, Cambridge, London, and New York. The goals of the organization include spreading understanding, love, and tolerance, as well as strengthening marriages and relationships.

The Society has hosted some of the leading figures in the world lecturing on their core values including Mikhail Gorbachev, Shimon Peres, Binyamin Netanyahu, Jerry Springer, Yitzchak Shamir, Bob Hawke, Javier Perez de Cuellar, Elie Wiesel, Simon Wiesenthal, Boy George, Diego Maradona, Rabbi Harold Kushner, and Professor Stephen Hawking.

If you would like further information about Rabbi Shmuley Boteach and the L'Chaim Society you can write to: Oxford L'Chaim Society, 6 East 39th St., 10th Floor, New York, NY 10016.

For information about Rabbi Boteach's books, lecture and media appearances, and for details about forthcoming Oxford L'Chaim Society events, you can check out the L'Chaim Society Web site at: *www.lchaim.org* or write to *info@lchaim.org*. Rabbi Boteach also publishes weekly essays on contemporary social and relationship issues over the Internet. If you would like to subscribe, please e-mail *info@lchaim.org,* or send in the following form.

Name . . . .

E-mail address . . . .

Address . . . .

Tel. . . . .